Playa del Carmen, Tulum & the Riviera Maya

EXPLORER'S GUIDES

Playa del Carmen, Tulum & the Riviera Maya

A Great Destination

FOURTH EDITION

Joshua Eden Hinsdale

The Countryman Press ✷ Woodstock, Vermont

Interior photographs by the author unless otherwise specified.
Frontispiece: Ricardo Vagg

Maps by Erin Greb Cartography, © The Countryman Press
Book design by Bodenweber Design
Composition by Eugenie S. Delaney

Published by The Countryman Press, P.O. Box 748, Woodstock, VT 05091
Distributed by W. W. Norton & Company, Inc., 500 Fifth Avenue, New York, NY 10110
Printed in the United States of America

10 9 8 7 6 5 4 3 2 1

Playa del Carmen, Tulum & the Riviera Maya
978-1-58157-276-6

This book is dedicated to my ever-supportive parents, my beautiful wife,
our amazing daughter, Maya (my favorite exploradora),
and our young son, Finn, who has never called milk
anything but *leche* his entire life.

Explore with Us!

What's Where At the start of the book you'll find an alphabetical listing of highlights, important information and other details that you may want to reference quickly to navigate the book, the Riviera Maya and its culture.

Geographic Orientation The cities and towns of the Yucatán Peninsula and the Riviera Maya are covered in this book starting with Playa del Carmen, the conceptual and physical center of the Riviera Maya. Subsequent chapters cover the Riviera Maya to the South and to the North of Playa, followed by other destinations nearby that are not technically a part of the Riviera Maya, including Cancún, Cozumel, and the Costa Maya.

Many locations are found along Highway 307, which parallels the coastline as it traverses the region from Cancún to the north down to Tulum and beyond in the south. Whenever possible, addresses are given using Highway 307 as a primary reference point, which is especially useful for self-guided travelers who choose to explore the region on their own.

The ★ symbol indicates the author's recommendations for the best restaurants, bars, attractions, and lodging places throughout the book.

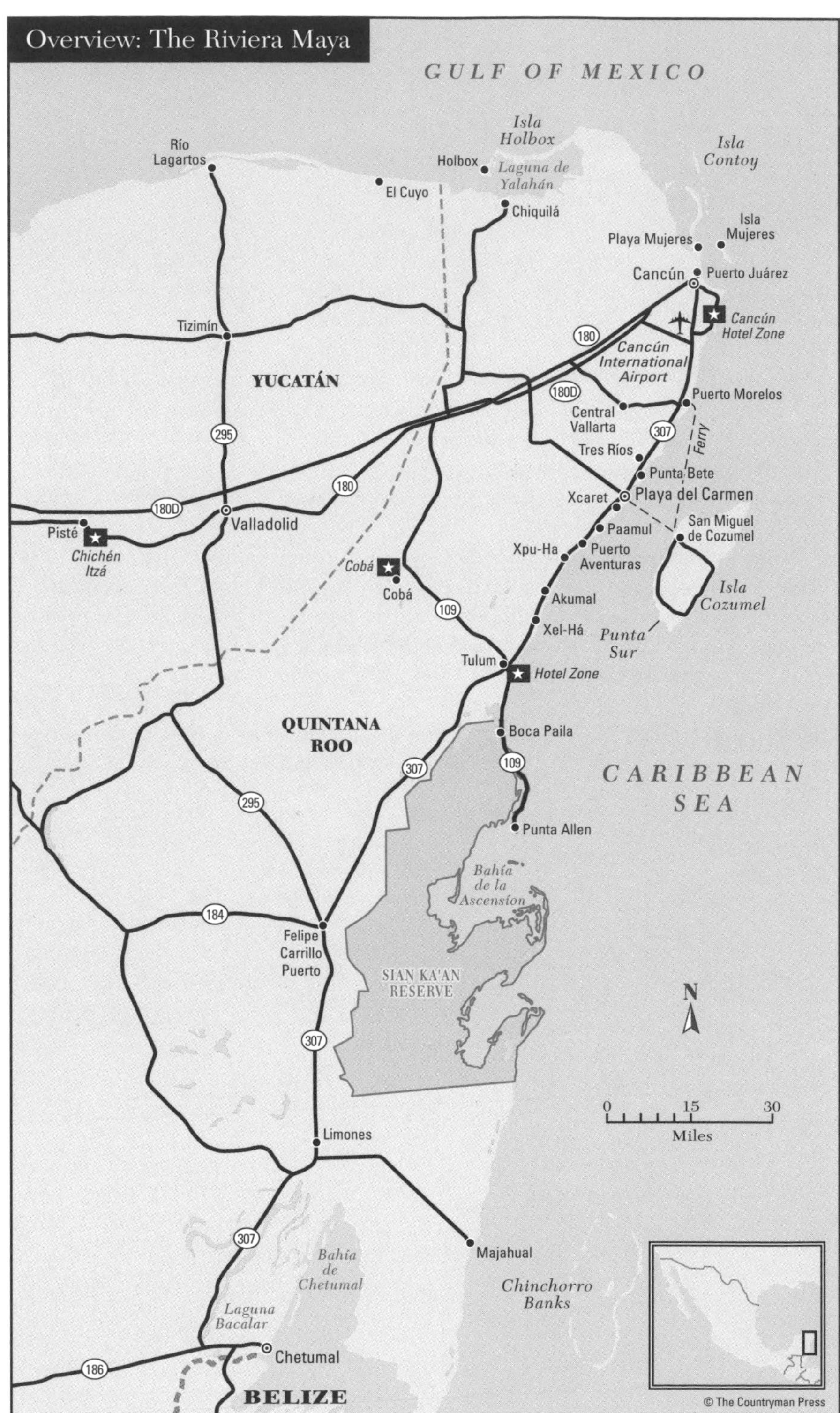
Overview: The Riviera Maya
GULF OF MEXICO
Isla Holbox
Isla Contoy
Río Lagartos
Holbox
Laguna de Yalahán
El Cuyo
Chiquilá
Isla Mujeres
Playa Mujeres
Cancún
Puerto Juárez
Cancún Hotel Zone
Tizimín
180
Cancún International Airport
YUCATÁN
180D
Puerto Morelos
Central Vallarta
295
307
Ferry
Tres Ríos
Punta Bete
180
Xcaret
Playa del Carmen
180D
Valladolid
San Miguel de Cozumel
Pisté
Paamul
Chichén Itzá
Xpu-Ha
Puerto Aventuras
Cobá
Cobá
Isla Cozumel
Akumal
109
Xel-Há
Punta Sur
Tulum
Hotel Zone
QUINTANA ROO
Boca Paila
109
307
CARIBBEAN SEA
295
Punta Allen
Bahía de la Ascensíon
184
Felipe Carrillo Puerto
SIAN KA'AN RESERVE
N
307
0 15 30
Miles
Limones
307
Majahual
Bahía de Chetumal
Chinchorro Banks
Laguna Bacalar
Chetumal
186
BELIZE
© The Countryman Press

Contents

Acknowledgments

I AM FOREVER GRATEFUL for my friends, family, and total strangers who have directly or indirectly led to or assisted with this project:

My mother introduced me to *Jonathan Livingston Seagull*, Willie Nelson, the beach, and a sense of wonder and delight with life. She encouraged me to explore the world, took motorcycle riding lessons with me when I was 15, cried when I left for college, and always made coming home a warm and wonderful experience.

My father taught me to water-ski, play baseball, and understand the stock market. He took me fishing, learned scuba so we could dive together, validated my wanderlust, and always led by example. He taught me that you can have an exciting life and still be responsible.

I met Andrea in Austin, Texas, and took her to Playa del Carmen hoping she'd fall in love with me (lucky for me, it worked). She travels with me when she can and understands that I still need to go when she can't. I carry her in my heart wherever I am. And when I return, she reminds me why there's no place like home. She is the most patient, most supportive, and most beautiful person I could ever know. Our daughter was born during a sultry summer in Austin, Texas, and was named Maya. We can't wait to teach her all of the wonderful things about the region and people that inspired her name.

Thanks also to my first dive buddies—Eric "Rico" Andrews, Keri Kennerly, Chris Glisan, Ellen Lock, and Amanda Miller; my colleague and friend George Hunter; my personal supporters Jeremy Reed, Sean Mitchell, Shawn Moran, Joy Taylor, Sam Shelby; my good-times friends Marshall York, Mike Leon, Sean Rasberry, and Derek Palisoul; our loving nanny Lesly Mendoza; Barry Diller; Jimmy Buffett; and everyone I've ever been to Mexico with or met while there. Special thanks to Chip Rankin for his destination insight and market intelligence.

I am thankful for the kindness, support, and assistance of the hundreds of hoteliers, restaurant owners, tour operators, bartenders, taxi drivers, and others who I met and learned from during my research. Thanks to the hotel associations, tourism boards, and other official organizations that offered information and support. And thanks to the people of the Riviera Maya, who smiled at me as I walked the beaches and streets of their hometowns.

Foreword

WHEN I WAS ASKED to write a foreword to this guidebook, I thought about how I could spend 10 years traveling through Mexico, with each day bringing a sense of discovery, new faces, and plenty of surprises. I have been visiting Mexico for more than 30 years and love it so much that I make my home in Los Cabos, where I run the Cabo Wabo Cantina, hang out, drink tequila, and jam with friends. Whether I'm down there or across the country in Playa del Carmen and the Riviera Maya, it's always great to be in Mexico.

Many people have discovered the charms of Mexico during the past 30 years, but I find that some things never change. I can still get the thrill of being the only gringo in a backstreet cantina and find adventure and exploration around every corner. Often, a sunrise means my day is ending, not beginning. For me, Mexico is a magical and mystical place. There is a timelessness and sense of a deep-rooted folklore that is personified in the people.

Most of all, I love the white-sand beaches, the music, the food, the fiestas, and enjoying time with family and friends. It's a place where the warmth of the sun is equaled by the warmth of the people. My family and I try new food, meet new people, and generally kick back on the world's greatest beaches. Mexico inspires me. It might mean a new song, a new idea, or a renewed outlook on life. Whatever it does to you, Mexico will remind you to enjoy life.

See you on the beach!

Sammy Hagar

Introduction

MY PARENTS FIRST TRAVELED to the Riviera Maya in 1980, when it was known only as the not-so-catchy "area south of Cancún." They went to Xcaret when it cost 25 cents and the road was yet to be paved. They went to Xel-Ha and Garrafon, in Isla Mujeres, and marveled at the tropical fish and the deserted beaches. They ate lobster on the beach in Cancún and snorkeled the virgin reefs of Cozumel. When they came home, they showed me their pictures and talked of their adventures, and I knew I'd go there one day.

My first experience with the Caribbean was in Belize, when I was 16. I went diving at Turneffe Island and was blown away by the color of the water, the number of fish, and the relaxing island lifestyle. A year later, I went on a dive trip to Cozumel with a group of friends from school. I loved the food, the freedom, and the excitement. We took the ferry to the then-tiny town of Playa del Carmen and could hardly find a place that was open to eat lunch.

For each of the next 10 years, I went to Mexico every chance I could, eventually leading group trips, selling travel packages, and making friends around the country. In college, I spent a year at the University of Costa Rica, studying Spanish and traveling around every weekend. After graduating from the University of Texas, I went to work for a Mexico-based tourism developer and worked on the early stages of the creation of Playacar.

I moved to Cozumel, worked in a hotel, and traveled the region extensively. I later moved to Cancún, worked for the *Cancún News* (the English daily newspaper, now closed), and made frequent trips to Playa del Carmen. In 1993, I visited the construction site of one of the first all-inclusive hotels, in Xpu-Ha, for a photo shoot, but I could never have imagined the development that would follow up and down the coast.

When I met the woman who later became my wife, the first trip we took together was to Playa del Carmen, where I hoped she'd fall in love with me. We stayed at a tiny pension along Quinta Avenida when it was still a dusty cobblestone street with just a handful of restaurants, shops, and bars. Lucky for me, the ploy worked, and later we named our first daughter Maya, after the region that we all enjoy together now.

Over the years, I have stayed active in the Riviera Maya community, splitting my frequent trips between Cancún, Cozumel, and Playa. As many others have, I've watched the area boom and grow, amazed with each trip at the new hotels, restaurants, and other attractions.

The region continues to draw me, almost magically, to its sandy beaches, taco bars, secret fishing holes, and buzzing nightspots. It is in my soul and has become a large part of who I am. I love being there, I love talking about it—and I love sharing it with other travelers.

LEFT: The hammocks at Xel-Ha are the perfect place for a nap. Philip Gamon

What's Where in Playa del Carmen and the Riviera Maya

AIRPORTS Most travelers will arrive in the Riviera Maya via the modern Cancún International Airport (CUN, www.cancun-airport.com). International flights also arrive at the smaller Cozumel International Airport (CZM), and transportation to the mainland is available via ferry. Charter and regional flights are also available at small airports in Playa del Carmen and on Isla Mujeres and Isla Holbox (see chapter 2).

ALL-INCLUSIVE At many hotels, everything a guest could require—including meals, alcohol and entertainment—is included in the nightly rate. Exactly what is included, and what level of service is offered, can vary from hotel to hotel (see chapter 5).

BEACHES White sandy beaches reign supreme in the Riviera Maya. However, visitors will encounter the occasional rocky beach, and many beaches are clearly nicer than others. In Mexico, all beaches are public property, although hotels and property owners along the beach are allowed to section off private areas and aren't required to provide beach access across their property.

BICYCLING Bike rentals are a popular recreation or transportation choice, particularly on smaller islands like Isla Mujeres and Isla Holbox and within larger master planned resorts. Many hotels offer courtesy bicycles for the use of their guests.

BOOKS Check out 11 great books—including tomes of history, mystery, madcap adventure and flirty Spanish language—recommended to complement your trip in chapter 13.

BOUTIQUE HOTELS The term *boutique* means many different things to many different people, and Mexico hoteliers are no different. However, in this book it generally refers to hotels that have a distinctive design or charm, offer quality service, have fewer than 50 rooms, and are not affiliated with a large conglomerate. There are many different flavors of boutique accommodation, especially in Playa del Carmen, Tulum, and Isla Mujeres.

LEFT: At dusk, jellyfish lanterns begin casting their magical, tropical glow throughout the Riviera Maya. Chip Rankin

Bicycling is particularly popular for getting around on Isla Holbox's car-less sandy roads.
Chip Rankin

BUS SERVICE Regular transportation is available in the region on the local bus system. For about $5, travelers can ride on air-conditioned buses one-way between Playa del Carmen, the Cancún airport, downtown Cancún, Tulum, and other area destinations (see chapter 2).

CAR RENTAL Travelers can rent cars at the airport or at tourist desks in Playa del Carmen, Cancún, Cozumel, and other destinations and resorts.

CARIBBEAN ISLANDS Three different island destinations located off the Yucatán Peninsula each sport a distinctive character and vibe. The more developed Cozumel and the enchanting Isla Mujeres can each be spotted from Playa del Carmen and Cancún, respectively, and both are accessible by ferry. The ferry to sleepy Isla Holbox lies three hours north of Cancún, prompting some visitors to opt for chartered air taxis.

CARIBBEAN SEA The striking turquoise waters of the Caribbean certainly sealed the region's fate when the Mexican government set about to create a new tourism destination in the early 1970s. Although Mexican and Mayan culture remain most dominant in the region, rivaled most closely by international influences, travelers can still find touches of the storied Eastern Caribbean waters throughout the Riviera Maya, particularly on Isla Mujeres and in Playa del Carmen.

CENOTES A rare geological feature of the Yucatán, a *cenote* (sen-NO-teh) is a freshwater sinkhole formed when the limestone ground caves in and fills with water from underground rivers. The U.S.-based National Speleological Society (www.caves.org/project/qrss) has an ongoing and well-advanced project to map the extensive network of freshwater caves (see chapter 10).

CHILDREN You don't have to leave the kids at home to have a fun vacation in the Riviera Maya. Many resorts have special facilities for kids, including playgrounds, kid-friendly meals, activities programs, and complimentary child care. In-room babysitting can be arranged through hotel concierges, who maintain a list of recommended caretakers. Smaller hotels can often arrange for a housekeeper to look after the kids while the parents enjoy a tour or day trip. Nature parks, theme parks, and zoos provide exciting daytrip opportunities. At the beach, kids enjoy collecting shells, watching the pelicans dive for fish, and building sand castles. In most areas there is little wave action, so introducing kids to the ocean is a breeze. In 2005, a playground was added to the town square in Playa, complete with a sandy play area, jungle gym, monkey bars, slides, and a great ocean view.

CONSULATE OFFICES The United States (www.usembassy.gov), Canada (www.canadainternational.gc.ca), and United Kingdom (www.ukinmexico.fco.gov.uk) all have consular offices in the region. All three have offices in Cancún, and both the U.S. and Canada maintain offices in Playa del Carmen. There is also a U.S. office in Cozumel.

CORAL Even though coral remnants that washed ashore give much of the region's beaches that bright white and sometimes almost pink hue, coral itself is not to be touched. The rare piece that washes ashore will easily cut up a bare foot. More importantly for those diving and snorkeling, coral is very fragile, and simple contact can break off a piece or cause a chemical reaction that kills the organisms that took hundreds of years to form and are a critical part of the earth's ecosystem. Learn more about coral protection and conservation from the World Wildlife Fund (WWF) at www.panda.org/corals.

CORAL REEF See Great Mayan Reef.

COSTA MAYA, OR THE MAYAN COAST The region known as Riviera Maya reaches its southern border in Tulum. The Mexican Caribbean coast that stretches from that point south to Belize is known as the Costa Maya. Quieter and slower than its neighbors to the north, it's noted for its many small, ecological themed hotels, large undeveloped areas and protected preserves.

CUBAN CIGARS As of press time, it is against the law for Americans to spend money on Cuban goods and services. While this technically includes Cuban cigars

This playground is in the middle of the town square in Playa del Carmen.

purchased in Mexico, a lack of records for these exchanges makes it a pretty appealing dalliance for many travelers while abroad (see chapter 4). Remember that while what happens in Mexico stays in Mexico, bringing Cuban cigars back home to the U.S. is another matter entirely.

CURRENCY The official currency of the Mexico is the peso. Although its value fluctuates daily against the U.S. dollar, there is rarely a notable difference in the rate during a visitor's trip. In tourist areas, prices are sometimes listed in American dollars and, since both currencies use the dollar sign ($), that sometimes breeds confusion. This book uses the dollar sign ($) to signify U.S. dollars and the word *pesos* when referring to Mexican pesos.

DIVING & SNORKELING The Mayan Riviera is one of the world's great destinations for saltwater and freshwater exploration. Check out chapter 10 for an in-depth discussion of dive sites, scuba certification schools, and recommended dive shops throughout the region.

DOLPHINS Travelers can sign up to swim with trained dolphins in a captive environment at Dolphin Discovery's centers (www.dolphindiscovery.com) in Puerto Aventuras, Cozumel, Akumal, and Isla Mujeres. Other programs are also available from Delphinus (www.delphinusworld.com) at Xcaret and Xel-Ha parks and Cancún's Dreams Hotel and Dolphinaris (www.dolphinaris.com) at Wet'n Wild (see chapter 8).

DRUG CARTELS With the election of a new Mexican president in 2012 and the subsequent change in policy, much of the shocking violence associated with Mexico's drug cartels has decreased. However, even during their height there were very few, if any, associated incidents in the state of Quintana Roo or the neighboring state of Yucatan. Although the country's remaining drug cartels undoubtedly have financial interests in Cancún and the Riviera Maya, as of press time almost all drug-related violence in Mexico has occurred near the borders and not in resort areas. Check with the U.S. Department of State at travel.state.gov for updates and, as always, don't go seeking out dark alleys in a foreign land.

DUTY FREE The notion of duty-free sales of alcohol, tobacco, and other taxable goods sometimes seems like a holdover from travel's more exotic heyday. But large shops selling duty-free goods can be found at the Cancún and Cozumel airports and many travelers continue to buy their allotment to take home. However, remember, if you're to traveling to the U.S. and will have to transfer to a connecting flight, TSA officials will not allow you to bring a liquor bottle in your carry-on baggage when you enter the terminal for your domestic U.S. flight. So be prepared to transfer your purchase to your checked luggage after you pass through customs or say *adios* to your new bottle of tequila.

ECOLOGICAL There are a number of small "ecologically" themed hotels and bed-and-breakfasts in the Mayan Riviera, particularly on Isla Mujeres, Isla Holobox, and south of Tulum. Although this doesn't always mean they are "green" hotels or offer any particular efficiency, they typically feature a stronger connection to nature and often demonstrate a more conscientious behavior.

EMERGENCIES Bad things happen, even in paradise, so it's good to know where you can turn. For emergency police, fire, or ambulance assistance, call 066 (the equivalent

Surf Before You Snorkel

Try these free online resources for more information about the Riviera Maya:

LocoGringo.com. This superb source for detailed aerial photos, virtual tours, and high-quality photos and descriptions of hotels, attractions, and beaches covers Playa del Carmen, the Riviera Maya, and surrounding areas. You can make reservations for hotels, condos, and villas as well as participate in its active message boards.

MayanHoliday.com. The author's blog and reservations site, regularly updated with news, travel tips, and features related to travel in Playa del Carmen and the Riviera Maya.

InTheRoo.com. This has lively discussion forums, an index of special offers, and comprehensive business directory for the Riviera Maya region.

RivieraMaya.com. The Riviera Maya tourism board's site has hotel and restaurant lists, plus attractions, travel stats, and tour info. Hotel reservations can be made online or by phone in the United States at 1–877–7-GO-MAYA (877–746–6292).

Playa.info. This site offers active message boards, detailed hotel reviews from recent travelers, a live webcam, and real estate information.

PlayaMayaNews.com. A community site for people living in or visiting Playa del Carmen, it provides local movie schedules, classified listings, human-interest stories, health advice, culture, and topics relevant to the local community. It makes an entertaining and interesting read whether you're actively planning a trip or just learning more about the area.

PlayadelCarmen.com. This commercial site lists area hotels and condos and features photos, videos, maps, destination guides, and message boards.

Friendly.com.mx. Explore hotels, restaurants, shops, and events that are gay-friendly, gay-owned, or otherwise have an appeal to gay visitors and locals alike.

TripAdvisor.com. The ubiquitous travel site has user reviews, candid photos, price comparisons, message boards, and reservation information for hotels throughout the Riviera Maya. The site is not specific to the region, so you will need to search to find a hotel in the region.

Travel.State.Gov. The U.S. State Department provides a wealth of travel information, covering documentation requirements, health, safety, and overseas services.

DestinationSoundtrack.com. Load up your playlist with the perfect songs about Playa, Cancún, the Riviera Maya, and vacations in Mexico.

of 911 in the U.S.) from any phone at no cost. You can also contact the Red Cross by dialing 065 from any phone. Local phone numbers are frequently changing, so if you are looking for other local emergency services and medical facilities, you can find them via the website addresses found on the last pages of this book, in chapter 13.

EUROPEAN PLAN (EP) The opposite of an All-Inclusive Plan, European Plan simply means at that hotel, rates only include accommodations. Food, drinks, and other activities require an extra charge. This is how most hotels in the U.S. operate. See chapter 5 for a detailed comparison.

EVENTS Holidays, festivals, celebrations, and other special events can add an entirely new dimension to your vacation. For specifics, check out the event calendar in chapter 13.

EXPATRIATE It's probably safe to say that at least one out of five visitors to Playa del Carmen contemplates tearing up his return ticket home. Ex-pats are the ones who did, or ultimately bought themselves a one-way ticket back.

FERRIES Overwater transportation to Cozumel and Isla Mujeres is available via modern ferries from Playa del Carmen and Cancún, respectively. Smaller ferries also provide service to Isla Holbox. For specifics, visit ferry operators Ultramar (www.granpuerto.com.mx) and Mexico Water Jets (www.mexicowaterjets.com.mx) and read the *Getting There* section for your respective island destination.

FIRE DANCERS Performing on the beach nightly at Fusion Hotel (www.fusionhotelmexico.com) and on Fridays and Saturdays at the Blue Parrot (www.blueparrot.com/fireshow) in Playa del Carmen, dancers twirl lit torches and lanterns through the night air, painting memorable patterns in the sky.

GAS STATIONS All full-service and owned by the government's oil distribution company Pemex, gas stations are plentiful along Highway 307 from Cancún to

Yo Amo Tacos is the perfect place to sit back with a drink and watch Playa's evening parade of passersby. Chip Rankin

Tulum. Travelers heading south of Tulum or west across the peninsula should plan to fill up at every stop. Prices run a little higher than in most U.S. cities.

GAY & LESBIAN In recent years, the number of gay-friendly establishments in the region has grown. It is not uncommon to see gay couples and patrons in the international Playa del Carmen (some gay people call it "gay indifferent" rather than "gay friendly") or bohemian Isla Mujeres. Even Cancún has had a gay nightclub for decades. Mexico itself has made headlines, legalizing gay marriage in Mexico City in 2009. Still, most of the country's residents remain very traditional and religious and it's always a good idea to exercise good judgment about public displays of affection when traveling in an unfamiliar area. For an up-to-date resource on gay-friendly events, restaurants, and hotels in Playa, visit www.friendly.com.mx; or check www.purpleroofs.com for gay-friendly accommodations across the region.

GOLF The arrival of the OHL Golf Classic in 2007 clearly signaled the region's arrival as a world-class destination for championship golf. Read up on the courses and the big names who designed them in chapter 11 and visit the Mexican Caribbean Golf Association online (www.cancungolf.org).

GREAT MAYAN REEF The largest coral reef in North America, second only to the Great Barrier Reef near Australia, is better known in scientific circles as the Mesoamerican Barrier Reef System. It begins off the coast of the Yucatan Peninsula near Isla Contoy and Isla Mujeres and extends south 197 miles past Belize, ending near the Bay Islands of Honduras. This living underwater environment is home to more than 600 species of fish and nearly 100 varieties of coral. Learn more about the Mesoamerican Reef Alliance's preservation and protection efforts at www.icran.org/action-mar.html.

GRINGO In Playa, as throughout Mexico, Americans are usually referred to as *gringos*. Though it may sound a bit harsh to some Americans' ears (it does have a negative connotation in some other Latin American countries), it isn't at all meant as a derogatory in Mexico. So don't take offense. To the Mexicans, using the word *Americanos* is confusing and a bit offensive to them, since all residents of North, Central, and South America could be considered "Americans." Also, since the full name of the republic of Mexico is Los Estados Unidos de Mexico, or the United States of Mexico, it's also not quite adequate to use the textbook translation of *estadounidiense*, which is essentially "United Statesian," for citizens of the USA. Americans are sometimes referred to as *norteamericanos*, which means "North Americans," but that's not quite accurate either since it fails to distinguish between the United States and Canada, and the latter's citizens are known simply as *canadienses*. So, embrace your inner "gringo" and don't consider it a negative label. In this book, the word American is used to refer to residents of the United States.

HIGH SEASON As in much of Mexico and the Caribbean, the peak season lasts from early February until early May. The two weeks over Christmas and New Year's also are very busy, and most hotels charge their highest rates of the year during that time.

HONEYMOONS From intimate boutique hotels, quiet beaches, and relaxing spa treatments to bustling restaurant scenes, plush resorts, and adventurous excursions, the Riviera Maya offers honeymoon options suitable for almost every couple.

Freshwater canals wind throughout Fairmount Mayakoba and neighboring resorts. Mayakoba

Many venues offer wedding planning services and they often also feature special packages for the newly married. But don't be afraid to custom-design a unique honeymoon that suits your unique tastes, style, and budget.

HORSEBACK RIDING Always a popular activity, especially for couples and families, horseback-riding options abound and there are many chances in the area to form that special bond with an equine friend. See chapter 7 for a couple of our recommendations.

HURRICANES With a season lasting from July through November, hurricanes have had untold impact on the Riviera Maya. Several storms, notably Hurricanes Emily and Wilma in 2005, caused enormous destruction to the beaches, buildings, and infrastructure. However, this damage has also led developers and the Mexican government to invest billions of dollars to improve and fortify the area. The greatest risk of storms typically occurs from late August through October, although this rule of thumb is unpredictable at best. Check the National Hurricane Center (www.nhc.noaa.gov) for recent activity and read about historical hurricanes in the area in the special sections throughout this book.

IGUANAS If you don't see an iguana on your vacation, you probably didn't leave your room (or the nightclubs) very often. Given the close proximity of the jungle, the prevalence of this scaly reptile, and its general indifference to people, is legendary. Iguanas are commonplace anywhere with significant vegetation. They're docile creatures, but look, don't touch. They can carry disease, and if you touch or harass them you'll probably get hurt or into a lot of trouble.

JUNGLE Despite the beautiful white beaches and the significant development around Cancún, Playa del Carmen, and Tulum, much of the region remains as the natural Yucatán Jungle. Besides iguanas, it's home to many species of flora and fauna, and at times can be unpredictable. The best way to experience it is as part of a tour or excursion (see chapter 8).

KITEBOARDING Navigating what is essentially a surfboard with a sail, novices and experts alike navigate the smooth waters of the Mexican Caribbean on kiteboards. Lessons are available, most notably with the legendary Ikarus (see chapter 8), and kiteboard rentals and limited instruction are often included at larger all-inclusive resorts.

MAYANS The original residents of a significant part of sub-tropical Latin America, the Mayans have left an indelible mark on the land. While the ruins of their former civilization are a large tourist draw, many of the local residents in the area are direct descendants of this people. Still known as Mayans, many still keep aspects of the culture and the language alive today. Much like in the region itself, stories and details about the Mayans can be found woven throughout this book. See chapters 3, 8, and especially 9 for details on their history and culture.

NIGHTLIFE Your options for nights on the town are primarily determined by your location. Playa has a robust nightlife, with options for dance clubs, lounges, casual bars, and dancing on the beach. And Cancún has built much of its reputation on the grand scale of its nightclubs. Smaller towns usually present more limited options, but there's almost always a spot to grab a beer or another nightcap of your choice.

NUDE BEACHES Mexican law prohibits going nude (including topless for women) in public—and this includes beaches as well. But there are several locales where officials look the other way, or pretend they do. It's generally acceptable, and common, to see women sunbathing topless in areas of Playa del Carmen's beach, particularly at the beach clubs just north of Constituyentes Avenue. Several remote beach hotels cater to naturalists of varying extremes.

OCEAN PRESERVATION AND PROTECTION Although it may be hard to imagine serious threats to our oceans while sunning along the Caribbean sun or swimming in its pristine waters, scientists estimate that, in the last 50 years alone, half of the world's coral reefs have been destroyed and more than 70 percent of the oceans' fish populations have been consumed or slaughtered through commercial fishing operations. National Geographic Society Explorer-in-Residence and renowned marine scientist Dr. Sylvia A. Earle advocates that our actions until 2020 will have profound impacts on the future health of the seas and the planet's ecosystems. Her frank, simple, and clear explanations of the damage, and what must be done to counter it, can be found in her 2009 book *The World Is Blue: How Our Fate and the Ocean's Are One*. It's fascinating and recommended reading for anyone moved by the beauty, wonder and diversity of life along the Great Mayan Reef.

Although nudity isn't officially legal, it's acceptable at some beaches in Tulum.

The beaches on Playa's main cove tend to clear out as the sun goes down.

OHL GOLF CLASSIC The only PGA Tour event in Mexico, the OHL Golf Classic (www.ohlclassic.com) is named after the developer of Mayakobá, its host resort. Televised across the U.S. since its 2007 debut, the tour is held on Mayakobá's El Cameleon course. Day passes start at $10, though a range of hospitality and accommodation packages are significantly more expensive.

PARKS Many destination-worthy parks are situated throughout the Riviera Maya, Cancún, and the Costa Maya. Options include seaside Mayan-themed adventures, water parks, crocodile zoos, and other showcases for local life. The best in the region are highlighted in chapter 8.

PETS Although Mexico allows visitors to bring dogs and cats into the country temporarily, if accompanied with the required paperwork, it's rarely a good idea. Many hotels and resorts do not permit animals and your pet will be at risk of catching diseases from local strays and other critters. Don't do it.

PESO See Currency.

PLAYACAR The master-planned development of Playacar features many large, all-inclusive beach resorts, private homes, and a golf course, and lies immediately south of the Paseo del Carmen shopping center and Playa's ferry dock. For travelers seeking all-inclusive comfort, with the option to easily wander into downtown Playa del Carmen, it can present a perfect destination choice. Learn more in chapter 5.

PLAYA DEL CARMEN The central destination that allowed the Riviera Maya to take root, "Playa" was once a sleepy fishing village with a ferry to Cozumel. It first caught on as a destination with European tourists, who along with divers from around the world, began frequenting the small hotels along the beach and prompting developers and entrepreneurs into larger and grander endeavors. It's expanded greatly and today is a full-fledged city. Despite its growth and popularity, downtown has retained elements of its fishing roots, blended with Mexican and international influences from Italy, Germany, the U.S., and South America.

PORTAL MAYA ARCH Unveiled on December 21, 2012 to mark the end of the Mayan long calendar, this 50-foot-tall arch is the newest landmark in Playa. Created by Mexican sculptor José Arturo Tavares, the bronze arch sits prominently just

Some Things are Still Cheaper South of the Border

Though the price of meals, drinks, and many everyday purchases are relatively close to what you'll find back home, some services are still a bargain south of the border. Here are a few ideas of how you can save some money while you're in the Riviera Maya:

New eyeglasses. Bring a written prescription or even a pair of well-calibrated glasses, and the technicians at area eyewear shops can match your prescription in a wide variety of frames and lenses for a fraction of what you'd pay at home.

Helpful guide at the corner *farmacia*

Manicures and pedicures. Want acrylic nails or just need a fresh mani/pedi? Prices are half or less of what you'd pay back home at salons catering to locals.

Watch repair. If you have an old watch that needs fixing and you've been putting it off, bring it on vacation. Drop it off one day and pick it up the next, and it'll be ticking like it was new. Watch shops in Playa are common a few blocks back from the beach, and the skilled craftsmen can fix almost anything.

Shoe repair. Shoes falling apart? Stop by a local shoe repair shop, and you can have new soles, heels, or other repairs done while you're away enjoying the ruins at Tulum. The price will be significantly less than it would be back home, and the craftsmanship is top-rate.

Prescription medications. Local pharmacies will gladly fill prescriptions from U.S. doctors. Don't have a prescription? In many cases, one can be issued on the spot, for a limited charge.

behind the city's main beach and the seaside Parque Fundadores. Learn more in chapter 3).

QUINTA Also known as Avenida Quinta, or Fifth Avenue in English, this is the proper name of the main tourist thoroughfare in downtown Playa. All locals and many tourists refer to it by the name Quinta. For purposes of clarity and consistency with other numeric street names, this book often lists it as "Fifth Avenue." However, if you want to speak like a local, or at least like a seasoned visitor, you'll want to say "Quinta." You're also likely to see it written as "5ta" (much like our "5th") on signs and printed materials while you're in Playa. Curiously, the name has no direct relation to the name of the state of Quintana Roo.

QUINTANA ROO Named for a key figure in the Mexican War for Independence, Andrés Quintana Roo, who hailed from the Yucatán Peninsula, this Mexican state was officially formed in 1974. It contains the entirety of the country's Caribbean coastline, including Cancún, Cozumel, the Riviera Maya, and the Costa Maya.

RELIGION Catholicism is the primary religion in the Riviera Maya, though many of the ancient Mayan rituals are alive and well, oftentimes intermingling with traditional Catholic practices. Services are offered in various denominations, and the larger hotels maintain a list of current services and worship schedules. Tourists are welcome at all ceremonies, provided they dress and act appropriately and show respect for the local customs.

Fifth Avenue has gone from a sandy path to the most famous street in the Mexican Caribbean in 25 years.

RIVIERA MAYA Stretching from Puerto Morelos to Tulum and encompassing Playa del Carmen, this region has surpassed Cancún itself in the number of hotel rooms and visitors. However, unlike Cancún's high-rises, the area's beloved low-rise development is spread out over a much greater and typically quieter area. English-speakers often refer to it as the Mayan Riviera, but this book has opted to use the local vernacular.

SEMANA SANTA "Holy Week" in English, this usually refers to the week prior to the Easter holiday, and often includes the week following it. Children in Mexico get two weeks off over Easter, and families often travel to the coasts during that time. Hotels and resorts frequently fill up completely during this period. When Semana Santa overlaps with the U.S. spring break season, expect rooms to be particularly hard to find.

SIAN KA'AN BIOSPHERE RESERVE Located south of Tulum and covering ten percent of the state of Quintana Roo, this federal land was set aside as a natural wilderness preserve (www.cesiak.org) in 1986. An official UNESCO World Heritage site (whc.unesco.org), it's home to more than 300 species of birds, 100 types of mammals, and a diversity of geographical features (see chapter 5).

SKY DIVING It's definitely an option off the shore of the former Mayan Empire. See chapter 8 for details on recommended outfitters.

SNORKELING See chapter 10, Diving & Snorkeling.

SPANISH Mexico's official language remains dominant in the Riviera Maya, even amongst Mayans. However, many Mayan words continue to be used and augment the local lexicon. Tourists can probably get by on English alone in Playa, Cancún, Isla Mujeres, and much of the Riviera Maya, but they may want to consider enrolling in a local Spanish language schools or program (see chapter 13).

SPRING BREAK From late February through early April, with a crescendo in mid-March, American college students visit Mexico in full force. Although they're typically focused on Cancún, there's some spillover to Playa, Cozumel, and other Riviera Maya destinations.

SUSTAINABILITY Green tourism, development, and sustainable operations are definitely important in the Riviera Maya today. Like the rest of the world, what they mean in practice remains open for interpretation (see chapter 5).

THEME PARKS See Nature Parks, Amusement Parks, and Zoos in chapter 8.

TIPS & GRATUITIES Outside of all-inclusive resorts, or unless your tab specifically lists *servicio* after the tax, tips are expected to be given to waiters (10 to 15 percent), massage therapists, tour guides, dive guides, and similar service providers ($10).

TOURS Numerous outfitters provide specialty tours throughout the region, and most can be booked at your hotel's tourist or concierge desk. The best tours are highlighted in chapter 8, and local specialty tours are featured in their respective geographic chapters.

UNDERWATER SCULPTURE GARDEN Artist Jason deCaires Taylor began an ambitious project in 2009, creating MUSA (www.MUSAcancun.com), an underwater garden of hundreds of sculptures of humans and common objects. Located near Isla Mujeres, 10 to 20 feet below the surface, MUSA (which stands for *Museo Subacuático de Arte*, or "Underwater Museum of Art") is a beautiful and eerie accomplishment. Made from a material conducive to coral growth, the statues are designed to encourage new growth, while also drawing visitors away from fragile natural reefs (see chapter 8 and www.underwatersculpture.com).

U.S. DEPARTMENT OF STATE As of press time, the U.S. Department of State (travel.state.gov) has issued no warnings to travelers visiting Mexico's tourism areas, including the state of Quintana Roo, home to Playa, Cancún, Isla Holbox, and the Riviera Maya.

WATER PARKS, XCARET, XEL-HA, & ZOOS See chapter 8.

WEDDINGS Countless opportunities for destination weddings, small and large, can be found throughout the Riviera Maya, and many hotels and resorts have specialists on staff to help you plan. Learn more about getting married in Mexico in chapter 13.

Learn about the cities of the Yucatán at this park in downtown Playa. Mike Stone

YUCATÁN Geographically speaking, "Yucatán" can refer to the overall peninsula or easternmost quadrant of Mexico that juts into the Caribbean Sea, the jungle that engulfs much of that area, or the Mexican state that borders Quintana Roo to the northwest. The word also can be used to denote traditional, cultural geographical features long associated with this lush and storied region of Mexico.

Before You Go

TRAVEL SHOULD BE EASY, it should be carefree, and it should be comfortable. Unfortunately, that's not always the case. Getting around, having the proper paperwork, and making sense of unfamiliar rules and regulations can cause a fair amount of stress during any vacation, and travel to the Riviera Maya is no different.

An old adage that scuba divers use is, "Plan your dive and dive your plan." This concept should be applied to vacation travel as well. Taking some time before your trip to learn a bit about the region where you are traveling and to create a plan for how you're going to get around is essential to enjoying your vacation to the fullest. After all, wouldn't you rather use your vacation time relaxing on the beach rather than visiting the consulate, searching for maps, or asking everyone you see for help?

ARRIVAL BY AIR

Most international visitors get to Playa del Carmen and the Riviera Maya by flying into the **Cancún International Airport** (CUN, www.cancun-airport.com), 45 miles north of Playa and 10 miles south of the resort city of Cancún.

Inaugurated in 1974, it's had regular renovations, leaving it in excellent condition. There are three terminals, and most visitors will arrive and depart at Terminal 3, which opened in 2007. It's quite modern and efficient, with Starbucks, Margaritaville Café, and other familiar conveniences.

CUSTOMS & IMMIGRATION

All visitors must have a valid passport book to enter Mexico. Before your arrival on an international flight, you'll be required to fill out a tourist card (good for up to 90 days) and customs form. Usually handed out on the plane, they're available at the airport.

As you deplane, stay with your group as you're funneled to Immigration. The wait can last a few minutes to nearly an hour, depending on flight schedules. Have your passport and your forms ready, and then remember to save your copy of the tourist card, which the agent will return to you with your passport. You must have it when you depart. If lost, there's a $40 fee, and you can expect a bit

LEFT: Guests at Mayakoba resorts can explore the reserve's canals on a 40-minute boat tour, which offers unique views of local flora and fauna. Mayakoba

Keeping You on Track

Exploring is fun, but so is knowing where you are. The famous creators of CancunMap series of maps/travel, Iowa couple Laura (a.k.a., "MapChick") and Perry have explored the region for more than 30 years and likely know more about its back roads, secret beaches, and hidden attractions than any non-local on Earth. They tag the area's top resorts, restaurants, beaches, and other highlights, but their true love is uncovering lesser-known attractions and off-the-beaten-path adventures. Maps contain their unique take on the area and their personal recommendations and advice. Their exhaustively researched and individually produced maps cover Cancún, Cozumel, Isla Mujeres, Playa del Carmen, Mayan landmarks, and the Riviera Maya, and sell for $10 each (www.CancunMap.com).

of an interrogation at the airport when you leave. After you claim any bags, you'll proceed to the customs checkpoint. Hand your customs form to the agent standing next to the vertical traffic light mounted on a pole about chest high. You'll be asked to push the button. Green means "go," and red means your baggage will be opened and inspected.

AIRPORT TRANSPORTATION

If your transportation's not prearranged through your vacation package, you'll find several options for getting to your hotel or wherever else you want to go.

A single taxi awaits arrivals at the Cancun airport in 1970. Cancun History Center

TAXIS

Taxi service from the airport is heavily regulated; only specially licensed cabs are allowed to pick up passengers. As a result, fares from the airport are higher than for the return trips to the airport. The official fare at press time from the airport to the Cancún hotel zone is $40, and a trip to Playa del Carmen will run you around $90 to $100 per vehicle.

A return trip from Playa should be about $40 to $50, but ask your driver for a price before you get into the cab.

SHUTTLE BUSES

Shuttle buses, called *colectivos*, are available for transportation to Playa del Carmen. You'll ride with other travelers, stopping at other hotels along the way, but it's a good way to save a few pesos. Fares to Playa del Carmen are $30 per person.

A *colectivo* charges per person and makes multiple stops.

CITY BUSES

Public bus service ($10) runs between the Cancún airport and the main Playa del Carmen bus terminal (Quinta and Juárez), a short walk or taxi ride to most Playa hotels. Purchase tickets just after you clear customs and immigration and before you leave the airport. Look for the booths advertising ADO, the company offering the service. Once you have your ticket, you'll be directed to the departure location. Any local will point the way, but make sure you're getting on the right bus, and don't be talked into paying additional fares for different services.

CAR RENTAL

If you plan to do much local exploring and prefer a self-guided trip over planned excursions, renting a car may be your best option. And since the price of car rental

Go Hog Wild in the Riviera Maya

For some travelers, taking a guided trip in a tour bus or even setting out on their own in a rental car is just too tame. For these intrepid travelers, renting a Harley Davidson may be the best way to visit the ruins, discover hidden beaches, and make a style statement, all while getting a tan. Harley Adventures (Highway 307 at Constituyentes Avenue, www.harleyadventures.com) offers 883 Sportsters, 1200 Customs, and Softtail Fat Boys for around $95, $145, and $195 per day. Riders are encouraged to exercise extreme caution while riding along busy sections of Highway 307 and any unpaved roads they encounter.

Approximate Fares from Cancún Airport to Area Destinations

	Colectivo/ Shuttle	Taxi (1–4 people)	Taxi (5–8 people)
Moon Palace	—	$50	$75
Cancún Hotel Zone	$15	$60	$100
Gran Puerto (Isla Mujeres ferry)	$20	$65	$105
Puerto Morelos	$25	$70	$95
Playa Mujeres	—	$80	$110
Mayan Palace	$25	$80	$110
Downtown Playa del Carmen	$30	$90	$125
Xcaret	$40	$120	$155
Paamul	$40	$120	$155
Puerto Aventuras	$40	$125	$155
Akumal	$50	$155	$190
Tulum	$50	$155	$190
Chiquila (Isla Holbox ferry)	—	$320	$390
Merida	—	$415	$520
Chetumal	—	$440	$590

for a day is about the same as taking a taxi from the Cancún airport to Playa del Carmen, it usually makes sense to pick up the car at the airport and drop it off on your way back. Alternatively, you can choose to get your car once you're at your hotel or drop it off early at one of your rental agency's offices in the Mayan Riviera.

When renting a car in Mexico, it's important to investigate your insurance options. You're required to carry at least liability, and it will be clearly marked on your rental contract. Collision and comprehensive add-ons are available and can add 50 to 100 percent to the car rental price. Verify in advance whether your existing car insurance or even credit card contract provides for rental car coverage, and ensure that the coverage extends to vehicles rented in Mexico. Many plans don't.

PLAYA COMMUTER FLIGHTS

Mostly used by private aircraft, the small airfield in downtown Playa del Carmen, a few blocks behind the Playacar Palace hotel, also has charter flights available through **AeroSaab** (www.aerosaab.com) to Cancún, Cozumel, Merida, Isla Holbox, and nearby destinations.

THE COZUMEL FERRY

If you hit the schedule just right, getting to Playa del Carmen from Cozumel can take even less time than arriving through Cancún. The **Cozumel International**

The ferry dock bustles throughout the day.

Airport (CZM) is smaller than Cancún's, with only two runways and a small terminal. As your plane slows to a stop on the runway, you'll think the wingtips are about to snip the treetops off the palm trees that line the strip, but it's a safe and modern facility, even if it lacks the pretensions of the more recently renovated Cancún airport.

As in Cancún, taxi service at the Cozumel airport is regulated, and taxi fare or shuttle service must be paid for at a kiosk in the airport. Visitors with little luggage looking to save a few bucks can walk off the airport grounds and hail a taxi on the street. An official taxi will cost you about $14 to the ferry landing, while a taxi hailed on the street will set you back only $7 or so. Either way, the ride is only 10 minutes and will take you through a quick tour of the town of San Miguel before letting you out at the base of the ferry landing, or *muelle* in Spanish.

Ferry schedules are clearly posted (www.mexicowaterjets.com.mx), and you'll have your option from a couple of different boats. Each boasts to be the newest and fastest, though any differences in the times are negligible. Seating more than

Cozumel Ferry Schedule

Cozumel to Playa del Carmen	Playa del Carmen to Cozumel
5:00 AM	6:00 AM
7:00 AM	8:00 AM
8:00 AM	9:00 AM
9:00 AM	10:00 AM
10:00 AM	11:00 AM
noon	1:00 PM
2:00 PM	3:00 PM
4:00 PM	5:00 PM
5:00 PM	6:00 PM
6:00 PM	7:00 PM
8:00 PM	9:00 PM
10:00 PM	11:00 PM

The schedule can vary by day. Check the daily schedule at the ferry dock (www.granpuerto.com.mx, www.mexicowaterjets.com).

The ferry boat to Cozumel takes less than 30 minutes.

200, ferries have air-conditioning, snack bars, restrooms, and both indoor and outdoor seating. The ride takes from 30 to 45 minutes, depending on the boat and the water conditions. On windy days the ride can be a little rough, so it's recommended that you use the restroom prior to boarding or before departure, in case it's too rocky to safely move around. Fares range from $12 to $14 each way, depending on how many boats are available. Roundtrip tickets are available and can save you the hassle of standing in line again, though it's generally not much of an issue.

Upon arriving in Playa, you'll walk down a metal ramp onto the wide concrete pier. If you've checked bags, they'll be delivered to you on the dock, near the ferry's bow. Tricycle taxis are available to help carry you and/or your bags to the street to catch a proper taxi or all the way to your hotel, if you're staying in the immediate downtown area.

ELECTRICITY

Electrical power is the same as it is in the States: 110 volts AC. Outlets are the same size, and most U.S. plugs will work without any problem. Some hotels do not offer polarized plugs (where one prong is slightly larger than the other), so if your important electronic gadget has a polarized plug, grab an adapter at your local hardware or discount store. Adaptors are very inexpensive and could save the day if you have an uncooperative outlet at your hotel.

WHAT TO BRING

The Riviera Maya isn't considered a remote location. You're usually never more than 30 to 45 minutes from a grocery store, pharmacy, clothing boutique, electronics store, hair salon, or even hardware store, and modern supplies are readily available.

Packing for a trip to Playa and environs is all about comfort and bringing what you want to have with you to make your trip perfect. Unless you're planning on a serious camping trip to Sian Ka'an or a long-distance jungle hike, you should consider your packing to be an exercise in preparing for a luxury getaway or what suits your comfort. What you need to bring is largely determined by where you're staying and what you plan on doing.

STAYING SAFE

Playa del Carmen is far from the sleepy fishing village where everybody knew each other and nobody locked their doors. It is still a happy little city, though, where a lot of people do know each other and not quite everyone locks their doors. Petty theft is the main problem, and tourists are advised to watch their belongings, lock their hotel rooms, and not leave valuables unattended on the beach or elsewhere.

For the most part, Playa is quite safe. It's best to not be on remote parts of the beach late at night, as incidents have been reported. Leave your jewels at home and, like anywhere else, don't flash large amounts of cash or be too showy with expensive equipment or electronic gadgets. Use the hotel safe whenever possible and don't leave valuables in plain view in your hotel room or rental car. Report suspicious activity at your hotel to the front desk, and be alert of your surroundings. Men should carry their wallets in their front pockets on crowded streets, and women should ensure their bags are fully closed and not swinging freely.

Although it isn't widely observed, there have been reports of drug running, gang activity, and associated crime and violence in the area. If you go looking for

Stay Out of Trouble

One good way to avoid run-ins with the local police is to not give them any good reasons to pull you over in the first place.

Never drink and drive. Nothing is more tempting to local officers than a rental jeep full of tourists with a cooler in the back seat and everyone holding Corona bottles as they drive down the road.

Wear your seatbelt. Just like in the U.S., there is a mandatory seatbelt law in Mexico. The beat cops in Playa del Carmen sometimes stand on the street corner, where it's easy to peer inside your car, so buckle up every time you get in the front seat of a car.

Pull over to use your mobile phone. Using a mobile phone or other similar gadget while driving is illegal in Mexico. It's also extremely dangerous when driving on unfamiliar roads, especially along Highway 307 and around downtown areas in Cancún, Playa del Carmen, or Tulum.

Words and Phrases

English	Spanish
Another one	Otra
ATM	Cajero automático
Bathroom	Baño
Beach	Playa
Beef	Carne de rés
Beer	Cerveza
Big	Grande
Boat	Lancha
Bottled water	Agua en botella
Breakfast	Desayuno
Bus	Autobús
Car rental	Renta de autos
Check/bill	La cuenta
Chicken	Pollo
Coffee with milk	Café con leche
Dinner	Cena
Downtown	El centro
Drunk	Borracho
Eat	Comer
Fishing	La pesca
Goodbye	Adiós, hasta luego
Good morning	Buenos días
Good night	Buenas noches
Happy	Felíz
Hello	Hola
How much	Cuánto
Ice	Hielo
I want	Yo deseo
Lime	Limón
Lobster	Langosta
English	Spanish
Luggage	Equipaje
Lunch	Comida
Money	Dinero
Money exchange	Cámbio de dinero
More	Más

English	Spanish
My name is	Me llamo
Nice to meet you	Mucho gusto
Orange juice	Jugo de naranja
Please	Por favór
Post office	El correo
Rain	Llúvia
Scuba diving	Buceo
Shrimp	Camarón
Shuttle bus	Colectivo
Sick	Enfermo
Silly tourist	Turista loca
Small	Pequeña
Sunscreen	Bronceadora
Swim	Nadar
Swimsuit	Traje de baño
Tax	Impuestos
Thank you	Graciás
Tip	Propina
Towel	Toalla
Waiter	Mesero
Walk	Caminar
Why	Porqué
You're welcome	De nada

TRY A LITTLE MAYAN

Hello, what's up?	Ba'ax ka wa'alik?
What's going on?	Bix a bel?
I'm fine.	Ma'alob.
See you later.	Taak tu lakin.
I'm just looking.	Chen tin wilik.
How much is it?	Bahúux leti'?
Tastes good.	Ki.'
Hot pepper	Lik
Juice	K'aab
Where	Tu'ux
Plaza	K'íiwik
Thank you	Dios bo'otik
You're welcome	Mixba'al

trouble, you'll have a better chance of finding it. Visitors are strongly advised to keep their noses clean and to stay well away from any obvious trouble or precarious situations. Don't travel into the destitute neighborhoods, especially at night. Don't associate with questionable individuals, and stay away from problem areas.

The Tourist Police hut (Quinta at 10th Street) is manned nearly 24 hours a day and most officers are bilingual and can help with any problems. They patrol the beach and the main roads in town and are well respected by locals.

There are dozens of budget hotels within a short walking distance of the bus station.

TIME ZONE

The entire state of Quintana Roo is on Mexico Central Time, which is GMT –6 hours, the same as U.S. Central Time. Mexico honors daylight savings time on a schedule similar to the United States., daylight savings starts the first Sunday in March (clocks move forward by one hour) and ends the last Sunday in October.

WEATHER

Month	High Temp.	Low Temp.	Ocean Temp.	Rainfall
January	80°F	66°F	75°F	3.75 inches
February	81°F	67°F	76°F	2.25 inches
March	83°F	70°F	77°F	1.75 inches
April	84°F	72°F	78°F	1.75 inches
May	87°F	76°F	80°F	4.75 inches
June	88°F	77°F	83°F	7.75 inches
July	89°F	77°F	85°F	4.25 inches
August	89°F	76°F	85°F	4.25 inches
September	88°F	75°F	84°F	9.00 inches
October	86°F	73°F	82°F	8.50 inches
November	83°F	71°F	81°F	3.75 inches
December	81°F	68°F	79°F	4.25 inches

History of the Playa del Carmen Region

> "In the beginning all was invisible. The sky was motionless.
> There was only water, the quiet ocean, the silence, the nights.
> Then there came the word."
>
> —From the *Popol Vuh*, sacred Mayan scriptures

PLAYA DEL CARMEN owes its growing popularity to the nearby resort town of Cancún, just 40 miles to the north, and Cozumel Island, just 12 miles to the east. The influence of these two towns has helped shape Playa since the days of the Mayans.

Playa del Carmen is named for Our Lady of Mount Carmel, the patron saint of Cancún. She was named for a town in Italy, which was the first place where a chapel was built in her honor, in 1263, before her ascension into heaven.

The first recorded visitors to the beaches of what is now Playa del Carmen came during the Early Classic Period (ad 300–600) of the Mayan civilization. Then called *Xaman-Ha*, or "waters of the north," Playa was a rest stop of sorts for travelers making their way from the great cities of the Mayan world to the island of Cozumel. These travelers readied their dugout canoes and prepared for the journey across the straits on the same shores that now house the restaurants, hotels, and nightspots of modern-day Playa del Carmen.

Cozumel, called *Ah Cuzamil Petén*, meaning "island of the swallows," by the Mayans, was a sacred site and home to Ix-Chel, the goddess of fertility and wife of Itzámna, the god of the sun. Young women across the Mayan empire, from present-day Yucatán, Honduras, Belize, and beyond, journeyed to Cozumel on a sacred pilgrimage to pay homage to Ix-Chel and pray for fertility and healthy childbirth.

In return for the dozens of shrines and temples that the Mayans constructed, Ix-Chel is said to have gifted the people with the graceful swallow, or *cuzamil*, which led the Mayans to give the island its name. Many of the temples for Ix-Chel have survived, including San Gervasio, which can still be visited today.

Meanwhile, on a sheltered sandbar known to the Mayans as *Kankun*, or "nest

LEFT: Mayan-inspired sculptures adorn many resorts. Philip Gamon

Growth

If you think the Riviera Maya's explosive growth came as a surprise to the Mexican government, think again. The growth plan was forecast in the mid-1970s by then-governor of Quintana Roo, Rojo Gomez. The following message was sent to President Luis Echeverria:

> *"We have prepared an integral plan for the development of the coasts of Quintana Roo, whose beauty is unparalleled and which has many attractive sites. It has beautiful beaches, clear ocean water, wild jungles and hidden Mayan ruins, which have yet to be explored because of lack of access. We have located 100 kilometers of coastline whose features promise a great future for tourism in the area."*

of snakes," the temples of El Rey were constructed as a ceremonial site and resting place for the society's nobles. The site is now adjacent to a golf course and across the highway from the Hilton Hotel, making it a popular destination for visitors to Cancún who want to see Mayan ruins but are not able to get to the more major sites in the region, such as Tulum, Cobá, or Chichén Itzá.

Cancún did not have many other sacred sites because it was so narrow and did not have good access to the mainland, though the ocean breezes and proximity to various shallow lagoons did make it a nice place to live for the natives who fished along its shores and harvested food from the mangroves.

During the post-Classic period (AD 1000–1500), the area around Playa del Carmen, Cancún, and Cozumel served as a major trade route and religious center, and the Mayan culture flourished and prospered. At its height, the walled city of Tulum contained splendors beyond belief, and the nearby town of Cobá was a spiritual center of the entire Mayan empire, with a population of nearly fifty thousand. Near the end of this period, the populations dwindled as the natives dispersed due to storms and wars and to seek gentler climates.

Juan de Grijalva, a Spanish explorer, passed close to Playa del Carmen in 1518 and then discovered Cozumel while en route to Cuba, several hundred miles to the east. He didn't stay for long, but word of his find traveled fast, and his countryman Hernan Cortez returned the following year, bringing Catholicism and little appreciation for the Mayan way of life. Cortez and his men demolished Mayan temples and built a Catholic church, and he also brought something else with him when he landed on Cozumel—smallpox. The disease spread quickly within the island's close-knit community, and the population was decimated, dropping from 40,000 to less than 200 within 50 years.

The first European settlement in the region was at Xel-Ha, just a few miles south of Playa del Carmen, which had been a Mayan outpost and is now an ecotourism theme park. Over the next two hundred years, the Spanish traveled throughout the Playa del Carmen area and the Yucatán, spreading Catholicism and disease as they went. Many Mayans resisted the new religion, and small communities retained their traditional ways and their sacred cultures. During the 1700s and 1800s, pirates set up shop on the nearly deserted shores of Cozumel, using it as a base for their marauding forays across the channel to Playa del Carmen and elsewhere around the region.

Meanwhile, trade continued in and around Playa del Carmen, given its location midway between the port city of Veracruz to the north and Honduras to the south. Local commodities, including salt and honey, were bartered for goods imported from other regions, giving the area a taste of the diversity, commerce, and—yes—tourism that would eventually secure its place in the Mexican economy.

John L. Stephens and Frederick Catherwood passed through the Riviera Maya in 1842 as part of their expedition to the Mayan ruins, documented in their excellent book, *Incidents of Travel in Yucatán*. In the book, Stephens writes about what they saw and the people they encountered while Catherwood presents exacting drawings of the ruins. The book is incredibly precise and detailed, and it's still used by scholars, archaeologists, and Mayan enthusiasts today.

In 1848 the Mayans and various Spanish refugees began to resist the Spanish occupation more aggressively, leading to an uprising known as the War of the Castes. During the struggle, a large group of the oppressed set out from the Yucatán town of Valladolid and traveled across the peninsula, settling in Cozumel, which led to a regrowth of the island's population. Other natives took cover in the ruins of Tulum, which made a great fortress given its walled perimeter. The town of San Miguel de Cozumel was officially established in 1840, and a couple decades later, United States President Abraham Lincoln pondered using the island as a place to send freed American slaves and even went so far as talking to the Mexican government about purchasing it.

Due to the remote location and its dense, inhospitable jungle environment, Playa del Carmen and the surrounding area kept a low profile for the rest of the 1800s. In 1902 the region was finally granted status as a territory of the country of Mexico, and it was named after Gen. Andreas Quintana Roo, of the Mexican army. That same year, on November 17, the town of Villa del Carmen was officially founded near the site of what is now Playa del Carmen's Leona Vicario Park. Charles Lindbergh stopped in Cozumel in 1928 in the storied *Spirit of St. Louis* plane. The island was used as a base by the U.S. Navy during World War II and was then abandoned again until the 1960s, when scuba adventurer and documentary film producer Jacques Cousteau visited the island with an underwater camera crew and began to show the world the beauties of the Great Mayan Reef (second in size only to Australia's Great Barrier Reef), which runs between Cozumel and Playa del Carmen for hundreds of miles.

Tulum was the most sacred site in the region for the ancient Mayans.
Riviera Maya Destination Marketing Office

Tourism visionary Fernando Barbachano purchased much of the land that currently makes up Playacar in 1966. The sale included nearly a

Where Did My Bathing Suit Go?

If you continually misplace something on your trip, don't blame your traveling companion—it may be an *alux* (pronounced "aloosh") playing pranks.

Aluxes are, according to Mayan superstition, mischievous elfin or childlike creatures that live in the tropical jungle and play tricks on those who don't believe in them or give them proper respect. Some stories claim that the aluxes were originally clay or stone carvings placed in the Mayan religious temples that later came to life.

Many Mayans and other locals claim to have had run-ins with aluxes. They can cause the phone to ring at odd hours of the night, and when it's answered, no one is on the other end. They can move objects around the room and sometimes even steal bits of food. To curry the favor of the aluxes, many people build them little houses or shrines on their property. Once appeased, the aluxes become good luck charms, helping to ensure a good harvest, bring about good fortune, and protect the believers from other dangers.

Many hotels in the Riviera Maya, even some large and well-established ones, have homes for the aluxes on-site, in hopes that appeasing them with a comfy dwelling will encourage them to be friendly, though they rarely talk about it. Ask your waiters and housekeepers, though, and chances are they'll know what you're talking about—and will probably have a story of their own to share.

mile of barren beachfront, stretching south from where the ferry dock now sits. The pricetag was a now-paltry $13,600, but it was a serious risk at the time. He subdivided the land and sold it in small parcels, the first of which sold in 1977 for $15,550, proving just how masterful his idea really was. The single most important factor in the development of the region came in 1967, when the Bank of Mexico and the country's tourism development commission identified Cancún as the location for one of its mega-development projects (along with Ixtapa, Los Cabos, Loreto, and Huatulco). In the original government documents, the area was called "Kan Kun," which quickly morphed into the more Spanish "Can Cun," and then eventually shortened to just "Cancún."

Bridges were built, sewer lines were laid, and electrical poles sprang up. The first Cancún hotels, opened in the early 1970s, were the Palacio Maya, Playa Blanca, Cancún Caribe, Camino Real, and Club Med. In 1970 a wooden boat dock was built on the central beach in Playa del Carmen, and shortly thereafter, ferry service started to Cozumel. In 1974 Quintana Roo was granted Mexican statehood and the Cancún International Airport opened for business, with a bamboo and palm air-traffic control tower and a single taxi waiting for arriving planes. Two years later, the city's Pok-Ta-Pok golf course opened with 18 holes, many with views of the ocean and minor Mayan ruins. Over the next ten years, Cancún grew from a coconut jungle visited only by traveling fishermen and a few loco gringos to a world-class tourist destination. The local population boomed as workers from across the country poured into Ciudad Cancún to find jobs and establish their families. The Playa del Carmen airstrip was laid in 1979 and the area's first hotel, the Balam Ha (where the Playacar Palace is now), opened the next year, and land along Fifth Avenue was given away to employees of the Calica mining company.

Cozumel experienced a growth spurt of its own, as recreational scuba diving became more popular and affordable and more and more divers came to witness for themselves what they had been able to see only on the Jacques Cousteau television show.

Despite a few bumps along the way, including lack of airline support, the devaluation of the peso, and a series of hurricanes, Cancún and Cozumel continued to grow and prosper. Somehow, though, Playa del Carmen lagged behind, as the city to its north and the island to its east developed more quickly. As the growth went on around it, Playa del Carmen was still known only as the ferry landing for boats traveling back and forth between Cozumel and the Quintana

2012: The Arrival of a New Mayan Era and Portal Maya

The Mayan calendar ended at 11:11 AM on December 21, 2012 (the winter solstice), coinciding with an extremely close alignment of the path of the sun and the galactic equator (the Milky Way's midpoint). In the years leading up to the event, many said it'd be the "end of the world," although the Mayans themselves had called it the dawn of a new "Golden Age."

In honor of the occasion, Mexican sculptor José Arturo Tavares was commissioned to create a new gateway to Playa that paid tribute to its Mayan ancestors and philosophies.

Debuting on that fateful December date late in 2012, Tavares's Portal Maya became a new landmark in in the heart of the square where the city began.

Commissioned to mark the dawn of a new Mayan era in 2012, the Portal Maya arch was created by Mexican sculptor José Arturo Tavares. Chip Rankin

Today, the 50-foot-tall, 50-foot-wide bronze arch frames the Caribbean Sea, telling of the region's ancient and modern influences. It depicts a man carried on a spiral of wind joining hands with a woman atop a swirl of water. At either side, the bases of the arch feature relief sculptures of larger-than-life figures, ranging from ancient Mayans, to noble fishermen, to bikini-clad beachgoers.

As much a sign of Playa's own growth and evolution as it is a Mayan marker, Portal Maya has become a magnet to those who see it. People move closer to take photos, inspect the sculptural details, watch the free evening Mexican and Mayan dance performances, and simply take in the view.

Portal Maya is grand and quirky, solemn and funny. It's not afraid to be itself, even if it may be doing so on a bigger budget these days. Even as it grows up and out into a new era, Playa remains a place unlike any other.

Roo mainland. A handful of fishermen lived in huts on the beach and a few optimistic entrepreneurs sold tacos and handicrafts to the hurrying travelers, but tourists and locals moved quickly through town on their way to the more established locales.

Playa was a tiny outpost in the 1970s. The church in the center of this photo is still there, at the northwest corner of the town square. Cancun History Center

In its hippie heyday, Playa del Carmen's visitors would while away the day along the beaches south of town. The small cove now occupied by the Gran Porto Real hotel was close enough to the town square to be convenient, but being just out of sight of the ferry dock made it the preferred place for those who liked to sunbathe au naturel. At night, tourists returned to the beach for the freewheeling and ultracasual nightlife under the stars, a refreshingly unpretentious antidote to the pulsating discotheques that were becoming so popular in nearby Cancún. During a full moon, locals and tourists alike congregated on the beach for a ceremonial "lunata" celebration, complete with bonfires, cold Coronas, and skinny-dipping—a tradition that must have made the Mayan gods smile (especially Ix-Chel, the goddess of fertility!).

But starting in the early 1980s, little by little, street by street, the tiny fishing village and ferry town began to grow. New shops, restaurants, and even a couple of hotels opened their doors, luring the passing visitors to stay a while. The first hotels were built of bamboo and palm fronds, with slatted wood doors—not to keep out thieves, but to prevent the wild pigs from entering and looking for food.

Disaster struck in September 1988, when Hurricane Gilbert slammed into Cozumel and the Riviera Maya with 170 mph winds, blowing the roofs off hotels, pulling trees out by their roots, smashing windows, and flooding the streets. Inside the storm, the barometric pressure was 26.23 inches, the lowest sea-level pressure ever recorded in the Western Hemisphere. The hurricane caused more than $80 million in damage in Cozumel alone, and it changed the face of the region for years.

In the early 1990s, Playa del Carmen became a regular stop for the cruise lines, exposing Playa to a new breed of revelers. Soon after, the

Ten "Old School" Spots for Nostalgic Riviera Maya Regulars

1. Antigua Posada Barrio Latino hotel (Playa del Carmen)
2. Blue Parrot restaurant & bar (Playa del Carmen)
3. Casa Denis restaurant (Cozumel)
4. CasaSandra hotel (Isla Holbox)
5. Costa del Mar hotel (Playa del Carmen)
6. Eclipse Hotel (Playa del Carmen)
7. La Habichuela restaurant patio (downtown Cancún)
8. La Rana Cansada hotel and La Ranita Bar (Playa del Carmen)
9. Ojo de Agua hotel and restaurant (Puerto Morelos)
10. Pension San Juan hotel (Playa del Carmen)

Local Lingo

Cenote: A rare geological feature of the Yucatán, a *cenote* is a freshwater sinkhole formed when the limestone ground caves in and fills with water from underground rivers.

Colectivo: A sort of taxi-bus combination, a colectivo is a van or similar vehicle used for local transportation. It has semi-fixed routes and is cheaper than a taxi.

Costa Maya: The coastline south of the Riviera Maya (which officially ends at Tulum).

Federal: Used when referring to Highway 307, a federal highway.

Ha: Mayan for "water." You'll see it used everywhere.

Mole: A chocolate-based sauce made with dozens of herbs and spices, used in traditional Mexican cooking.

Muelle: Spanish for "dock," it's commonly used when referring to the ferry landing, which is also called the "embarcadero."

Nopales: Sliced cactus from the nopal tree, it's used locally in breakfast juice and can be served grilled or sautéed with any meal of the day.

Palapa: Thatched palm used to make roofing in the Riviera Maya. The tight weave keeps out rain and has to be replaced every couple years. The word is also used generically to refer to any structure that has a thatched-palm roof.

Pan dulce: Literally "sweet bread," it's used to describe a variety of delicious locally made breakfast pastries. For a quick start to your day, order a *café con pan dulce*.

Parada: Spanish for "bus stop."

Playa: Meaning "beach" in Spanish, this is the short name used locally when referring to Playa del Carmen.

Playacar: A name created in 1992 to refer to the tourist development located just south of First Street and the ferry dock.

Propina: Spanish for "tip." Make sure you check your bill to see if tip has already been added: *propina incluida*.

Quinta: Spanish for "fifth," it's the name used for Fifth Avenue, the main tourist strip in Playa del Carmen.

Riviera Maya: The name used to refer to the area from just south of Cancún to Tulum. The actual boundaries tend to change a little bit, depending on whom you talk to. The phrase was coined in the early 1990s and is sometimes said in English, "Mayan Riviera."

Tacos al pastor: Pork tacos cooked on a vertical spit, seared with licking flames and served with pineapple slices.

Tiempo compartido: Spanish for "time share." If a deal is too good to be true, like a Jeep rental for $20 a day, chances are it's part of a *tiempo compartido* offer.

outdated Cozumel ferry boats were replaced with sleek and modern jet-powered watercraft, which made the trip from the island faster and easier on the stomach and brought in even more visitors.

Guadalajara-based tourism giant Grupo Sidek purchased thousands of acres of land along the shoreline just south of the ferry landing, with designs to develop the area that had been dubbed "Playacar." First came the Continental Plaza (in 1992; now the Playacar Palace). Later that year, the Diamond Resort (now the Allegro Occidental) was inaugurated, marking the first opening of an all-inclusive resort in the Riviera Maya. A golf course opened in September 1994, and then hotel after hotel rose from the jungle, changing the face of the community forever.

On the other side of the ferry dock, development continued as well, but government-imposed density restrictions kept away large-scale hotel projects, and small, family-run inns dominated the landscape. From 1990 to 1997, the local population grew from 2,000 to 20,000, and 100 new families were moving to town each month, establishing Playa del Carmen as Mexico's fastest-growing city, a title it held for most of the first decades of 21st century.

The main road paralleling the beach, Quinta Avenida, or Fifth Avenue, became the town's principal street and was lined with restaurants, shops, hotels, and other businesses catering to the tourist trade. Favored by European backpackers and U.S. and Canadian budget travelers, Playa del Carmen began to make a name for itself on the international travel scene. Known as the place where the hippie lifestyle was not only accepted but celebrated, "Playa," as the in crowd called it, had arrived.

In 1999, the area's mayor, Miguel Ramón Martín Azueta, worked to popularize the term Riviera Maya for the land between Cancún and Tulum, which had previously only been referred to as the Cancún–Tulum Corridor.

A larger-than-life, record-spinning neon Jesus absolves partygoers at La Santanera.
Chip Rankin

By the late 1990s, Quinta had extended more than a mile north of the ferry dock, and much of it was closed to vehicular traffic, creating a pedestrian-friendly walkway that developed a unique character unknown in other parts of the world. In the early 2000s, Quinta stretched past Constituyentes Boulevard (between 18th and 20th Streets), and the area was dubbed "La Nueva Quinta," sometimes called "Little Italy," "Upper Playa," or simply "The New Playa." Italian-style cafés stood next to taco stands that stood next to gourmet steakhouses, creating a town with a truly eclectic and international flair. The beach north of Constituyentes also saw some changes. A second ferry dock was built, two large-scale resort hotels were constructed, and a couple of beach clubs sprang up, offering food and drink service, *palapa* and chair rentals, and towel service for the cruise passengers, day-trippers, and guests from hotels that aren't on the beach.

As the upscale all-inclusive hotels of Playacar introduced the town to more affluent travelers, the tone of the village continued to change. The thatched-roof bus station was rebuilt with electric displays and molded plastic seats. Across the street, McDonald's opened up, then a couple of Starbucks, and up and down the coast, more and more resorts were carved from the jungle. Renovations began on Quinta as work crews buried the utility lines and paved the gravel road with cobblestones, giving the road a bit of colonial inspiration to go along with its nouveau chic attitude.

Hurricanes Emily and Wilma, both devastating storms with deceivingly demure names, tested the region's will in the summer and fall of 2005, when they sliced similar paths across Cozumel, Cancún, and the Riviera Maya. Emily raged with sustained winds of 135 mph, shearing off rooftops, leveling trees and signs, shattering windows, rearranging beaches, and sending sixty thousand tourists scrambling for shelter. Wilma completed the one-two punch by hammering the area three months later with 150 mph winds and a storm surge topping 11 feet in Cancún. Tourists were confined to shelters for days, and it took some nearly two weeks after the storm to finally get a flight back home. Hotels in Cancún were hit the hardest, though all along the Riviera Maya there was extensive flooding and wind damage. Some hotels closed for days, while others took weeks or even months to reopen.

The region bounced back, though, as the communities worked together to rebuild and restore the splendor of the area. In fact, the town's resilience through adversity seemed to prove its staying power, as the condo boom kicked into high gear in early 2007. One of Playa's original hotels, the Corto Maltes, turned to condos. The El Faro Hotel, site of the landmark lighthouse did the same. Up and down each block, workers could be seen converting hotels to condos and building new structures where there were none. The area north of Constituyentes saw an especially strong push, with new developments going up on nearly every block. Most complexes were small, with no more than 12 or 14 units, but others are much larger, threatening to change the face of the town.

Quinta features a growing mix of international chains and local businesses. Chip Rankin

In 2009, another challenge to the area arrived in the form of the H1N1 "Swine Flu" scare, which kept international tourists away, drove occupancy levels to rock-bottom levels, and even caused many hotels to close, at least temporarily. Later in the year, though, the tourists returned.

A massive beach renovation effort pumped in thousands of tons of sand from the ocean seafloor, building up the beachfront and widening it in many areas, which helped to reverse the

Hurricanes of the Riviera Maya

1951, Hurricane Charlie: Made landfall in the Riviera Maya with 125 mph winds.

1955, Hurricane Janet: Walloped the tiny town of Xcalak and Chetumal.

1967, Hurricane Beulah: Came ashore as a category 2 storm, causing widespread damage.

1980, Hurricane Allen: Weakened as it approached the region, sparing it from harm.

1988, Hurricane Gilbert: Smashed into Cozumel with 170 mph winds and a 15-foot storm surge, caused more than $80 million in damage on the island alone, stranded a 125-foot Cuban freighter (the *Portachernera*) on the beach in Cancún, and killed more than 300 people after it crossed the Yucatán and hit northern Mexico.

1995, Hurricane Roxanne: Slammed into the Riviera Maya with 115 mph winds.

1998, Hurricane Mitch: This massive storm was expected to hit the area but curved away. An American tourist was killed in a boating accident near Cancún related to the rough water.

2003, Hurricane Claudette: Skirted the area with tropical storm–speed winds before continuing on to Texas.

2004, Hurricane Ivan: Made a beeline for the Yucatán, causing heavy rains and high waves along the coast, before curving north and slamming Florida.

2005, Hurricane Emily: Struck Cozumel as a category 4 storm, then crossed the Riviera Maya near Puerto Aventuras, causing widespread damage, some severe, though the area recovered after a quick cleanup.

2005, Hurricane Wilma: Just three months after Emily, Wilma became the most intense hurricane ever in the Atlantic Basin. The eye lingered over Cozumel and Cancún for nearly a day, causing severe damage to waterfront areas and flooding much of the region.

2007, Hurricane Dean: Made landfall in the middle of the night just north of Chetumal and Majahual, south of the Riviera Maya, as a Category 5 storm. Nearly 150,000 residents evacuated to shelters. Some small towns were cut off for days and about a third of the hotels in Tulum received at least moderate damage.

2008, Hurricane Dolly: Before it was a full-fledged category 1 hurricane, the weak tropical storm crossed directly over Cancún with no noteworthy damage.

2010, Hurricane Alex: Still a tropical storm when it crossed the Yucatán Peninsula, Alex did only minor damage before it entered the Gulf of Mexico, became a category 2 storm, and slammed into northeastern Mexico.

2011, Hurricane Rina: The fourth major hurricane of the 2011 season formed in the Caribbean Sea south of the Yucatan Peninsula. Though it barreled toward Cancún and the Riviera Maya, it suddenly weakened to a tropical storm before hitting the coast.

2012, Hurricane Ernesto: Ernesto hit the town of Mahahual with a fairly light touch, bringing lots of rain and knocking down some trees and power lines.

The old and the new mingle peacefully in Cozumel.

effects of storm erosion and made the beaches wider and more beautiful than ever.

Playa del Carmen celebrated the end of the Mayan long calendar on December 21, 2012. Leading up to the event, many pointed to the date as an end-of-the-world prophecy. However, scholars of the Maya (and those who listened to them) knew the date represented a grand new era of rebirth. To mark the occasion, the debuted Portal Maya, a grandiose, 50-foot bronze arch commissioned from Mexican sculptor José Arturo Tavares. Rising from the town square just behind the city's main beach, the curving structure ties the story of the Maya to the Playa del Carmen of today.

By the middle of 2014, the Riviera Maya had surpassed Cancún in the number of hotel rooms available and was celebrating its status as one of the top international tourist destinations in the world, with about 41,000 hotel rooms and 4.1 million visitors a year—30 percent of whom are European. Expatriates from more than 45 countries around the globe call Playa del Carmen home, and the town seems to thrive on the notoriety.

And through it all, Playa has stayed true to its roots, somehow preserving its almost magical charm and exceptional character. It is still a place where travelers from around the world come together to lounge on the beach, toast the day with a cold beer, sip a hot cappuccino, and celebrate life. And in a town where backpackers from crowded hostels, newlyweds from fancy all-inclusives, and European trendsetters from chic new condos all cozy up to the same bars, it's easy to understand why Playa so easily works its way into your heart.

Acanto Boutique Condo Hotel's rooms and suites surround a peaceful courtyard steps away from the heart of Quinta. Acanto Boutique Condo Hotel

The ruins of Xaman-Ha can still be seen in modern-day Playa del Carmen. The main temple is along the beach just south of the Playacar Palace hotel and is now a popular spot for wedding ceremonies. Many other shrines dot the Playacar development, including the golf course. And though it may be hard to envision a time when the Mayans carved their dugout canoes from local trees and plied the waters to Cozumel, today's visitors to Playa will undoubtedly feel a sense of the grand history, the sacred importance, and the incredible natural beauty that have lured visitors to its sandy shores for thousands of years.

As one longtime local resident puts it, "No one knows what makes Playa so special, but everyone seems to return."

1

Playa del Carmen

PLAYA DEL CARMEN is in the geographic center of the Riviera Maya and the region's principal city. It's the seat of the municipal government and is home to the area's primary lodging, dining, nightlife, and shopping options.

Playa, as the locals call it, is the only town in the region whose development fills the land between Highway 307 and the beach. Within the past decade, it has even spilled onto the west side of the now elevated highway, an area that has seen development including major shopping centers and local housing. Its growth shows no signs of slowing down.

No longer a sleepy fishing village, Playa has grown into a cosmopolitan beach resort, while somehow staying true to its roots, typified by its laid-back lifestyle, low-rise development, international flavor, and casual come-as-you-are vibe. Visitors will find small local inns next to luxury villas, taco shacks next to steakhouses, and dusty cantinas next to stylish lounges. The mix of people and cultures, the variety of tourist offerings, and the welcoming spirit of the locals make it a unique travel destination, not just in Mexico, but in the entire world.

A WALKING TOUR OF PLAYA DEL CARMEN

Take a walk through some of the older parts of Playa del Carmen and glimpse samples of the town's Mayan past, its dynamic present and its international-flavored future.

600 Years of Arrivals & Departures

Start at the very center of the Riviera Maya—the gazebo in the town square where Quinta Avenida (Fifth Avenue) meets Juarez Avenue. Stand in the center of the gazebo and gaze out at the bustling plaza, with its park benches, flowering plants and shade trees (notice the painted white trunks), and the massive new 50-foot-high Portal Maya sculpture arch in front of the beach. Walk toward the water and

LEFT: Downtown Playa from 22nd to 12th Street. Reina Roja Hotel

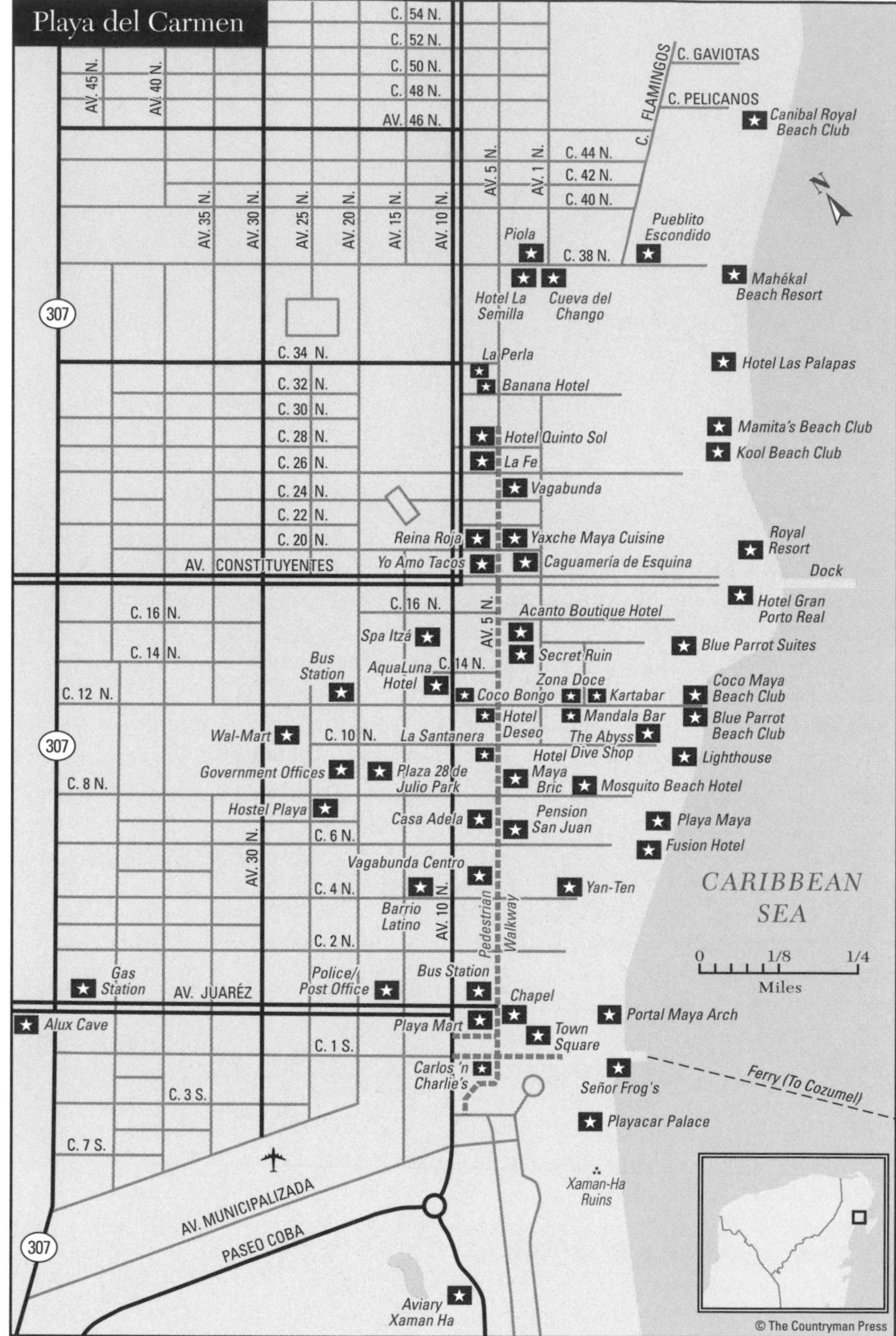
Playa del Carmen
C. 54 N.
C. 52 N.
C. 50 N.
C. 48 N.
AV. 46 N.
AV. 45 N.
AV. 40 N.
C. GAVIOTAS
C. FLAMINGOS
C. PELICANOS
Canibal Royal Beach Club
C. 44 N.
C. 42 N.
C. 40 N.
AV. 5 N.
AV. 1 N.
AV. 35 N.
AV. 30 N.
AV. 25 N.
AV. 20 N.
AV. 15 N.
AV. 10 N.
N
Pueblito Escondido
Piola
C. 38 N.
Mahékal Beach Resort
Hotel La Semilla
Cueva del Chango
307
C. 34 N.
La Perla
Hotel Las Palapas
C. 32 N.
Banana Hotel
C. 30 N.
C. 28 N.
Hotel Quinto Sol
Mamita's Beach Club
C. 26 N.
La Fe
Kool Beach Club
C. 24 N.
Vagabunda
C. 22 N.
C. 20 N.
Reina Roja
Yaxche Maya Cuisine
Royal Resort
AV. CONSTITUYENTES
Yo Amo Tacos
Caguamería de Esquina
Dock
C. 16 N.
Acanto Boutique Hotel
Hotel Gran Porto Real
Spa Itzá
Blue Parrot Suites
C. 14 N.
Bus Station
AquaLuna Hotel
Secret Ruin
C. 12 N.
Zona Doce
Coco Maya Beach Club
Coco Bongo
Kartabar
Hotel Deseo
Mandala Bar
Blue Parrot Beach Club
Wal-Mart
C. 10 N.
La Santanera
The Abyss Dive Shop
Lighthouse
Government Offices
Plaza 28 de Julio Park
Hotel Maya Bric
Mosquito Beach Hotel
C. 8 N.
Hostel Playa
Pension San Juan
Casa Adela
Playa Maya
C. 6 N.
Fusion Hotel
Vagabunda Centro
C. 4 N.
Yan-Ten
CARIBBEAN SEA
Barrio Latino
Pedestrian Walkway
C. 2 N.
0
1/8
1/4
Miles
Gas Station
Bus Station
AV. JUARÉZ
Police/Post Office
Chapel
Alux Cave
Playa Mart
Portal Maya Arch
C. 1 S.
Town Square
Carlos 'n Charlie's
Ferry (To Cozumel)
C. 3 S.
Señor Frog's
Playacar Palace
C. 7 S.
Xaman-Ha Ruins
AV. MUNICIPALIZADA
PASEO COBA
Aviary Xaman Ha
© The Countryman Press

The town square in Playa del Carmen borders the beachfront.

consider buying a cup of fresh fruit (cantaloupe, watermelon, mandarins, mangos, cucumbers, and coconuts), topped with chili and lime for $2. If you're already thirsty for a cold beer or frosty margarita, the *palapa* bar at the beachfront is a good place to watch the action on the beach while sitting in the shade. Head south from the bar and you'll see a low-rise cement building on your right, serving as navy barracks and topped with radio antennas. The soldiers at the entrance are armed with machine guns and are usually willing to pose for a picture.

It's all smiles in the Riviera Maya. Penny Atkinson

Keep going south to the ferry dock, which was first built in 1969–70 and has regular departures for Cozumel Island, located 11 miles offshore. Peek inside the Sr. Frog's Bar and check out the VW bus turned into a DJ booth and the swinging barstools modeled after lifeguard throw buoys. Turn right and head uphill toward the Carlos 'n Charlies restaurant. Cut left a half-block up, at an arched passageway between two shops, and walk towards the Playacar Palace hotel. This was the first "large" hotel in town and was called the Continental Plaza when it opened. You'll see a small Mayan shrine on a little ridge to your right, but keep walking parallel to the creek and a block past the hotel to where the road takes a sharp left toward the beach and you'll see an even bigger one.

This is the Xaman-Ha ("Waters from the north") structure, an important ceremonial shrine discovered in 1528 by Francisco de Montejo (the same Montejo whose name was given to a local beer from Merida that's sold around town). Mayan women would pray here before heading across the straits to Cozumel in their dugout canoes to worship Ixchel, the goddess of fertility. A placard at its base tells more of the story. Follow the trail around the ruin and cut back toward the tennis courts, heading back north on Coral Negro Street through a quiet residential area with million-dollar homes straddling the creek, which varies from dry to several feet deep, depending on recent rainfall. Go past the guard post and peek over the rail to your left to see a cave that has been carved into the creek bed. Access was blocked off in the late '90s, but it's still interesting to look down and ponder what sort of ancient Mayan rituals may have taken place there 600 years ago. Curve to the left and follow the short street to the next intersection, where you'll see a statue standing at the corner. Turn left here and then take an immediate right on the first street, and head west on a short road that dead-ends into the fence at the head of the runway of the Playa del Carmen Airport, built in 1979.

A small Mayan shrine is tucked away in this alley off Fifth Avenue.

Turn right here and you'll be heading north on 15th Avenue, flanked by an elementary school on your right. The first intersection is Juarez Avenue. Turn right onto Juarez and head back in the direction of the beach. This is a hectic street with mopeds and taxis buzzing by, plus buses arriving and departing at the ADO bus terminal that will be on your left, which is the former site of the town's original tortilla factory.

Keep going straight and you'll arrive at the tiny Playa del Carmen chapel, which was erected in 1964 and underwent major renovations in 2007 to build the water bridge, add the rear glass wall, and resurface the exterior whitewash. Respectful visitors are welcome to step inside the church and enjoy the ocean view behind the altar and a calming respite from the bustle of the town square. No padded kneelers are present, as worshippers simply kneel on the floor. No photography is allowed and donations placed in the receptacle by the door help with regular upkeep.

This may be a good time to stop at the Playa Mart shop, located at the same intersection as the bus station, for a bottle of water, quick snack, or maybe an enormous velvet sombrero and a bottle of mezcal with a worm at the bottom. Next, you'll want to head north on Quinta, the main pedestrian thoroughfare through the heart of the tourist zone. On your right, you'll see a religious shrine of another kind—the local McDonald's. Take note, though, even this American hamburger joint has a thatched-palm roof, as if that somehow helps it blend in. An ATM is on this same block, if you're feeling low on cash. Stay on Quinta for two blocks, enjoying the rush of locals mixed with guests of nearby hotels, day-trippers from the all-inclusive resorts along the coast, and cruise ship escapees stretching their legs. Chances are good you'll be offered fake Cuban cigars, drink specials, a date with someone's sister, or a prescription for Valium if you hang around very long. You might also see flute-toting musicians, a parrot "driving" a remote-control car, or a tiny colorful monkey on someone's shoulder—all willing to pose for a picture for a few pesos.

Sneaking Around

The second intersection is Fourth Street and you'll want to turn right here, heading downhill toward the beach. On your left, you'll pass a convenience store and an old painted sign for the Yan-Ten Beach Club. The facility is mostly defunct now, but it avoided the condo rush because it hides a large freshwater *cenote*, making it nearly impossible to build around. Enter through one of the corridors leading behind the convenience store, or even go straight into the Yan-Ten entrance to catch a glimpse of the *cenote*, currently occupied by a family of resident turtles and used as an aqua playground for the families living on the property.

Playa del Carmen's original church is in the town square.

Backtrack a bit up Fourth Street and go past Quinta this time. On this block, you'll discover a castle-like structure that was built as the town's first indoor shopping mall in the early 2000s, though it was so ill-conceived, with no parking and a maze-like interior, it lasted only a few months before closing down. Keep heading uphill on Fourth Street to 20th Avenue and turn right.

Keep going another block to the city hall municipal building. Turn into the main structure on your left, and enter the courtyard to view a nice fountain backed by a huge colorful mural depicting life through the years in Playa del Carmen. The park across the street has a walkway with goal-post-like arches bearing the names of various towns within the Playa del Carmen municipal district, plus upright rocks displaying the state song and others showing how to count to 20 in the native Mayan language. Depending on the day, there may be a free show at the amphitheater on the northeast corner of the park. Head back toward the beach on 10th Street and look for the Santanera bar on your right, which offers sweeping views of the beach and of the action along Quinta below it. Continue down 10th Street toward the beach and the lighthouse that crowns the beachfront condo complex.

Walk out on the beach and look beyond the waves and you can see the hotels that make up Cozumel's northern hotel zone. Walk to your left on the beach and you'll find the Blue Parrot Beach Club, where you'll see topless sunbathers of every shape and size and maybe catch a glimpse of the fire dancers rehearsing for their weekend night shows. Cut up through the complex next to the dance floor, past the reception area, and out to the street.

Playa's Past & Present

You're now at the eastern end of the 12th Street Party Strip, or *Zona Doce*, as I like to call it, though locals haven't progressed from called it simply "la doce." Head uphill past Mezcalinna's, Kartabar, Mandola, Di Vino, and the other patio lounges that make up Playa's trendiest district. Turn right back onto Quinta and head north for a couple of blocks.

Once you're back on Quinta, between 12th and 14th Streets, look on your right for a statue of a Mayan god, with feathered headdress. It marks a small passageway that leads to a nearly forgotten Mayan ruin, about the size of a Volkswagen Beetle. It sits behind a chain-link fence, marked with a signpost from the National Institute of Archaeology, but is otherwise nondescript, with little to explain its history or any other fanfare. Still, though, it's fun to see and try to envision how the native Mayans may have used it. Perhaps it had something to do with the gulley that you can see if you follow the hallway to the right of the ruin, past some of the town's least-trafficked storefronts.

Keep heading north on Quinta and you'll approach a tree on your right,

Most people never realize this lagoon exists.

The Mexican flag flies proudly over the municipal building in downtown Playa del Carmen. Brian E. Miller Photography/www.lomimonk.com

heavily adorned with glass orbs and rings of lights, first put there when the UltraFemme and UltraJewels shops opened in late 2007. It's especially nice to see at night, when it provides a warm glow visible from blocks away. The big intersection ahead is Constituyentes Avenue, marked with a large Olmec head (the predecessors of the Maya) statue in the center of the traffic circle. Across the street is Yo Amo Tacos, which serves good tacos and great margaritas. Take a picture with the giant cow, which is Playa's version of Kip's Big Boy. The structures to the north of here didn't exist ten years ago and now constitute the area known as the "New Playa," "Little Italy," or the "International District," depending on who you talk to.

If you're not tired yet, keep walking north on Quinta. The primary tourist district continues for another 20 blocks or so, with dozens of restaurants, bars, and shops ripe for exploring. Turn right anywhere along this stretch and you're only two blocks from the beach. This is where Mamita's Beach Club and other popular wave-watching spots can be found.

After all that walking, I think it's time for a Corona. Or a margarita, or a piña colada . . .

Checking In

Best places to stay in and around Playa del Carmen

For some travelers, selecting a hotel is part of the fun of a visit to Playa del Carmen. There are more than 450 hotels offering some 41,000 rooms in the Riviera Maya, with many of them in the greater Playa area. Within a 2-mile radius, visitors can see more than 100 hotels, many of which, while not necessarily large, would be perfectly suitable for most needs. (Many of the area's hotels—about 75 percent—have 30 rooms or fewer.) Though many people choose to book a hotel prior to arriving, for most of the year it's completely possible to show up without a reservation and take a stroll around town looking at different properties and current prices before making a final decision. Most hotel operators will happily give travelers a quick tour of their property and rooms, and sometimes will be willing to negotiate a discounted price.

Accommodations range from student hostels and inns with very few amenities that cater to budget travelers to large self-contained resorts with first-class facilities and services. "Concept hotels," such as Hotel Deseo and Reina Roja, offering trendy accommodations (and typically nightlife) in uniquely designed surroundings, have become an integral part of the local hospitality landscape.

Many hotels offer a wide range of room choices, with simple beach cabañas, modern hotel rooms, and luxury villas within the same resort. The most important considerations are location (on the beach, on Quinta, or in town), budget, and desired atmosphere (romantic, singles, quiet, traditional). The selections in this chapter are organized into three different price-range categories—budget, midrange, and luxury—and within each category there are a wide range of choices to please a wide range of tastes.

This statue on Constituyentes honors the Olmec, who lived in the region even before the Maya.

BUDGET HOTELS

Generally located a few blocks from the beach, between the town square and 30th Street, these properties are considered to be clean and safe but don't have many of the amenities that many travelers are accustomed to. Most don't have swimming pools, beautiful views, or on-site restaurants, and the rooms may not have in-room bathrooms, air-conditioning, or balconies. Prices range from $15 for a bed in a hostel dorm room to $75 for a well-kept room in a family-run inn with ceiling fan, purified water, and in-room safe. These hotels are popular with budget travelers, students, and short-term visitors who just need a place to stay for a couple of days while traveling through.

The 16-room Italian-owned ★ **Barrio Latino Hotel** (Fourth Street between 10th and 15th Avenues, www.hotelbarriolatino.com) is a popular base for Europeans, student travelers, and those who could stay at one of the more luxurious properties around town but choose the smaller inn for its local charm, traditional character, and family-like service. Just 1½ blocks from Quinta, the hotel provides quick access to the town's restaurants and nightlife. Rooms are secure and clean, with private bathrooms and ceiling fans. Many have air-conditioning. The owners can book most of the same tours that the larger tour agencies can, but they return their sales commission to their guests, resulting in a nice discount.

With fewer than 20 rooms, a common terrace, and a rooftop sundeck, the three-story **Hotel Banana** (Quinta at 32nd Street, www.hotelbanana.net) has the feel of a large and friendly home. Set in the middle of the action, it's a few blocks from Kool and Mamita's beach clubs. The young and outgoing staff can make local recommendations and plan day trips.

There's always something going on at **Siesta Fiesta** (Quinta between

Eighth and 10th Streets, www.siesta fiestahotelplaya.com), a hot spot in the middle of Playa's busy pedestrian walkway, which can be a good or bad thing. A restaurant and bar in the cozy courtyard features several hours of live music each night and a large-screen TV for live sporting events and recorded concerts. Vacation camaraderie is especially strong here, making it a great spot to meet and socialize with other travelers.

The friendly, family-run, 12-room ★ **Pension San Juan** (Quinta between Sixth and Eighth Streets, www.pension sanjuan.com) is located right on Quinta. There is an incredibly charming outdoor kitchen for guest use on a terrace overlooking Quinta, which gives you the sense that you're in your own private café.

Xtudio Comfort Hotel (Quinta between Fourth and Sixth Streets, www.xperiencehotelsresorts.com) promises clean, comfortable stylish rooms and a friendly staff at a simple price. Rooms are large and the décor is simple, but modern. Guests have privileges at the rooftop deck at Xtudio's sister property, Hotel Illusion.

The small, 16-room, **Hotel Alux** (14th Street between 10th and 15th Avenues, www.hotelalux.com) features contemporary Mexican design and hacienda-inspired furnishings—a good choice for visitors who don't mind being a couple blocks removed from the action.

A longtime favorite for budget travelers, the 36-room **Hotel Vista Caribe** (Quinta at Sixth Street, www .hotelvistacaribe.com) has a great location on Quinta only a block from the beach and boasts a small swimming pool and flower garden.

The family-owned 29-room **Maya Bric Hotel** (Quinta between Eighth and 10th Streets, www.mayabric.com) is a good spot to meet other divers if you need a dive buddy. The hotel also used to go by the name of Tank-Ha, the name of a local dive center formerly located on site. There is a shaded pool for basic dive instruction and divers can book their trips onsite.

With its stucco walls, *palapa* roof, green grass, and stone walkways, **Luna Sol Hotel** (Fourth Street between 15th and 20th Avenues, www.lunasolhotel .com) charms from the moment you see it. Each of the 16 rooms opens onto a grassy courtyard.

The 14-room **Koox City Garden Hotel** (Constituyentes at First Street, www.kooxhotels.com) was formerly known as Posadas Las Iguanas and still retains much of its small-town charm. The relaxing pool is located amidst a

The Pension San Juan is a budget-minded hotel on Fifth Avenue.

tropical garden filled with flowering plants.

Students, singles, and extreme budget travelers also have some great local spots to choose from. Located about a half mile from the beach and directly across from the Walmart, the inexpensive **Hostel Playa** (25th Avenue at Eighth Street, www.hostelplaya.com) is a good alternative for students and budget travelers who want a safe spot without frills. Rooms feature brightly colored natural wood and have mosquito netting, orthopedic mattresses, and clean bedding. Guests can use a fully equipped kitchen and a common living room with sofas, TV, and DVD player. At night, the central lounge area takes on an almost magical atmosphere, conjuring visions of a granola-traveler's version of the Hogwarts dining room, as small groups gather around tables drinking beer, digging through guidebooks, and sharing tales from the road. Cash only.

Named for Cuban Revolutionary Che Guevarra and topped with a lively rooftop bar under a *palapa*, student favorite **Hostel Che** (Sixth Street between 15th and 20th Streets, www.hostelche.com.mx) primarily offers dormitory sleeping with bathrooms in the suites, basic kitchen and laundry facilities, a lounge area with TV, and a computer with free Internet access.

Centrally located, the popular **Hostel Rio Playa** (Eighth Street between Fifth and 10th Avenues), located one block from the beach and a half-block from Quinta, is also a great spot to meet other travelers, with a rooftop pool and bar. It offers private rooms and 14-person mixed and women-only dormitory rooms.

Bright and vivid **Tres Mundos Hostel** (North Sixth Street between 20th and 25th Avenues, www.tresmundoshostel.com) offers mixed and women-only dormitories and private rooms in a location five minutes away from Quinta and a block away from Walmart.

MIDRANGE HOTELS

Located on or near Quinta, or even on the beach, these hotels are sufficient for most travelers. Many have swimming pools, restaurants, bars, and other amenities. They generally have air-conditioning, and all have private bathrooms. Prices range from $80 for a standard hotel off the beach to $120 for a property with a premier location (on Quinta or the beach), air-conditioning, and upgraded amenities. They are popular with travelers who want to stay somewhere comfortable with a local feel, without spending too much money.

The friendly and centrally located ★ **AquaLuna Hotel** (10th Avenue and 14th Street, www.xperiencehotelsresorts.com) features ten rooms just a block away from the action on Quinta. All rooms have king-sized beds and are decorated with a Mediterranean-Caribbean aesthetic. Rooms are all non-smoking, The affordable hotel offers comfort, convenience, and style at a very affordable price.

Also from Xperience Hotels and Resorts, **Hacienda Paradise** (10th Avenue between 20th and 22nd Streets, www.xperiencehotelsresorts.com) boasts 33 rooms filled with hardwood furniture typical of the traditional Spanish haciendas. Patios or balconies overlook the garden and swimming pool. A favorite hotel amongst travelers seeking style and comfort at a friendly price, the hotel is also home to the restaurant Nuestra Casa and a spa. Rooms are all equipped with wifi, cable TV, ceiling fans, and safes that can easily hold a laptop.

20 Popular Spots for Student Travelers

1. 100% Natural restaurant (Cancún & Playa del Carmen)
2. Antigua Posada Barrio Latino hotel (Playa del Carmen)
3. Babe's Noodles & Bar (Playa del Carmen)
4. Banana Hotel (Playa del Carmen)
5. Blue Parrot bar (Playa del Carmen)
6. Weary Traveler hostel (Tulum)
7. Casa Tequila—La Tequilaria Shop & Bar (Playa del Carmen)
8. Coco Maya Beach Club (Playa del Carmen)
9. El Fogon restaurant (Playa del Carmen)
10. El Oasis Mariscos restaurant (Playa del Carmen)
11. Hostel Playa (Playa del Carmen)
12. Hostel Rio Playa (Playa del Carmen)
13. La Zebra Beachfront Cabanas & Cantina (Tulum)
14. Litros bar (Playa del Carmen)
15. Mezcalinna bar (Playa del Carmen)
16. Pizza Pazza restaurant (Playa del Carmen)
17. Screamink Tattoos (Playa del Carmen)
18. Señor Frog's bar (Playa del Carmen)
19. Hostel Che (Playa del Carmen)
20. Vagabunda restaurant (Playa del Carmen)

The 29-room ★ **Fusion Hotel** (Sixth Street at the beach, www.fusionhotelmexico.com) has a great beachfront location, just a block from the most bustling part of Quinta. The rooms are oriented around a central courtyard and are reminiscent of a Spanish villa, with winding staircases and meandering sidewalks. The lively beach club features seaside drinks and dining and a nightly fire show.

Opened in 1984, ★ **La Rana Cansada** (10th Street between Quinta and 10th Avenue, www.ranacansada.com) is one of Playa's oldest and most beloved hotels. Loyal guests return year after year for the consistently comfortable colonial-style accommodations, central location, true beach town ambiance, and friendly service from

The beach at the Fusion Hotel has drinks and snacks during the day and a fire dancer show each evening.

Construction walls promise to be a frequent site along Quinta as old hotels and storefronts make way for new hotels, shops, and attractions. Chip Rankin

the Swedish hosts and Mayan staff. Just a couple blocks from the beach and a half-block from Quinta, the hotel has 15 simple, individually designed rooms (upgrades with air conditioning are available), a community kitchen, and a lounge area.

Illusion Boutique Hotel (Eighth Street between Quinta and the beach, www.xperiencehotelsresorts.com) from Xperience Hotels offers 41 spacious guest rooms featuring marble floors and bathrooms adorned with precious ticul stone mined in the region. All rooms either overlook a central courtyard or the Caribbean Sea itself, just a half block away.

One of the original beach hotels in Playa, the modest 38-room colonial-style **Costa del Mar** (First Avenue between 10th and 12th Streets, www.hotelcostadelmar.com) has kept up with the times but has retained its simple and relaxing nature. The beachfront El Pirata serves draft beer and snacks at a wooden bar with swinging bar stools. Directly adjacent to the Blue Parrot bar (see Drinks & Dancing), guests have ready access to the nighttime revelry. Rooms near the beach can be a bit loud at night, so choose one near the street if you want to go to bed before the clubs close.

The artsy 18-room **Eclipse Hotel** (First Avenue between 12th and 14th Streets, www.hoteleclipse.com) has themed rooms, including the two-story Robinson Crusoe Suite, the De Luxe Suite, and the Caribbean Palapa Suite. Each eclectic and casually rustic room features original decor and artwork, a unique floor plan, wooden furnishings, and other extras, including some with air-conditioning. The courtyard has some large palm trees, hammocks, and gardens. It is a favorite of traveling artists, young couples, backpackers, and others who enjoy character and charm in their accommodations.

With shaded hammocks set amidst a lagoon-like sunken garden and waterfall, **★ Luna Blue Hotel & Gardens** (26th Street between Quinta and 10th Avenue, www.lunabluehotel.com) evokes a lost-in-time quality not always easy to find in a modern resort destination. Formerly known as the Zanzibar, it was completely renovated in late 2005, partly with the help of Hurricane Wilma and partly with the help of the ambitious new owners from San Francisco, who have worked to constantly update and refine the hotel, both inside and out.

Even though it's right on Quinta, the similarly named **Hotel Lunata** (Quinta between Sixth and Eighth Streets, www.lunata.com) also seems somewhat secluded once you pass through its narrow entrance, adding an air of seclusion and sophistication not found in other downtown hotels. The decor is contemporary hacienda style, designed by architect Angel Isles, with archways, earth tones and blues, river stones, dark woods, iron, and tile. The hotel has the feeling of an old-style guesthouse, with only ten rooms, each with its distinct charm.

Quirtky and rustic, **SHALALA Casa Hotel** (38th Street between Quinta and First Avenue, www.shalala hotel.com) features five bungalow rooms around a funky outdoor area. Each room is unique, with a rustic design belying the comfort to be found in sheets with 1,500 thread counts.

Magic Blue Boutique Hotel (10th Avenue between 10th and Twelfth Streets, www.hotelmagicblue.com) offers a modern tropical atmosphere, relying on dark woods rather than the stucco or concrete that is frequently seen in the region. With 44 rooms arranged around a large grassy area, swimming pool, and bar, the open grounds offer a more relaxed feel than many of the more tightly laid out properties in downtown Playa.

Recently renovated, the Italian-owned **Hotel Quinto Sol** (Quinta at 28th Street, www.hotelquintosol .com) is a Mediterranean/Mexican hacienda-style hotel in the heart of Quinta's international section. The midsize hotel has much of the same style and class as some of the area's more expensive hotels, yet its prices are more moderate.

Located above a busy restaurant and bar, the 14 rooms and penthouse suite at ★ **Posada Freud** (Quinta between Eighth and 10th Streets, www.posadafreud.com) define funky chic. Request a room with air-conditioning.

LUXURY HOTELS

The best of the best, these hotels and resorts cater to international travelers accustomed to the finer things. Most big hotels have multiple swimming pools, restaurants, bars, fitness rooms, business centers, and concierge service. The smaller concept hotels are lighter on on-site amenities, but high on style and status. All generally have efficient air-conditioning, satellite TV, spacious rooms, well-designed bathrooms, guest balconies, and on-site restaurants, and many also have room service, Internet access, and other amenities associated with a first-class hotel. Room rates range from $125 per night for a highly rated tourist-class hotel up to more than $500 per night for a room at a top-of-the-line all-inclusive resort.

Constructed on the former site of Playa's original nudist beach, the family-friendly, all-inclusive, 287-room ★ **Gran Porto Real Playa del Carmen** (Constituyentes Avenue at the beach, www.realresorts.com) was the first large-scale hotel built on the town's main tourist strip rather than Playacar. It has Italian and Mediterranean decor and overlooks a waveless cove at the southern end of Playa's central beach. There are five restaurants, four bars, a nice pool, a car rental desk, a day spa, and a kids' club. Guest favorites

Ocean Safety

Many beaches along the Riviera Maya use a colored flag system to alert swimmers of the ocean's condition:

Black: No swimming allowed. Used to denote swift current, dangerous tides, lightning, or other serious problems. Seldom seen and should be taken very seriously.

Red: Caution urged. Dangerous conditions possible. Used to mark crashing waves, presence of rocks, or other potential hazards. Common at high tide or on windy days. Good swimmers can still enter the water but should be careful.

Yellow: Stay alert. No known issues, but swimmers should stay aware. Most common flag flown in the area. Used on all but the calmest of days. Competent swimmers should not be dissuaded from enjoying the water.

Green: Ideal conditions. Safest swimming possible. Seen only on the best of days.

include the 24-Hour Room that's always stocked with snacks, drinks and even bottles of booze, and the thatched-roof beach bar, with rope-swing barstools and a view of the entire main bay. This is also one of the very few hotels with a view of the sunset over the ocean. It's perfect for guests who like the full range of services offered by a large-scale resort but want to be in the middle of the Playa del Carmen bustle rather than tucked away in Playacar or farther out in the Riviera Maya.

Its sister property across the street, the adults-only ★ **The ROYAL Resort Playa del Carmen** (Constituyentes between First Avenue and the beach, www.realresorts.com) is even more upscale. With 518 rooms and a grandiose portico reminiscent of Cancún or even Las Vegas, it is by far the largest hotel on the Playa del Carmen side of town. The sand on the beach is great, the water is calm, and it's one of the better beaches in the area. In fact, it's the site of many weddings, which make for a fun distraction for the sun-worshippers that always inhabit the waterfront area. It has six restaurants, four bars, a massive pool, an ultra-luxe day spa, a *temazcal* sweat lodge, and a full fitness center, which offers daily spinning and pilates classes. Next door is Mamita's Beach Club, a popular day-tripping site for cruise passengers and trendy beach-goers. Guests lounging poolside or beachside will enjoy butler services that include cleaning sunglasses, cold towel services to battle the heat, a choice of 20 varieties of suntan and sunscreen lotions, and the delivery of newspapers, magazines, and books in varied languages. The ROYAL is among the first resorts in the region to offer online check-in 24 hours before arrival, allowing guests to choose their room from available options the day before they arrive.

Located in the newly bustling northern part of Quinta, the independently owned, adults-only ★ **Casa Ticul Hotel** (Quinta between 38th and 40th Streets, www.casaticul.com) opened in early 2008. Though named after an old Yucatan city south of Merida known for clay pottery and leather shoes, the environs here are decidedly more contemporary. A cozy lobby feels like a stylish home in 1930s Europe and the quaint courtyard, small pool, and sundeck look especially charming after the sun goes down. Thoroughly modern, the 20 rooms feature dark wood furnishings, luxury bedding with pillow-top mattresses, and nice bathrooms with rain showers. A great stretch of beach is 2½ blocks away.

Marking a new milestone in downtown Playa del Carmen itself, the new 332-room **Hyatt Playa** is located along 460 feet of white sand beach immediately north of The ROYAL (scheduled to open in 2015). It's notable as the first large American resort brand within Playa's city limits.

Sometimes it seems that all smaller Playa hotels aspire to belong to the new guard of concept hotels, but there are some noteworthy standouts.

Built around a central pool and swanky bar, ★ **Hotel Deseo** (Quinta and 12th Street, www.hoteldeseo.com) offers 15 very minimalist, but very cool, rooms. Think Miami Beach meets Beverly Hills meets Riviera Maya. The walls are crisp white, and lounge music is piped in from the hotel bar. On the nightstand, you'll find incense, earplugs, and condoms. The beds are amazingly comfortable, and the rooms have stage lighting, so you can create your own shadowbox show, if you're so inclined. It's a good place to meet other travelers, and it's always a plus when there's a happening bar right outside your door. Best bet for the young and single crowd.

Charming, romantic, and intimate, ★ **Acanto Boutique Condo Hotel** (16th Street between First and Fifth Streets, www.acantohotels.com) is situated in the very heart of Playa, tucked around the corner from Quinta and

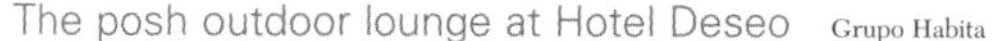
The posh outdoor lounge at Hotel Deseo Grupo Habita

Hit the Beach

Playa, plage, spiaggia, beach: However you say it, and in whatever language, the white powdery beaches of the Riviera Maya are undeniably—and justifiably—the region's main draw. Though not quite as flourlike as the shoreline in Cancún, the crushed-shell beaches in and around Playa del Carmen are world renowned for their softness, white color, and cleanliness.

The moon rises after a fun day at the beach.

All ocean beaches in Mexico are considered federal property and are open to the public. No hotel, landowner, beach bar, or other entity may legally restrict access to the beach. That being said, it is common for hotels to cordon off an area for the exclusive use of their guests, and this is generally accepted, as it seems to do more good than harm for the most number of people. All-inclusive hotels, for instance, may serve food and drinks on the beach, and it is helpful to their servers if their guests are slightly removed from other beachgoers. Some beach bars set up a perimeter around their beachfront tables and do not allow minors to enter and can even have a cover charge, but the area cannot extend all the way to the water line, so nonpatrons can still freely pass by without being hassled. In some spots, resorts have set up a roped-in area where their guests can use beach chairs and beach umbrellas without being hassled by passing vendors or other nonguests.

Amazing beaches abound in the Riviera Maya. Riviera Maya Destination Marketing Office

Licensed vendors can set up chairs and shaded *palapas* and can legally charge for their use. The general rule is, unless you're staying at the hotel that owns the facilities, you are not allowed to use them. Still, though, many tourists successfully beach-hop and visit a number of different beaches and rarely have problems using any lounge chair they happen by. Sometimes ordering a drink can earn you access to a good beach spot, and having a beach towel that matches the color of the ones the hotel provides helps, too.

Many of the main beaches, including the beach just north of the ferry dock in Playa and along the shallow cove of Akumal, are secured by federal lifeguards, who are well equipped and well trained to handle most emergencies. The nature parks, including Xcaret, Xel-Ha, and Tres Rios (see chapter 8), have private guards on duty to keep an eye on bathers and assist with any problems. With the lack of undertow, little poisonous marine life, clear water, and well-marked swimming areas, accidents are relatively uncommon, though, and the beaches are considered quite safe.

Some areas, though, do require a bit more caution. Keep an eye out for submerged rocks, shallow reefs, and off-course WaveRunners. Be careful also to avoid the black spiny sea urchins, floating debris, and diving into shallow water. If you're exploring remote areas, it's a good idea to stay in a group and not wander off alone. It's also important to keep in mind that although the Riviera Maya is generally safe and most of the people are friendly and welcoming, every town has its bad apples, and you don't want to encounter them. Even though the beaches are government property, locals may not take too kindly to tourists wandering too far from the beaten path and encroaching on their home territory. Be careful not to enter private property that is adjacent to the beach and be respectful of locals who have claimed a beach area for themselves.

A lifeguard stand on Playa's main beach shines in the moonlight.

Petty theft can be a problem anywhere, including on the beach. Keep a watchful eye on your belongings if you stray from them or, better yet, take turns playing in the waves and leave someone on the beach to watch your things. And don't assume that just because you're on a remote spot and can't see anyone that no one can see you. Stories abound of snorkelers who come back to their beach blankets after a stint on the reef only to find their bags pilfered. Though some may choose to deny that there could be crime in paradise and instead blame the pesky and ever-curious white-faced monkeys, the thieves' penchant for cash, MP3 players, smart phones, and digital cameras leads me to believe the culprits are looking for more than bananas.

The city police in Playa del Carmen sometimes patrol the popular beaches of town on ATVs. They are mainly looking for rowdy drunks and local drug users, so the average tourist, even a Corona-guzzling one, is almost never bothered. In some areas, generally remote beaches, the Mexican Navy performs foot patrols, presumably checking for drug runners and drop-off sites. Be respectful, and they will pass by with just a friendly wave.

Playa del Carmen's most popular beach zone is just north of Constituyentes Avenue and the ROYAL Playa del Carmen hotel (18th Street) all the way to 40th Street. This includes the KOOL, Mamita's and Canibal Royal beach clubs.

set just one block from the beach. It offers easy access to the original heart of Playa del Carmen as well as Quint's popular new international stretch. Traditional décor conceals modern comforts and amenities, including a rooftop patio overlooking the sea. The boutique hotel features 1-, 2-, and 3-bedroom accommodations, including units with full kitchens, that surround a central courtyard and splash pool. Although the hotel is only a couple of blocks away from the bustling nightlife of 12th Street, you wouldn't know it when you turn the corner onto its quaint and quiet street. The smoke-free hotel welcomes families and couples and provides beach club access, free wifi, and international calling.

Simple, fresh and elegant, the bed and breakfast ★ **Hotel La Semilla** (38th Street between Fifth Avenue and the beach, www.hotellasemilla.com) features nine carefully curated guestrooms furnished from the spoils of Mexico's many once-grand haciendas. Modern comfort melds with a "Rough Luxe" design that is completely unique in Playa, but also manages to fit right in. Amenities are limited to the plush rooms, a covered outdoor kitchen and dining room overlooking the jungle, and a stunning garden courtyard. You'll think you're a guest at someone's meticulously designed home.

The boutique beachfront ★ **Mosquito Beach Hotel** (Eighth Street, www.mosquitobeachhotel.com) oozes a hip and cool style and comes complete with an on-site Mayan spa, sleek furnishings, premium bedding, and an exclusive design that exudes a sense of privilege and superiority, right down to the trendy red and black lounge chairs along the hotel beach. With the closing of its sister property on Quinta, the original Mosquito Blue Hotel, to make room for a shopping center, this hotel is now the sole property carrying the Mosquito name.

Mannequins at play at the Reina Roja bar.

One of Playa's tallest buildings, the literally over-the-top **Hotel Reina Roja** (20th Street between Quinta and 10th Avenue, www.reinarojahotel.com), glows red from the outside, and approaching visitors will spot it a block away. Mexican-owned, the hotel evokes Amsterdam's red light district, with bondage mannequins on display and a crimson glow that's replicated in the guestrooms. A party hotel for party people, it features a large bar, popular with the locals, and a massive rooftop bar with city views and a swimming pool. Five themed rooms—including the "After Hours Room," with DJ booth, disco lights, dance floor, and outdoor smoking area—are available for the extra indulgent. This isn't a exactly a "cozy" place, but it's very high in gimmick value, making it good for wooing a date or looking like you're in-the-know.

Adults-only **Be Playa Hotel** (26th Street between Quinta and 10th Avenue, www.beplaya.com) offers sleek and stylish rooms, complete with a large bathtub in each room. The

Local Lingo—Out on the Town

2 x 1. Look for this sign at the entrance to a bar, and you'll know that their two-for-one happy hour has begun! Don't see the sign? Try asking the bartender for "dos por uno" anyway—you might get lucky.

Anejo con coca. Anejo is a golden blend of aged rum, and it goes great with Coke, making it a bit of an upgrade from a standard rum and Coke. To order one in a loud bar, grasp your chin and move your hand downward, as if stroking a beard. Then, with the same hand, hold your pinkie under your nose for a moment, then wipe it away, as if you're snorting a powdered Colombian export from under your fingernail.

Barra libre. Some bars offer *barra libre* nights, where your cover charge includes open bar, or basically all you care to drink. This normally includes bottled water, so it's a good chance to hydrate as well.

Cantinero. Spanish for "bartender."

Chela/chelada/michelada/chamochela. *Chela* is colloquially used to mean "beer." A *chelada* is a beer served in a glass of fresh lime juice and salt. For a real local treat, try a *michelada*—a *chelada* plus Worcestershire, Tabasco sauce, and tomato juice. A recent twist, a *chamochela*, adds a tamarind-like fruit called a chamoy to the traditional *michelada*.

Consumo minimo. Translating from Spanish into "minimum consumption," it's a common policy at popular bars and clubs, where instead of a cover charge, your entry fee includes drink coupons equivalent in value to the amount you pay to get in. Such a policy keeps out patrons who just want to socialize and dance but not buy anything.

Cuba libre. "One revolution is still necessary: the one that will not end with the rule of its leader," wrote Cuban spiritualist Jose Marti, describing his desire for a free Cuba, which in Spanish is *Cuba libre*. It's also the name used locally for a rum and Coke served with a wedge of lime. In the Riviera Maya, bartenders will still understand if you just order a "Cuba."

Desechable. Remember, no bottles on the street, so if you want your drink to go, ask for it in a *desechable*, and it will come in a Styrofoam cup. Many bars also have a stack of them at the exit, so if you've got one for the road, leave your glass behind.

En las rocas. Spanish for "on the rocks." Try your margarita *en las rocas* and earn a bit of respect from your *cantinero*.

Frog's/Carlos. Abbreviated versions of Señor Frog's and Carlos 'n Charlie's, it's how the locals refer to the popular drinking establishments.

Lager. Used when ordering a Dos Equis (XX) beer in the green bottle, as opposed to the XX Amber, which is the dark beer in the tinted bottle. You can also hold your index fingers together to form an "X" in front of you, then pump your hands twice, indicating *dos equis*, or "two Xs." To order two or more Dos Equis, first flash the number of drinks you want with your fingers, then proceed to make the "X" sign.

Nohoch. The Mayan word for "big." Order your favorite cocktail *nohoch*, and it'll be served in a tall glass.

rooftop bar offers a sleek, stylish pool, dining area, and the expected stunning Caribbean views.

Guests traverse a wooden bridge from Quinta to reach the calmer lobby of the upscale ★ **Blue Parrot Fifth Avenue** (Quinta between 10th and 12th Streets, www.blueparrot.com), an extension of the local Blue Parrot brand. Eighteen spacious, Asian-inspired rooms are adorned with ornate *palapas* and are perched above a decorative pool. The scene is much more serene and sophisticated than at Blue Parrot's beachfront location, where guests have privileges at the Blue Parrot beach club.

The 22 units at the affiliated **Blue Parrot Suites** (First Avenue at 14th Street, www.blueparrot.com) have Bahamas-like contemporary rattan decor, with modern amenities and name-brand furnishings. A bit removed from the rest of the beachfront Blue Parrot complex, it is quite calm and relaxing. There is a small pool, and the beach is only a block away. Check in at the Blue Parrot bar on 12th Street 1½ blocks away.

★ **Playa Palms** (First Avenue between 12th and 14th Streets, www.playapalms.com) was known as the Blue Parrot until 2007, and this essentially remains the hotel at the Blue Parrot bar. As such, it offers the quintessential Playa del Carmen experience. It's more of a tropical community center than a hotel. Housed in a condo-style complex a block away from the reception and bar area, the 39 luxury rooms are spacious studios and suites with contemporary/tropical décor. A few have oceanfront views, but most are set back a bit from the beach, looking across at other units, with a partial ocean view to one side. There is a narrow pool between the buildings and a welcomingly shady courtyard. There is also a small group of rustic beachfront bungalows just north of the beach bar.

The décor is reminiscent of a Mexican hacienda, but with many modern upgrades. It has multiple sundecks where sunbathing in various states of undress tends to occur and is particularly popular with gay travelers.

Evoking the tone of a crisp Miami Beach escape, **The Palm at Playa** (Eighth Street between Quinta and 10th Avenue, www.thepalmatplaya.com) has 69 rooms surrounding a smart-looking courtyard filled with palm trees. Rooms are modern and quite comfortably luxurious. The de rigueur rooftop deck comes complete with pool, bar, and lounges.

Also offering minimalist rooms and a swanky lobby, and channeling the spirit of Fashion Week, **In Fashion Hotel Boutique** (North 12th Street between Quinta and 10th Avenue,

The Playa Palms hotel is on the beach and just a block from Fifth Avenue.

The second-story pool at the In Fashion Hotel Boutique In Fashion Hotel

www.infashionhotel.com) was designed to please the critical tastes of traveling divas, trendsetters, and other fashionistas. Across from Coco Bongo, the hotel has a swimming pool on the second level and overlooks the nightly street party on *Zona Doce*. Original paintings, sculptures, and photography are featured throughout this venue that's part Mexico City, part New York.

The new **Soho Playa Hotel** (10th Avenue and 24th Street, www.sohoplayahotel.com) is another stylish boutique hotel with a crisp, modern tropical design that would be at home in South Florida, Buenos Aires, Ibiza, or Los Angeles. In addition to comfortable rooms and a rooftop pool and bar, Soho Playa features a unique artist in residence program, focusing on and displaying the works of different local artists throughout the year.

The upscale **Hotel El Punto** (Quinta and Eighth Street, www.hotelelpunto.com) uses deep reds, dark wood, and natural stone to offset its elegant, understated style. A rooftop bar and tapas restaurant overlook the ocean.

Other area hotels celebrate the local, relaxed character of traditional Playa or the region in general. One of Playa's original hotels, ★ **Hotel Las Palapas** (34th Street at the beach, www.laspalapas.com) is still one of its most revered. It's a bit north of the main strip, so the beach is a touch more secluded, with no rocks, making it a great place to play in the water. There is a shady pool, Mayan-inspired lawn art, and an interpretive walking trail through the jungle. The hotel's 75 rooms are housed in spacious individual *cabañas* near the beach or in two-story villa-like buildings around a pair of grassy courtyards. The beachfront rooms don't have air-conditioning, but most of the rest do.

Appearing a bit Mediterranean, with cool blues and whites, the **Playa Maya Hotel** (on the beach between Sixth Street and Eighth Street, www.playa-maya.com) can be reached only by the beach, making it one of the few places in town where you get to feel the sand each time you come and go. Family-owned, the hotel has 20 rooms, giving it an intimate and relaxed feeling

Many of the guests at the Playa Maya Hotel visit each year. Playa Maya Hotel

absent at some of Playa's more-trendy options. A small pool makes for a nice dip, though the beachfront is the main attraction. It's one of the best in the area, with sandy water access, generally calm waves, and plenty of bikini-clad (or not) people-watching. A casual seaside restaurant serves up delicious coconut shrimp, fish ceviche, and other seafood and Mexicanzona doce dishes.

This eight-villa collection of **Blue Pearl Suites** (First Avenue between 10th and 12th Streets, www.theblue pearl.com.mx) feels more like a private apartment complex than a hotel. Located just a half-block from *Zona Doce,* it somehow retains its privacy and serenity. The owners, a charming couple from Mexico City, moved to Playa to live out a stress-free life, focusing on conservation, recycling, and natural living. All units feature local handcrafts, natural fibers, and hammocks.

Beachfront **Mahékal Beach Resort** (38th Street and Quinta, www .mahekalplaya.com) is laid out like an old Mayan village, with low-rise, thatched-roof *cabañas* housing most of the rooms. One of the original hotels built in the area and renovated for a new concept, it retains its local charm while keeping the facilities up-to-date. It is one of the last hotels on the northern edge of town, offering a remote sense of privacy.

★ **Villas Sacbe** (First Avenue between 12th and 14th Streets, www .villasacbe.com) offers privately owned one- and two-bedroom condos, each with its own unique and trendy decor. The complex has a narrow, meandering pool and Jacuzzi, and it's a great place to stay in luxury and still be close to the *Zona Doce*.

Even though it's on a busy intersection blocks from Playa's busy International District, **Arena Blanca** (38th Street between Quinta and 10th Avenue) offers solitude and relaxation just inside its locked gates and stone walls. A small table seems to float like an island in the center of the swim-

It May Be Paradise, but It's Still the Jungle

Even though Playa del Carmen and the Riviera Maya are exotic and wonderful beach vacation destinations, they're still relatively undeveloped and are in close proximity to the jungle. Set your expectations accordingly.

You should also remember that there are hassles and frustrations inherent to any travel situation. You're on vacation to have fun and celebrate life, so try not to let little challenges you encounter bother you.

If a chicken walks into your beachfront restaurant and pecks at your crumbs, don't get mad—take a picture. If a gecko streaks across the wall of your hotel room, don't call the front desk—give him a name and consider him your pet. If your shower runs out of hot water, don't complain to the concierge—it's good for your sunburn. And most importantly, if you find yourself at odds with your travel partner, it's time to hit the nearest bar, order a margarita, feel the warm breeze, and remember why you came here in the first place.

ming pool, visible from each of the 11 rooms in the three-story, classic Spanish building. Units, with domed brick Catalan ceilings, premium linens, tile floors, and marble countertops, are individually owned. Make reservations on sites like VRBO.com or the locally operated www.PlayaisFun.com.

Asian design influences abound at the ★ **Aldea Thai Resort** (28th Street and the beach, www.aldeathairesort.com), including ornamental statues set throughout the grounds. Thatched roofs, dark stone tiles, exposed natural wood beams, and sleek accents ensure a modern and upscale tropical environment.

On a corner, just a block off Quinta, the 45-room **La Tortuga** (10th Avenue and 14th Street, www.hotellatortuga.com) offers stylish rooms and a private and upscale ambience.

Local Flavors

Taste of the town—restaurants, cafés, bars, bistros, etc.

Playa del Carmen offers an incredibly wide variety of cuisine types and dining establishments. From hole-in-the-wall taco shacks offering complete meals for less than $5 and traditional Mexican steakhouses serving fine cuts of Angus beef and live lobster to stylish lounge-style restaurants serving Mediterranean and international cuisine, Playa is sure to please.

Restaurants have a tendency to come and go in Playa, especially on the very busy and popular Quinta, where property owners routinely raise their rents. Even with all this change, much also remains the same, and many old favorites remain. In truth, it's hard to go wrong with having dinner in Playa and strolling down Quinta. In fact, walking around and considering the options just might become one of your favorite evening rituals.

Breakfasts are normally inexpensive, with many restaurants posting their specials on a chalkboard out front. Choices include traditional Mexican

Not sure what to eat? Walk down Fifth Avenue for some ideas. Ricardo Vagg

dishes such as *pan dulce* (sweet pastries), *huevos rancheros* (ranch-style eggs), and *huevos Mexicanos* (Mexican-style eggs), and there are also American favorites such as pancakes, omelets, and steak and eggs and European choices such as bagels and lox, croissants, and crêpes.

Lunch is generally quite casual, with many travelers choosing to eat fresh seafood, sandwiches, or burgers on the beach or next to their hotel pool. Most restaurants in town are open for lunch, too, with happy-hour specials starting early and plenty of seats available at the sidewalk restaurants along Quinta.

Once the sun goes down and the stars come out, the lights of the restaurants, bars, and shops of Playa's main street start to twinkle, and candlelight glows from many eateries. The town begins to feel a bit like an international bazaar, with the restaurants competing for your business, hawking their specials, offering free drinks with a meal purchase, and tempting diners with live music, wafting smells, and attractive hostesses.

Choosing where to eat is sometimes half the fun, with many visitors making several laps along the almost 2-mile-long street, checking out the night's offerings and taking in the scene. Many restaurants put together sample entrées and place them on display next to their menus, showing you the exact size of their plump steaks, lobster tails, giant shrimp, or fish fillets. Each block has several options to choose from and one famous block, on Quinta between 28th and 30th Streets, has 12 restaurants, including seven intimate eateries in a row, each three-tables wide and two or three rows deep, ranging from a Mediterranean restaurant offering lamb and hookah pipes to an Asian noodle house to an Argentinean steakhouse.

If you're not sure what you're in the mood for or if you have a group of travelers with varied tastes, you're in luck, since many of the restaurants have extensive menus, spanning the range from tacos to pasta, from fish to steak, and from pizza to burgers.

Restaurants in this book are labeled as inexpensive, moderate, or expensive. The average meal price at an inexpensive restaurant is less than $8 per person. Moderate restaurant meal prices range from $8 to $20. Expensive restaurants offer meals starting at $21.

All of the locations in the *Budget Dining* section are ultracasual eateries catering to locals, students, and other budget travelers. They're good places to sample the local fare and use your Spanish. They typically don't accept credit cards and may have restrooms that aren't up to the cleanliness standards of some travelers. Even so, they're regulated by the health department and serve only purified ice and water.

BUDGET DINING

★ **El Fogon** (30th Avenue between Fourth and Sixth Streets, in front of Harmon Hall) serves a mixed-grill plate (*parrillada mixta*) big enough to serve three people. Try the fried nopal cactus.

A favorite with locals and ex-pats, the *palapa*-shaded ★ **Vagabunda** (Quinta between 24th and 26th Streets, www.vagabundaplaya.com) and its sister location ★ **Vagabunda Centro** (Quinta between Fourth and Sixth Streets) serves traditional American and Mexican breakfasts, crêpes, omelets, pastas, and cappuccino.

The surf-and-skate-inspired **Burro Playero** (Plaza Pelícanos at Eighth Street between 10th and 15th Avenues, Mamita's Beach Club at 28th Street and the beach, and Centro Maya at 50th Avenue and Highway 307, www.burroplayero.com) offers a fresh spin on Mexico's traditional standby favorite, with clever, taco-packaged options for an international audience.

You can also eat seafood with the locals at **Coctelería el Paisano**

Grab a cheap bite at La Vagabunda.

Peso-Pinching Activities

Traveling on a budget? Try these free and fun activities:

- Take free salsa lessons Tuesday and Thursday at 7 PM at La Bodeguita del Medio (see Dining).
- Walk along the interpretive nature trail at the back of the parking lot of the Las Palapas hotel (see Luxury Hotels).
- Visit the Xaman-Ha ruins in Playacar, just south of the Playacar Palace hotel (see chapter 5).
- Head to the beach and build a sandcastle in the shape of the great pyramid at Chichén Itzá.
- Get up early to watch the sun rise over the Caribbean. Some people like it even more than watching a sunset.
- Take advantage of the free appetizer/drink coupons offered by many restaurants along Quinta in Playa del Carmen.
- Stroll the park across from the municipal building, and learn to count in Mayan from the educational displays.
- Grab your snorkel and take a dip in Manatee *cenote*, across from Blue Sky Resort in Tankah (see chapter 5).
- Watch the fire dancers perform their nightly show on the beach in front of Hotel Fusion (see Drinks & Dancing) at 10 PM.
- Join the locals for a street party in Cozumel, complete with live music, each Sunday evening in the town square.
- Snorkel the protected cove at Akumal Bay and see moray eels, stingrays, and barracuda lurking in the shallows.

Veracruz (Avenue Juárez, just west of Highway 307), specializing in shrimp cocktail but also serving fried fish, ceviche, and other dishes. It's located away from the tourist zone, and you're likely to be the only travelers there. Most of the waiters don't speak English, but don't let that keep you away. Chances are you'll be able to communicate enough to order, or someone at the restaurant can help translate.

El Faisán y El Venado (Highway 307, just north of Avenue Juárez) is a popular local spot for tacos, quesadillas, and seafood. At midday, workers fill the plastic tables and order from the *comida corrida* menu, which offers hearty meals prepared and served quickly.

Just like the busy taco stands near where the locals live, the popular **Yo Amo Tacos** (Constituyentes at Quinta), Spanish for "I Love Tacos," serves fresh, hot tacos al pastor (cut right from the fire), beef tacos, and cheese tacos. Tables along the patio overlook the traffic circle near The ROYAL Resort.

The casual Argentinean-owned ★ **Tango Taco** (10th Street between

Get a cup of fresh fruit (with salt and lime) for $1 at the town square.

Dine for Less Than $15/Day

Breakfast—Tequila Barrel: Huevos rancheros served wfith refried beans, toast, and coffee ($5).

Lunch—Cart next to the town square bus station: Plump chicken tamales steamed in banana leaves ($2/each).

Dinner—Vagabunda: A value-conscious restaurant in the heart of New Playa. Fresh tacos with tangy salsa. ($4.50).

Drinks—Pick up a quart of beer from a grocery or convenience store and sit on the seawall in the town square, watching the world go by.

10th Avenue and 15th Avenue) serves up Argentinean meats, Mexican tacos, and amazing prices (huge grilled steaks go for about $10) just a block off Quinta.

Killer Taco (First Avenue between 10th and 12th Streets) a good place for cheap tacos on the way to or from 12th Street. The menu is written on a chalkboard and features beef tacos, quesadillas, burritos, and even pork tacos al pastor, cut right from the spit. Everything on the menu is $5 or less. They don't sell alcoholic drinks, but feel free to pick up a beer at one of the area convenience stores and bring it in to consume with your meal. Cash only. Open late.

BRO-chetas (28th Street and the beach, www.brochetas.mx) serves up delicious skewers of meats—including steak, chicken, and seafood at reasonable prices; located across from Mamita's Beach Club.

If you're tired of tacos, slices start at $1.50 at **Pizza Pazza** (Quinta at 14th Street; 10th Avenue between Eighth and 10th Streets), and drink combos are available. Open late, they're a favorite for satisfying after-party munchies. Open late.

MEXICAN & MAYAN

Feeling more like a private party at a stately hacienda in rural Mexico than a beach town restaurant, ★ **Casa Adela** (Quinta between Sixth and Eighth Streets, www.casaadela.com) offers some of Playa's best Mexican food and a warm and inviting atmosphere that makes diners want to linger and soak it all in. Upscale Mexican cuisine, mole enchiladas, and seafood top the menu. Diners are drawn to the combination of traditional and whimsical décor, but it's the food that brings them back for a second time. Seating is available indoors or outside on the pedestrian walkway.

Occupying a prime corner at the northern edge of the Paseo del Carmen Mall, **Carlos 'n Charlie's** (10th Avenue at First Street, www.carlosandcharlies.com) could be called the anchor

Mayan Cuisine

Contributed by Destination Riviera Maya *magazine*

Traditional Mayan cuisine integrates the delights of land and ocean: the beans, vegetables, and fruits cultivated, mixed with the products of fishing and hunting as part of the customs of a centuries-old society. Corn, chocolate, honey, and turkey not only are the main ingredients of delicious meals and beverages but also are an integral part of Mayan religious rituals, where chocolate became known as the "drink from the gods." Numerous spices such as peppercorn, coriander, achiote (similar to paprika), and cinnamon are used to make *recados*, special seasoning pastes that enliven chicken, fish, or beef dishes. Some traditional Mayan dishes include the following:

Cochinita pibil. The word *pibil* means "to roast in a hole," and luckily, modern cooks have devised a method that requires no shovel. The dish is typically made with pork and marinated with red *recado* and bitter orange. It is wrapped in banana leaves with onions and steamed or roasted, and then served with onions marinated in vinaigrette.

If you like it spicy, ask for *salsa habanero*. Brian E. Miller Photography/www.lomimonk.com

Poc chuc. Char-grilled pork marinated in sour orange with black beans, purple onion, tomato, and Mayan spices.

Papadzules. Tortillas stuffed with hard-boiled eggs and covered in a pumpkin seed and tomato sauce.

Frijol con puerco. Pork and black bean stew served with chopped radish, onion, tomato, and pieces of lime, eaten with a corn tortilla.

Relleno negro. Turkey, ground beef, and hard-boiled eggs in a blackened chile sauce.

Tikinxic. A whole fish marinated in achiote and sour orange with tomato, white onion, and green pepper slices, then wrapped and grilled in a banana leaf.

Panuchos. A fried tortilla filled with refried beans, pieces of turkey or chicken, lettuce, tomato, onion, and avocado.

tenant of the entire shopping plaza. This Mexico standard offers consistently good Mexican food, seafood, and pasta, though the main draw is the lively atmosphere, unique decor, and friendly waiters.

★ **La Cueva del Chango** (38th Street between Quinta and the beach, www.lacuevadelchango.com), or the "Monkey Cave," is an eclectic spot that manages to be rustic, funky, and romantic all at the same time—perfect

Bikes are a popular transportation choice for tourists and locals in the Riviera Maya. Chip Rankin

for a special occasion or just a night out. The menu features several cuts of steak, fish, shrimp, fajitas, and other Mexican specialties. The candlelit tables are in a jungle-like setting, making it very soothing and exotic. The restaurants features vegetarian and vegan menu options.

With an eclectically eye-catching design, the open, two-level Mexican gastropub ★ **Caguameria De Esquina** (First Avenue and 20th Street, www.caguameriadeesquina.com) easily attracts interest. It also pleases the stomach with unique dishes that began with traditional Mexican fare and went forward from there. The menu includes pan-tostadas, lobster burritos, *chanclas* (part pizza, part taco), sandwiches, and more.

With its Spanish-tiled roof and strolling mariachi bands, ★ **La Parrilla** (Constituyentes between Quinta and First Street, www.laparrilla.com.mx) puts diners in the mood for good Mexican meals, and it delivers. The best dishes include beef fajitas, grilled shrimp, and *chiles rellenos*, and there are also fresh salads and vegetarian dishes. Save room for the flambé desserts and flaming coffees, prepared tableside.

Offering seating along the sidewalk, in a spacious red interior or on a second-story terrace overlooking Quinta, ★ **Yaxche** (Quinta at 22nd Street, www.mayacuisine.com) is one of Playa's most respected restaurants. It serves authentic Mayan cuisine, including fish, chicken, and turkey, all cooked with native methods using traditional spices. Yaxche is the Mayan name for l*a ceiba,* a green-leafed tree believed to bring good luck. Try the Mayan Kiss after-dinner drink, made with Xtabentún and Kahlúa.

★ **La Perla Pixán Cuisine and Mezcal Store** (34th Street between Quinta and Tenth Streets, www.laperlaplaya.net) offers up traditional Oaxacan dishes and unique mezcal combinations in a simple, but charming covered outdoor restaurant. Although just a few doors down from Quinta, the

Authentic Mayan food with an upscale style at Yaxche

restaurant gives off a remote and even slightly mystical vibe. It's enough to make you wander if there are any magical ingredients in those fine mezcals and tasty original sauces (which include flavors like prickly pear and habanero, mole with almonds, and cheese sauce with mezcal).

Situated in the garden of the small SHALALA Casa Hotel, ★ **Fonda Regina** (38th Street between Quinta and First Avenue, www.shalalahotel.com) serves up fresh Mexican breakfasts made from local ingredients and drawing from Caribbean and Latin American influences.

Both locations of **Mi Pueblo** (Quinta and Eight Street, Quinta and 34th Street, www.mipuebloplaya.com) serve up fresh and delicious traditional Mexican fare. The newer northern location is particularly spacious, with a large outdoor patio surrounded by overgrown jungle.

A sports bar and Mexican cantina, **Pez Vela** (Quinta at Second Street, www.pezvela.com) has several settings in one spot: There is a bar with swinging bar stools, a central dining area with plastic tables, a few sidewalk tables, and some TV-front tables, perfect for watching live sports games, which seem to always be on. The menu, which includes tacos, grilled shrimp, and burgers, is inexpensive and good for the price. For the best deal, order beer by the bucket (five bottles).

Aldea Corazon (Quinta and 14th Street, www.aldeacorazon.com) offers a modern, refined spin on traditional Mexican cuisine and margaritas. Opt for a table in the back of the restaurant in the peaceful jungle garden next to the *cenote*.

Other popular stops include **Origenes Cocina & Bar** (Quinta at 38th), which uses traditional spices to prepare its contemporary Mexican cuisine, and **El Templo** (Eighth Street between Quinta and 10th Avenues), which serves typical Mexican dishes on a large second-story terrace on a busy side street, an ideal spot for relaxing and sipping a cold beer.

ITALIAN

At La Fe Restaurante (Quinta between 26th and 28th Streets) you'll think you've been transported to an Italian beach town and stumbled upon a friendly neighborhood restaurant where everybody knows each other. Tables line the sidewalk and covered terrace and are filled each evening with local and visiting Italians sipping imported wines, munching on fresh bread, and feasting on pizza, pasta, and seafood dishes. The boisterous late-night crowd spills well into the blocked-off road, turning the bar scene into a bit of a street party, with techno music booming and gelato, cappuccino, wine, and tequila each being enjoyed in abundance. Italian and French voices are much more common than English or Spanish, but everyone is welcome to join in the fun.

Serving three meals a day, the sidewalk café ★ **Il Baretto** (Quinta at 26th Street, Quinta at Eighth Street) is also somewhat of a headquarters for the Italians residing in Quinta's international neighborhood. More than just ex-pats appreciate Il Baretto's pasta, pizza, seafood, and beef menu items, though. The restaurant also serves imported coffee drinks, espresso, and cappuccino and is known for sumptuous desserts.

An old Playa favorite, ★ **Ristorante Da Bruno** (Quinta at 12th Street, www.dabrunoplaya.com) is known for both its authentic Italian menu and its premium people-watching perch in the heart of Quinta. The owners and chefs are Italian, the pasta is made in-house, and the food tastes fresh and hearty. Top dishes include gnocchi, pizza, ravioli, antipasti, prosciutto, mahimahi, lobster, and, of course, tiramisu.

Another local favorite, the tiny

Don't sit; swing at the bar at Pez Vela.

Fast Food in Paradise

Face it: After a few days of beer drinking, taco eating, and sensory overload, it's nice to be in the familiar confines of a McDonald's, Starbucks, or another American chain.

Although all chains offer the same fare you know back home, the McDonald's outlet across from the bus station at Quinta and Eighth Street, where Quinta leads south from the town square, is worth a peak. It may be one of the company's few franchises to sport a *palapa* roof.

Burger King
Quinta at Eighth Street

McDonald's
Quinta at Second Street
Highway 307 by Chedraui

Starbucks
Quinta at 10th Street
Quinta at 28th Street

Subway
Constituyentes at 10th Avenue
Paseo del Carmen Mall

sidewalk restaurant **Romagna Mia** (Cozumel Avenue (First Avenue) between 30th and 32nd Street) near Mamita's Beach, serves traditional Italian cuisine, including pasta carbonara, strozzapreti, gnocchi, and lasagna. Try the ham and cheese *piaditas*—an easy dish to share.

A new Italian favorite in Playa, **Cenacolo** (Quinta and 28th Street, www.cenacolo.com.mx) offers a modern Italian gastronomical journey based on traditional Italian philosophies in a sleek, upscale, and modern setting.

Enjoy modern Italian dishes in Playa international district at **Negroamaro Italian Restaurant and Bar** (Quinta between 34th and 38th Streets), where pastas and breads are baked fresh daily.

Piola Playa del Carmen (38th Street and First Avenue, www.piola.it), the local outpost of the beloved Italian pizza and gnocchi chain, service up fresh slices, noodle dishes, and Tiramisu in a crisp modern setting. The restaurant is set back, slightly behind some natural jungle.

Long a destination restaurant in Cozumel, Cancún, and Isla Mujeres, **Rolandi's** (Paseo del Carmen Mall, www.rolandirestaurants.com) outpost in Playa offers a casual ambience with an upscale flair. Wood-oven pizzas highlight the menu, along with pastas and desserts.

INTERNATIONAL

An elegant bar and eatery, ★ **The Glass Bar** (Quinta at 12th Street, www.theglassbar.com.mx) has cushioned chairs, linen tablecloths, and personable waiters. The menu features Italian and Mediterranean food, pasta, fish, steak, and an extensive wine list, featuring selections from Mexico, the Mediterranean, and beyond. Outdoor seating is slightly less exclusive, but still very upscale and comfortable, offering a great view of the goings-on along Quinta. Credit cards accepted.

Known for its gourmet Argentinean cuisine and large wine list, ★ **Ula Gula** (Quinta at 10th Street) features white linen tablecloths, candlelit tables,

Nightlights of Playa del Carmen

Each night, many points of light blink into existence up and down Fifth Avenue, in hotels, and along the beach. They give Playa a new overlay, setting the stage for romance, laughter, and interpersonal adventure.

Jellyfish Lamps. Carved from gourds and melons, these showstopper lanterns adorn shops, restaurants, and hotels, collectively giving Playa a distinctive sense of place. Made by hand, they feature illustrations, shapes, or other carvings. Multi-colored glass pieces are often inset into carved pockets, allowing vivid hues to jump out. The strings of shells hanging from many of the lamps earned them their name.

Catholic Votive Candles. These tall candles—usually displaying important religious figures such as Jesus Christ, the Virgin Mary, or other key sainted figures—are traditionally lit in prayers, as devotions and in remembrance of departed family. Christmas Lights. Good old-fashioned twinkle lights make for festive restaurant décor year round. You might spot them in plants and trees or adorning restaurant arches. Bring a string from home to hang in your hotel room to create instant, magical mood lighting.

Wall Sconces & Tin Lamps. Often spied in courtyards, restaurants, lobbies, and condos, these artistic clay, metal, and wooden shades make popular design accents. Bright lights tucked inside shine through small, intricate holes and patterns in the shade itself, creating brilliant points of light amid an ambient, low-lit setting.

Moroccan Lanterns. Similar to the sconces and lamps, these more elaborate hanging lanterns feature more ornate and precise patterns, as well as colored glass panes. They tend to show up as signature décor elements, particularly in bars and restaurants seeking to evoke an exotic flavor.

Restaurant Table Candles. Short, stubby red table candles and local homemade varieties, give you firelight to call your very own while dining in many of the city's sidewalk restaurants.

Many shops on Fifth Avenue feature colored lamps.

Torches. Typically perched above the fray, on the beach or along private hotel paths, these flames add a further flare of excitement to your evenings.

Fire Lanterns. Featured in the infamous fire dancing shows, these lanterns are literally set aflame and swung at the end of chains. During their performances, dancers paint vivid, overlapping circular patterns in the air and around themselves.

and a sultry but casual terraced dining room over Quinta. It is a favorite of trendy locals, American ex-pats, and visiting diners from around the world who value luxury. Downstairs from the restaurant, there's a tiny lounge on the street corner decorated in white and tan. It has a trendy vibe, with an interior decorated with candles, and a nice, romantic view of Quinta.

A French-owned gourmet restaurant and wine bar, ★ **Byblos** (10th Avenue at 24th Street) is one of the few other spots in town where you can enjoy a delicious dinner in an air-conditioned dining room with white linen tablecloths and exceptionally high service levels. Menu highlights include carpaccio, foie gras, pasta, risotto, grilled fish, flambéed lobster, veal chops, rabbit, New Zealand beef and lamb, duck, apple tarts, and crêpes flambéed with Grand Marnier.

You've heard of cave diving, but ★ **Alux** (Avenue Juárez between 65th and 70th avenues, just west of Highway 307, www.aluxrestaurant.com) offers cave dining. Housed deep within a natural cave, formed thousands of years ago, and featuring live music nightly, it makes for a romantic spot for dinner or a drink. The food is not the best, but the novelty of the experience more than makes up for it. Local promoters occasionally host all-night rave parties here, which can get extremely crowded and are best avoided if you're prone to claustrophobia.

Cool colors, flowing tapestries, dim lamplight, and flickering candles highlight the decor at the Mediterranean-style ★ **Kartabar** (12th Street at First Avenue, www.kartabar.com). The menu features Lebanese and Mediterranean cuisine and seafood, including beef carpaccio, Provincial Mussels

Kartabar is one of several trendy lounges on 12th Street.

(baked with Parmesan, garlic, olive oil, bread, olives, and parsley), calamari, falafel, stuffed grape leaves, tabouli, shrimp stew, lobster ravioli, and mahimahi. It's also a great spot for an after-dinner drink, a puff on a hookah, or a romantic tête-à-tête. The scene is somewhat social, but folks tend to keep to their groups more than not. Things really get going around midnight, when the dinner crowd yields to the late-night lounge scene, steeped in style and exclusivity.

With fewer than ten tables located away from the beaten path, the upscale eatery ★ **Oh Lala Cuisine by George** (14th Street between 10th and 15th Avenues, www.ohlalabygeorge.com) works hard to deliver an exceptional meal and experience. The attentive staff, fresh delicious dishes, and modern space make it worth seeking out.

Located on a charming street, across from Açanto Boutique Condo Hotel, the cool and upscale **Plank** (16th Street between Quinta and First Street, www.plank.mx) offers fresh USDA certified beef, chicken, and fish, as well as grilled vegetables and gourmet flatbreads, cooked on wooden and Himalayan salt planks.

Much more casual and lively, ★ **Karen's Seafood, Steak House and Pizzas** (Quinta between Second and Fourth Streets, www.karens.com.mx) has nightly live music and one of Playa's most all-encompassing menus. Crowds tend to linger in the fun and joyful atmosphere, so getting there early for a good table is recommended.

A swanky lounge/restaurant with indoor seating, candlelit tables, comfy sofas, and sidewalk tables facing Quinta, **Di Vino** (Quinta at 12th Street, www.divino.com.mx) offers upscale selections like grilled fish, steak, and lobster. As the night goes on, diners swap out for drinkers, and the lounge scene begins. The swank factor multiplies, and the indoor couches become the favored seats, making an ideal spot for candlelit canoodling. Food is served until late at night, but you'll see more swizzle sticks than butter knives as the night goes on. It's also a great spot to woo a date or show your feelings for your special someone. Credit cards accepted.

Boasting an "eat, drink, lounge" concept, the fusion restaurant **Amaris** (Paseo del Carmen Mall, www.amaris.com.mx) features decor and cuisine from Asia, Central America, and the Mediterranean. It has a marble bar, plasma TV, and indoor/outdoor seating. Best bets are the chicken satay—grilled chicken strips with peanut sauce.

Spanish-style tapas and cocktails are served with ocean views at **La Azotea Bar & Tapas** (Eighth Street and Quinta, www.hotelelpunto.com) atop Hotel El Punto. By day, the restaurant serves snacks and cocktails to folks who stop by and look out over the Caribbean Sea. At night, stylish patrons lounge amidst the deep red lighting, nosh on tapas, and enjoy being seen.

The upscale **La Caprichoza** (Quinta between 12th and 14th Streets, www.lacaprichoza.com) offers fish, lobster, steaks, pasta, and fresh salads. Located upstairs, the restaurant's soothing, welcoming atmosphere (including live music most nights) makes you want to take a break from Quinta and stay a while.

The primary draw at **Los Tulipanes** (Quinta at 14th Street, www.lostulipanesplaya.com) is the lounge-like atmosphere and soothing decor. Candlelit tables, soft music, and icy margaritas beckon passersby to stop in and stay for a while. Stop in for a drink before or after dinner.

Duck into the casual **Chic Pea Falafal and Lemonade Bar** (38th Street between Quinta and First Avenues) for light Middle Eastern food and delicious lemonades, including varieties flavored by blackberry, basil, lemongrass and ginger, and strawberry.

Despite its name, **Boston Grill Wine & Cigars Bar** (Quinta at 14th Street, www.bostongrill.com.mx) serves meals below a canopy of trees and has live music, a swing bar, and a handful of candlelit tables spilling out to the curb, making it one of the more relaxing spots along this busy strip. Guests are encouraged to linger and light a cigar after their meals.

Situated off Quinta's international stretch, the French kitchen and Caribbean art gallery **Cocotte Cita** (38th Street between Quinta and First Avenues, www.cocottecita.com) draws locals and visitors for fresh and rich French cuisine. After sunset, the casual daytime sidewalk café turns into a more romantic setting alongside a small *cenote.*

Como Como (10th Avenue between 12th and 14th Streets, www.comocomo.mx) offers rich Mediterranean flavors that keep ex-pats and international locals coming back.

Keep kosher at **Chabad Lubavitch** (10th Avenue between Sixth and Eighth Streets, www.jewishplaya.com), a local synagogue and restaurant. A kosher delivery service is also available.

ASIAN & SUSHI

With two locations, ★ **Babe's Noodles & Bar** (Quinta between 28th and 30th Streets; 10th Street between Quinta and 10th Avenue, www.babesnoodlesandbar.com) offers inexpensive and well-portioned Asian and Thai dishes for lunch and dinner. They serve chicken, beef, pork, vegetarian dishes, coconut rice, spring rolls, and egg rolls.

The Buenos Aires–based **Sushi Club** (Tenth Avenue and 26th Street, www.sushiclubweb.com) can be found in an uber slick space on the ground floor of the Be Playa hotel. The restaurant offers sushi as well as a mix of Japanese and Asian fusion dishes.

Sushi Itto (Paseo del Carmen Mall; 10th Street at First Avenue, www.sushi-itto.com.mx) offers fresh sushi, plus a variety of cooked rice and noodle dishes, at its two locations. The shrimp and rice is especially good. Delivery available.

Locals and visitors enjoy consistently good Thai food, including Pad Thai, curry, chicken satay, and pork dumplings at **Gluay Muai Thai** (38th Street, between Quinta and the beach), a crisp, modern, and casual eatery.

Officially part of The ROYAL, the Asian fusion restaurant **Asiana** (Constituyentes Avenue and First Avenue, www.realresorts.com) is also open to non-resort guests. It serves lunch and dinner in a bright, modern environment with strong lime green accents.

STEAK

With its wide and undulating staircase opening up on a prominent corner of Quinta, ★ **Madre Tierra** (Quinta and 14th Street) is hard to miss. The steakhouse, which also has an extensive seafood menu, exudes a warm and inviting atmosphere that reaches out from its open and minimalist second story *palapa* and into the street below.

The two-level **Sur Steakhouse** (Quinta at Calle Corazon, between 12th and 14th Streets) offers fan-cooled dining overlooking Quinta. The Argentinian grill is big and open and has a décor that's slick and mod, with indirect lighting, soothing lounge music, and a strong Mediterranean vibe.

A Sunset Facing East?

Since the Riviera Maya faces east, it is not known as a good place to witness a tropical sunset. If your beach vacation just won't be complete without watching the golden orb disappear into the horizon, there's still hope. Try these five tips for catching a sunset in the Riviera Maya.

- Take a champagne sunset cruise aboard the *Fat Cat* 41-foot catamaran in Xaac Cove near Puerto Aventuras and watch the sun sink into the Caribbean (www.fatcatsail.com).
- Walk to the point at the north end of Playa del Carmen Cove, in back of the Gran Porto Real hotel, and watch the sun go down next to the lighthouse.
- Climb to the top floor of the Paseo del Carmen mall and enjoy a rare sunset over downtown Playa and the jungle beyond.
- Take a day trip to Isla Cozumel and stay for sunset, then take a late ferry back to the mainland. Since the town's main beaches and town square face west, the sun sets over the ocean, just like in the postcards.
- Travel to the still unexplored Isla Holbox, northwest of Cancún, where you can watch the evening sun settle into the Gulf of Mexico from the sleepy beach. (see chapter 7).
- For the ultimate unobstructed sunset view, schedule a sundown skydive and look down, not up, at the setting sun (see chapter 8).

The beach behind the Gran Porto Real is one of the only spots in town to watch the sun set over the water.

It's all about the steak at **El Diez Argentine Grill** (Quinta at 30th Street, www.eldiez.com.mx). The Argentinian Parrilla specializes in steak, but pizza and seafood can be ordered from El Diez's sister restaurant next door.

SEAFOOD

Located next to the Playa town square, gourmet ★ **La Casa del Agua** (Quinta at Second Street, www.lacasadelagua.com) features European and Latin fusion cuisine, including fresh fish, shrimp, and shellfish, plus Angus beef and a few traditional Mexican dishes. Water features decorate the dining room, and candlelit tables are covered in white linen, giving it a contemporary, romantic feel.

Created by emerging culinary sensation Enrique Olvera, the local restaurant sensation ★ **Maiz del Mar** (Quinta and 30th Street, www.maizdemar.com) sources its dishes from the local area, with a focus on sustainability and high-quality dishes. It derives its inspiration from the traditional cooking found along Mexico's ample coastlines.

One of Playa's older restaurants, the two-story ★ **Blue Lobster** (Quinta at 12th Street, www.bluelobster.com.mx) opened in 1991 and specializes in live lobster and seafood (including a daily $19 lobster special), plus such unusual dishes as octopus puffs, fish with curry and anisette, and coconut shrimp. Key lime pie is popular, and there's live music in the evenings.

Located by the highway and away from the heart of the tourist zone, inexpensive ★ **El Oasis Mariscos** (22nd Street and Highway 307) remains popular with the local expats and natives. It features shrimp tacos, fish tacos, ceviche, and other seafood and Mexican dishes. The *palapa*-style dining room is large, and the decor is decidedly Mexican. If you don't speak Spanish, a waiter or staff member can likely help you decipher the menu.

Another spot popular with expats in the know, ★ **Los Aguaschiles** (Constituyentes between Quinta and First Avenues) offers great seafood, tacos, and ceviche, with an array of delicious sauces and drink specials. You can't go wrong with one of the ceviche plates or Los Aguaschiles's fresh takes on the traditional tacos.

Join the locals at the vibrant ★ **La Bamba Jarocha** (30th Avenue between 36th and 38th Streets), a bit off the main tourist trail. It's safe and friendly, and the waiters will be happy to help you order. Favorites include fried or grilled fish, seafood cocktails, fresh oysters, and paella. A traditional baked rice dish called *arroz tumbada* is served on Sunday only.

A sidewalk serenade at Blue Lobster restaurant

Poised on a high profile corner of Quinta, **Almirante Pech** (Quinta and 30th Street) will catch your eye because it just looks so cool. The new concept from the folks at Diablito Cha Cha Cha serves contemporary seafood and Mexican fusion cuisine. Even if you don't eat there, you'll likely be drawn to having a drink at the bar.

Formerly known at Big Lobster, **Caribbean Lobster** (Quinta between Fourth and Sixth Streets, www.caribbeanlobster.com.mx) offers beers, whole fish, fajitas, surf and turf, and, of course, lobster. Friendly waiters provide a bit of entertainment during your meal.

Local favorite **Las Brisas** (Fourth Street between Quinta and 10th Avenue) specializes in shrimp cocktail and ceviche, and also serves fried fish and grilled shrimp. Seating is in an open, covered dining room, allowing the breeze to flow through.

CAFÉS & LIGHT FARE

Facing the Olmec statue and fountain at a busy intersection, ★ **Ah Cacao** (Constituyentes at Quinta, www.ahcacao.com) makes all sorts of chocolate delicacies, including hot/cold drinks, to-die-for brownies, ice cream, cookies, and old-fashioned chocolate bars. It also has gourmet coffees from around Mexico. Stop by and ask for a sample. Popular with locals and tourists, new locations of Ah Cacao have begun popping up along Quinta.

Open for breakfast, lunch, and dinner, ★ **100% Natural** (Quinta between Eighth and 10th Streets, www.100natural.com.mx) is one chain restaurant that feels completely local. There are several different eating areas, from the sidewalk and tables next to a waterfall to covered tables with ceiling fans upstairs. The menu has omelets, enchiladas, sandwiches, seafood, steak, and other dishes. The fresh fruit juices and smoothies are delicious and good for what ails you. Special concoctions exist that claim to lower cholesterol, boost energy, cure hangovers, and improve memory. The prices are good, and the food is always fresh and delicious.

Hungry but don't want to go out?

Playita Express offers restaurant food delivery to hotels, condos, and other locations throughout Playa del Carmen. The service works with almost 100 local restaurants, including Yo Amo Tacos, El Oasis Mariscos, Rolandi's, and even McDonald's and Subway. There's a 15 percent service fee, and tips are not included. Delivery is available from 11 AM–9 PM. For more information, visit www.playitaexpress.com.

Off the beaten path, both locations

100% Natural restaurant has fresh fruit smoothies and healthy meals.

of **El Nativo** (Benito Juarez Avenue between Highway 307 and 55th Avenue; 30th Avenue between Constituyentes and 20th Streets) are popular local spots for fresh smoothies and juices.

★ **Chez Céline** (Quinta and 34th Street, www.chezceline.com.mx) is a perfectly traditional yet modern French bakery, boulangerie and pâtisserie with patio and indoor seating. In addition to sweets, pastries, frozen lemonades, teas, and coffees, the café also has a full sandwich and salad menu. If you're taking your food and treats to go, head directly to the counter to order. If you plan to eat there, grab a seat and a server will find you.

The tea trend hasn't skipped Playa, but the city's indisputable center of teatime is **The Little Teapot** (Quinta between 26th and 28th Streets). With a rough luxe décor offset by bright green-and-white striped walls, the shop has 150 teas stored in white tins on its wooden shelves. Get your teas to go, or enjoy on site with a freshly made cupcake.

Bars & Nightlife

When the sun goes down, the action on Quinta heats up. Tourists hit the town with their sun-kissed skin and newly purchased tropical outfits to enjoy the evening breeze, have dinner, gaze at the twinkling lights, and then, quite frequently, have a few drinks. Fortunately, there are plenty of options for nightlife on and around Quinta and the beach. Whether you're looking for a casual beach bar, live tropical music, TV sports, or a cosmopolitan discotheque, you'll find what you're looking for in Playa. There are clubs and bars all along Quinta and at various spots along the beach. Many travelers will take a few laps around town to see what's going on before settling on a place to go. As the night goes on, the crowd thins a bit, becomes less populated with Americans, and funnels to the after-hours clubs, some of which continue serving drinks until sunup.

The most popular area for nightlife is 12th Street, sometimes known as the *Zona Doce*, where bars and clubs line both sides of the road all the way from 10th Avenue to the beach. An eclectic crowd assembles from midnight to 2 AM at the tiny hole-in-the-wall bar between the main entry to La Santanera and the pizza shack next door. They serve beer in giant Styrofoam cups and have only a couple of tables, with the crowds spilling over into the street for a nightly impromptu street party.

DRINKS & DANCING

Look for the brightly lit Vegas-style sign facing 12th Street and you'll find ★ **La Santanera** (Eighth Street between Quinta and 10th Avenue, www.lasantanera.com), which is frequented by the cool kids from Mexico City and around the world. But don't worry, even this place has an unpretentious and down-to-earth atmosphere and a rooftop patio bar. Relocated to the former site of Playa's dearly departed hotspot Hotel Básico, the club decor seems to pay equal homage to Mexican professional wrestling, the Catholic Church, and the killer views of Playa below. As they enter, visitors pass an almost two-story neon Jesus slyly spinning a

Top 10 Songs to Add to Your Playlist

The right song can help secure a memory, make good times even better, and share an experience with friends. Try some of these to capture the spirit of the Riviera Maya:

"Margaritaville" by Jimmy Buffett. Said to have been written on a flight from Cozumel to Houston, it's a song about a mythical island at the bottom of a Cuervo bottle.

"Mexico" by James Taylor. This is a classic tale of an extended vacation: "The sun's so hot, I forgot to go home."

"Stays in Mexico" by Toby Keith. A countrified reminder to keep your vacation exploits to yourself.

"Mexico" by Nash Girls. Young women having fun at the beach.

"Married in Mexico" by Mark Wills. A south-of-the-border romance complete with beachfront nuptials.

"I Got Mexico" by Eddy Raven. Sometimes, that's all you need.

"Blame It on Mexico" by George Strait. "Too much guitar music, tequila, salt, and lime." I know I've used this excuse before.

"Ten Rounds with Jose Cuervo" by Tracy Byrd. Crazy things can happen with tequila, especially after 10 rounds.

"Mail Myself to Mexico" by Buddy Jewell. Vacation fantasies go postal.

"One Step Closer to Cancún" by Elmer Thudd. Inspirational song about an upcoming vacation.

turntable displaying the phrase "All is forgiven." The first level is like a traditional open-air bar, with views over Quinta below.

Upstairs contains the crowd of dancing, socializing, and margarita-drinking patrons. DJs spin the latest tunes, including American pop, Mexican rock, tropical music, and a bit of funk. The crowd is a good mix of locals and visitors, gay and straight. Opens at 8 PM, but it doesn't start hopping until at least midnight. Last call is 4 AM.

The Riviera deftly combines culture, cuisine, recreation, and really big margaritas into one fun resort destination.

Mucha Ropa, Mucha Ropa!

The equivalent to the English "take it off, take if off," *mucha ropa, mucha ropa* is just as cliché and out of fashion. In the Riviera Maya, the main gentleman's clubs are in Playa del Carmen, along Highway 307. They are generally considered safe for tourists, though like anywhere, it's best to keep your wits and not do anything that you think could get you in trouble. That being said, the law allows for quite a bit, and you're sure to find your choice of willing participants—for a price.

One such club is **Baby's Hot** (Highway 307 at Sixth Street). A small hangout for locals, it doesn't see many gringos and can seem a bit rough around the edges to many foreigners. Cover charge is posted at $25, but they're flexible if they think you'll spend some money once you're inside, especially if you threaten to go down the road to visit their competitors instead. A few blocks south is **Marlin Men's Club** (Highway 307 and Avenue Juárez, www.marlinmensclub.blogspot.mx). It's the most stylish of the nonmembership clubs, featuring a pool table, laser light show, massages, escort girls, show girls, table dances, private dances, and multiple stages. Cover charge is negotiable. Farther down Highway 307, across from the southernmost entrance to Playacar, is **Chilly Willy's**, a *palapa*-roofed sister club to the longtime nudie institution in Cancún. Cover charge is posted at $20, and the club seems to open only certain times of the year.

Each club offers table dances in a private curtained room for $15–20, payable directly to your dancer of choice, waiter, or floor manager (who is eager to assist with your selection). More intimate encounters can be arranged for an additional fee (around $200 for the complete package), and each club has private rooms for rent by the hour.

Drinks are relatively inexpensive, though if a dancer asks you to buy her a drink, the fee is significantly higher—up to $15 for a single cocktail—so unless you're ready to drop a lot of money, you're probably best off saving your pesos for a dance since it's roughly the same price. Cash is the preferred payment method, so bring some bills and stay aware of your surroundings.

All taxis know these clubs well and will often recommend one to you since they get a kickback for dropping people off there. Negotiate your price in advance (it shouldn't be more than a few dollars from any Playa del Carmen or Playacar hotel), and if you want to try to get in without paying a cover, have them drop you off a block or two away so you're not obligated to your taxi driver in any way. No need to have your cabbie wait for you; there are plenty waiting outside when it's time to leave.

Be smart. Be safe. Have fun.

The opening of ★ **Coco Bongo Playa del Carmen** (12th Street between Quinta and 10th Avenue, www.cocobongo.com.mx) in 2008 marked Playa's unofficial departure from its hippie heyday and ushered in a new era of mass international tourism that continues to reshape this once-sleepy fishing town. Though smaller than its sister club up the coast in Cancún, it's still Playa's largest, most modern, and most extravagant nightspot. In fact, is should be viewed more as a

One last Corona before catching the plane home

tourist attraction that you must experience than as simply a nightclub. Live performances, including lip-syncing celebrity lookalikes, flair bartenders, DJs, dancers, and—most notably—high-flying acrobats keep the audience entertained all night long, making it feel like New Year's Eve every night of the year. Smoke machines, a video wall, laser light show, balloon drops, confetti explosions, and compressed air blasts help ensure that there's always something pumping energy into the crowd. Cover charge is $70 and includes open bar with domestic beer and liquor drinks. Open nightly from 10:30 PM to 5 AM.

Coco Bongo is by far Playa del Carmen's largest nightclub.

The king of *palapa* bars in Playa, **Blue Parrot** (12th Street at the beach, www.blueparrot.com) was once a sort of community center, with a hotel, popular lounge chair-laden beachfront, lively meals, and flowing beers. It's still a haven by day. Though at night, it's something a shadow of its former self. At times it is one of the best parties in town, though the dancing typically takes place inside the complex, rather than along the beach. The main oval-shaped bar is about 100 feet long and is ringed with swinging bar stools, plus several tables and chairs leading all the way to the water's edge. Food is served

5 Welcoming Hotels for Gay & Lesbian Travelers

Although gay travelers are generally welcomed throughout the region, these spots make a particular effort to attract and engage gay travelers. For more gay-friendly options visit www.friendly.com.mx and www.purpleroofs.com.

1. **Aventura Mexicana hotel (Playa del Carmen)**—Gay men from around the world often mix with straight couples and European travelers at this 48-room hotel with a rooftop Jacuzzi and sundeck.

2. **Hotel Secreto (Isla Mujeres)**—Same sex couples fit right in at this stylish, private island boutique.

3. **In Fashion Boutique Hotel (Playa del Carmen)**—Aspiring to be all things fashionable, this new hotel highlights art, fashion, and a minimalist style and markets itself to the "Project Runway" set.

4. **Viceroy Riviera Maya (Punta Bete)**—This small upmarket resort caters to couples and well-educated travelers from North America and regularly welcomes gay and lesbian travelers. It holds strong appeal to couples, so unless you're traveling with a group that has rented out some or all of the resort, it's unlikely to be a good venue for meeting new romantic prospects.

5. **Mosquito Beach Hotel (Playa del Carmen)**—This stylish beachfront boutique is a popular choice for gay travelers.

until 6 PM. In a nod and thrust to traditions past, local fire dancers perform on Fridays and Saturdays around 10 PM, flinging sparks and ash dangerously close to the thatched roof. Although no longer nightly, the show still entrances the crowd, made up of Americans, Canadians, locals, and other people from around the world. The show is amazing, though, with attractive young performers showing off their skill and daring. Open bar is available or visitors can just pay an entrance fee starting around $10. A covered lounge area offers romantic cushioned seating areas on top of the sandy beach and a stage, where a DJ spins throbbing electronic beats sure to set the mood for a fun night.

Popular with day-trippers, cruise passengers, Mexico first-timers, and vacationers at hotels in the adjacent Playacar development, ★ Señor Frog's (Plaza Marina, at the ferry dock, www.senorfrogs.com) is always a good bet for good cover bands, reggae music, audience-participation gags, goofy contests, and a bit of risqué fun. It is built out over the sand and has a great view of the Palace Resort beach and the ferry dock. There is live music nightly and DJ dancing until the wee hours, and there are many audience-participation opportunities, including sexy body contests, drinking contests, and sing-alongs. The menu features Mexican standards, plus pasta, seafood, and burgers.

Situated next to Coco Bongo, and almost as popular, Palazzo (12th Street between Quinta and 10th Avenue, www.palazzodisco.com) is a more traditional nightclub than its neighbor. Upon entering the club, visitors travel to the second floor, so they make their grand entrance with the dance floor below them, filled with light shows, dancing, drink specials, and frenzied patrons. Open Thursday through Saturday from 10:30 PM and 6 AM.

La Bodeguita del Medio (Quinta between 36th and 38th Street, www.labodeguitadelmedio.com.mx) is a Cuba-themed restaurant during the day and evening, but its crowd gets more rowdy and the music gets louder as the night goes on. Live salsa music is featured most nights. For a break from the crowd, seek respite on the back patio overlooking a steep, rocky arroyo, and ask for a marker to add your name to the wall of fame. Originally founded in Havana, Cuba in 1942, where it earned fame as one of Earnest Hemingway's favorite watering holes, it boasts a slightly kitschy decor with Cuban art, flags, and paraphernalia. There are daily drink specials and free salsa lessons Tuesday and Thursday at 7 PM.

Beach club by day and night club by night, **Coco Maya Beach Club** (14th Street at the beach, www.cocomayabeachclub.net) is an alternative to the sometimes over-hyped scene at the Blue Parrot next door. No fire dancers here; just hip DJ music, a handful of couches arranged around the dance floor, and a few additional sitting areas set up in the sand. At the main bar, drinkers vie for the bartender's attention while a movie projector plays old Mexican classics on a wall nearby.

With its rainbow flag and suggestive name, **Playa 69** (Quinta between Fourth and Sixth Streets, www.rivieramayagay.com) is far from being subtle about being Playa's dedicated gay bar. There's live and recorded male entertainment, and it's a great spot to meet gay and free-spirited locals, ex-pats, and travelers from around the world. Starting around midnight, the scene lasts until about 4 AM.

TRENDY LOUNGES

Crimson-red nightlife hotspot Mandala Bar features many pan-Asian design motifs and symbols in both Playa del Carmen and Cancún. Chip Rankin

During the day, ★ **Mandala Bar** (12 Street at First Avenue, www.mandalanightclub.com) may look like it closed down a month ago, but at 10 PM, the red leather couches are pulled from storage and set up along the street and the music starts to pump, making this one of the hipper places to linger over cocktails. The multi-level bar is popular with revelers from around the world, with a vibe that's more Miami Beach–chic than Playa-casual. The centerpiece is a large dance floor that fills up as the night goes on. The sexy crowd is far less pretentious than one would guess by appearance alone. Cover fee is charged most nights after the club begins to look full, though a little finagling can usually get you in for free.

At the ★ **Deseo Bar** (Quinta between 10th and 12th Streets, www.hoteldeseo.com) you can indulge in ultra-hip lounging in an atmosphere as nontraditionally Mexican as the $10 martinis they serve. You'll feel cool as soon as you crest the top stair that leads to the bar from Quinta. It's a lot like being in L.A. or Miami when

A rustic beach near Tulum

10 Tips for Enjoying Your Trip

Rent a car. Being mobile and free gives you a whole new perspective on a destination. You won't need it the whole time, but get one for a few days and explore the coast on your own. Pack a cooler, beach towel, map (freebies are available at the airport and most hotels), and mask/snorkel, and hit the road. Make sure to hit Tulum, hidden beaches, and lost-in-time villages.

Learn a little Spanish. A little goes a long way, and it helps you feel like you belong. It's also a nice gesture to make to your Mexican hosts, who will appreciate the effort and are usually happy to take some time to teach you new words. For bonus points, learn a little Mayan. Even saying "hello" or "thank you" in the native language is a sure way to get smiles from the locals, many of whom speak it fluently.

Take care of yourself. Don't get dehydrated or sunburned. Drinking plenty of purified water will keep your energy level up and can prevent serious illness. Don't be stingy with the sunscreen, either: a trip-ruining sunburn can happen in less than an hour if you're not used to the sun and you don't protect yourself. And while you're at it, put on insect repellent before heading out at night. While others are scratching their ankles, you'll be enjoying your margarita.

Order the whole fish. Native to the region, this dish has been a favorite for hundreds of years. The fish is scaled and gutted but left whole, and it is then lightly fried and usually served with tomatoes and onions. It's a good dish to share, with each diner forking off the pieces he or she wants. Even the skin is crispy and tasty, full of healthy fish oils.

Request a mariachi song. Sure, you can hear them playing at the table across the way, but there's nothing like being surrounded by the band as they play at your very own table. It makes for great photos, also, so request a song, try to sing along, and take some fun pictures. Tip $3–5 per song.

Check out the late-night scene. Sitting at a rope-swing bar stool and dancing under the stars is a longtime Playa tradition, and it's alive and well at the Blue Parrot (see Drinks & Dancing). The party gets going after midnight, and on Fridays and Saturdays you can catch their famous fire dancers putting on a show, followed by DJ music and dancing inside the club. Into a more relaxing scene? Linger over a glass of wine at the Glass Bar (see International Dining), savor mojitos at Diablito Cha Cha Cha or practice your lounging skills at Kartabar (see Trendy Lounges). Not tired yet? Head to La Santanera (see Drinks & Dancing) and learn to dance like a local.

Stroll along the beach. Leave your sandals behind, and take a long walk on the powdery white-sand beach. If you're staying in Playacar, head south toward Xcaret and follow the beach until a rocky point bars your way, and you'll find a secluded and picturesque spot to rest before heading home. If you're staying near Quinta, head north past Mamita's Beach Club all the way to the Reef Club hotel and the deserted beach beyond (Playa Chun-Zumbul).

Visit a *cenote*: These freshwater sinkholes, unique geographical features, are a lot of fun. The refreshingly cool water feels great after a day in the sun, and the virtually unlimited visibility makes you feel like you're floating in space. Hidden Worlds (see chapter 7) is the most expensive, but it's also the best.

There are many postcard-worthy sites throughout the Riviera Maya. Gary Walten/locogringo.com

Snorkel or scuba dive on the Great Mayan Reef. Take the plunge for a chance to see colorful corals, tasty-looking lobsters, stern-looking barracuda, slippery eels, majestic turtles, and hundreds of tropical fish.

Get up early. Though the sun sets over Quintana Roo mainland, it rises over the Caribbean. Combined with the solitude and quiet of the early-morning hours, watching the sunrise is a spiritual and calming way to start your day. Next, head to your favorite café for a cup of coffee and some *pan dulce* (sweet pastries) as you watch the shops open up and the tourists start their rounds.

Paper lanterns adorn a store front on Quinta. Chip Rankin

you're at Deseo, but without the attitude. The glimmer of the pool, the glowing lights from the rooms ringing the deck, and the projection TV on the wall next door set a surreal stage for some serious lounging. Most of the patrons are hipsters from Mexico City, and they all seem to know each other, but find your spot at the bar, at a poolside bed, or at one of the lounge chairs near the hotel rooms, and you'll fit right in.

Across the street from the entrance to the Blue Parrot, ★ **TriBeCa** (12th Street at First Avenue, www.tribecaplaya.mx) gets busier as it gets later. It has a nondescript, cool, modern nightlight décor that could easily be found in Miami. Like many of the clubs along the *Zona Doce,* the club is largely open, both making a show for the passersby on Twelfth Street and, for those in the club, making a show of the passing crowd outside. International DJs spin lounge and chill-out music while patrons dance on the tables, conspire at dark tables, and enjoy watching the busy street scene. Open 5 PM–4 AM daily, but if you (and your friend) don't want to go home, you may be able to snag one of the hotel rooms at 3Beca Hotel above the bar.

See and be seen at the swanky open-air **Diablito Cha Cha Cha** (12th Street at First Avenue, www.diablitochachacha.com) while you sip mojitos, cuba libres, daiquiris, and other tropical drinks. The lights are dim, but the people-watching is still second-to-none, as the well-heeled, international set grooves to African and Latin rhythms while showing off their trendy vacation duds.

CASUAL DRINKS

Primarily a local hangout, ★ **Litros** (First Avenue between 10th and 12th Streets) offers 33-ounce beers for $3 and equally large mixed drinks for $7. It's a good spot to sit on the sidewalk and watch the crowd gather for the Blue Parrot. The small indoor area has funky lighting and Mexican rock music. Can't finish your drink? It's okay to get it to go, as long as it's in Styrofoam.

Requesting a Mariachi Song

The strolling mariachis you see in the restaurants, walking down Quinta, or sometimes even on the beach work for tips. The typical price per song is $3–5, but ask ahead to be sure. Duos can cost less, and larger groups cost more. Not sure which song to request? Here are a few longtime favorites to choose from:

"El Son de la Negra." This raucous song is often the first song played when the mariachis make their grand entrance; it's also a lively, uplifting song to play anytime the room needs a lift.

"La Bamba." Everybody knows the words—at least some of them. This is an uplifting song of hope and can really get the crowd going.

"La Cucaracha." The sad tale of a bad day for a cockroach. It's a funny and entertaining song that's easy to sing along with. Kids love it, too.

"Las Golondrinas." A sad song known to bring grown men to tears. It tells the tale of the swallows flying on and is often played when someone is gone or going away.

"Las Mananitas." This is the song played for birthdays and celebrations. Request it for a friend who is celebrating something special.

"Maria Isabel." An easy song to sing along to, it tells the story of lovers on the beach. It has a happy tropical sound that you'll remember for a long time and is especially popular in Cozumel.

A good time to request "Vamos a la Playa"

Visitors looking for a shady spot to sip a cold drink can discover what the guests of the La Rana Cansada hotel already know. ★ **La Ranita Bar** (10th Street between Quinta and 10th Avenue, www.ranacansada.com) will find themselves at home at this traditional rustic Mexican setting that says "beach town cantina." Patrons can sit at the bar, in the lounge area, or out in the courtyard, surrounded by flowering tropical plants.

A good spot to watch a live sporting event on TV, ★ **La Taberna** (Fifth Street between Quinta and 10th Avenue) has a wall of computer workstations, with Internet access going for $1.50 an hour. There are dart boards, pool tables, and multiple TVs, and there's also cold air-conditioning, so it's a good spot to go after a long day at the beach, when you just can't bring yourself to sit at a patio bar. They serve good tacos, burgers, grilled chicken, nachos, steak, quesadillas, and seafood cocktails.

The American-dominated happy-hour favorite ★ **Big Al's and Redneck Steve's Beer Bucket** (10th Street between Quinta and 10th Avenue) offers loud pop and rock music, beer specials, mixed drinks, and a come-as-you-are attitude. Seating is on the ground floor or on an upper deck overlooking the street. While not a great place to impress a date, it's a fun place to party with friends and make some new ones. As the night goes on, the scene gets a little crazier, making for a fun night on the town. They play U.S. sports on TV for the playoffs and other key games.

Help Support the Playa del Carmen Fire Department

The local fire department, Bomberos de la Riviera Maya, frequently sets up a kiosk in the Playa del Carmen town square near the ferry dock. They sell hats and T-shirts with the department logo to raise funds to buy updated equipment for the rescue squad. The department's various firehouses welcome guests who want to take pictures and are eager to exchange patches with other fire departments around the world.

The Tequila Barrel (Quinta between 10th and 12th Streets, www.tequilabarrel.com) is a Playa classic. A dark wood bar gives a traditional hacienda feeling to the interior, while a large-screen TV near the back plays sports and news. When nothing good is on TV, there is live music. Sidewalk tables spill out onto Quinta, making this a great spot to sip a cocktail and watch the parade of people walk by. The bartenders are friendly and welcoming, and the bar stocks more than 85 types of tequila, plus a huge selection of

The Tequila Barrel has sidewalk tables and a back room with sports betting.

Common Beers of the Riviera Maya

Bohemia. Served in a dark bottle with gold foil on the neck, Bohemia is a bit more expensive than other beers. With a robust taste, it's a bit of a status symbol.

Bomemia Dark. Introduced to the Riviera Maya in 2008, this darker cousin of Bohemia offers a richer head and creamier, almost stout-like finish.

Corona. Though it's brewed in Mexico, it seems to be more common in the States. Not all bars carry it, so if you're normally a Corona drinker, it may be time to expand your horizons. Normally served with a slice of lime.

Dos Equis. Advertised on billboards throughout the region, Dos Equis (XX) comes in lager (green bottle) and amber (tinted bottle). The lager is much more common and goes better with lime.

Leon Negra. Somewhat of a microbrew, this dark and flavorful beer is locally brewed in Mérida, the capital of the state of Yucatán. Sometimes hard to find.

Modelo Especial. Sold by the bottle or in single cans in the convenience stores, this light-bodied lager is favored by many locals and goes nicely in a beach cooler.

Montejo. Crafted at the same Mérida brewery as Leon Negra, this beer adds a touch of class to your bar visit when it's available.

Negra Modelo. A dark beer sometimes sold at a slightly higher price than others, it's normally served in a glass and goes great with steak.

Noche Buena. From the makers of Bohemia, this dark seasonal brew is available only in the winter holiday season. The name means, essentially, "Christmas Eve."

Sol. Commonly found at beach bars and nightclubs, Sol is what most Corona drinkers opt for when their usual beer is not on the menu. Frequently served with lime.

Superior. Served in a dark tinted bottle, which helps keep it from getting skunked in a cooler on a sunny day, this full-bodied beer is sold at a discount in grocery stores and is available mostly at bars favoring locals.

Tecate. Most commonly served in cans, Tecate is best enjoyed with plenty of salt and lime. Popular at sports bars.

Victoria. Brewed by Grupo Modelo, the same company that makes Corona and local favorites, this is a hoppy pilsner that isn't generally exported, so it's fun to see it and try a few.

Want your beer to go? Ask the bartender for a *vaso desechable* and walk out with your drink in a plastic cup.

imported cognacs, whiskeys, and Scotches. The kitchen serves up traditional Mexican and American breakfasts, plus burgers, wings, fajitas, and other bar foods. The bar's website has a live web cam and archives photos taken at the bar each night.

The quiet **Bottega Vino Bar Con Cocina** (Quinta between 38th and 40th Street, www.bottega.mx), from the chef at Como Como, specializes in good wines and shared plates in a relaxed, low-key environment.

Dancing on the Sand: Top Spots to Have Sand between Your Toes and a Drink in Your Hand

Blue Parrot, 12th Street at the beach. Get there early to reserve a coveted waterfront table. If you fall out of your chair, you'll land on powder-white sand.

Fusion Beach Bar & Grill, Sixth Street at the beach. This relaxed beach bar offers a festive but laid-back alternative to the Blue Parrot down the beach. Most nights, fire dancers perform on the beach, at 10:30 on weeknights and midnight on weekends.

Mamita's Beach Club, 28th Street at the beach. Who says you can't go dancing during the day? The folks at Mamita's prove that getting your groove on by sunlight can be just as fun as by moonlight. The party gets going in the early afternoon, peaks just before sundown, and then quickly dwindles. Arrive early to claim a coveted beach bed.

Señor Frog's, Plaza Marina, at the ferry dock. Built above the beach at the base of the ferry dock, this resort-town stalwart packs in a primarily American clientele in search of good Mexican food, pop music, and sometimes love. Dancing patrons can get their drinks to go and boogie on the beach below.

This courtyard bar and restaurant **Siesta Fiesta** (Quinta between Eighth and 10th Streets, www.siestafiestahotelplaya.com) is a popular meeting spot where travelers congregate to watch live sporting events on the big-screen TV and listen to live music (several bands per night). After the live music, the staff puts live sports or recorded concerts on the TV, and the party keeps going. There are tables near the stage, several bar stools, and sidewalk tables for those seeking a bit more peace and quiet. Vacation camaraderie is especially strong here, making it a great spot to meet other travelers. Food is available all day long. There is also a quaint hotel offering comfortable and affordable accommodations.

Giving a little taste of the jungle to the sidewalk bar scene, **Living Garden Bar** (Quinta between 14th and 16th Streets) opened in 2007 and quickly developed a loyal following. Some tables front Fifth Avenue, but others are set back in a tree-covered setting, surrounded by tropical plants, dappled lighting, and jungle décor. It's a nice place to chill out for a while and grab a snack. The temperature seems to drop about ten degrees as soon as you step inside.

The hole-in-the-wall **Karaoke Bar** (Sixth Street between Quinta and 10th Avenue) is a fun spot to have a few beers and do something you wouldn't do back home—sing in front of a crowd of strangers! The song list features popular hits in English and Spanish.

Mezcalinna Bar (12th Street between the beach and First Avenue, www.mezcalimperial.com) offers cheap drinks if you don't want to pay cover for a club. Enjoy your drink in the crowded bar, or get it to go and join the street party.

Situated above Mezcalinna, up a narrow staircase, is the highly eclectic, open-air **Dolores YucaBar** (12th Street and First Avenue). The bar itself seems to be an evolving mix of concepts, including cheap liter-sized drinks and Christmas lights strung though the tree branches. The bar has a mixed crowd of locals and tourists and is often, but not always, a go-to favorite of gay partygoers.

BEACH CLUBS

The bustling ★ **Mamita's Beach Club** (28th Street at the beach, www.mamitas beachclub.com) attracts a trendy crowd that gathers every afternoon to soak up the sun and sip cold beers and frosty margaritas. It's usually packed with day-trippers, cruise passengers, and sun worshippers staying in Playa but not on the beach. There's a small pool and several *cabaña*-style beach beds, available on a first-come, first-served basis. A DJ spins lounge and pop music suitable for bar-top dancing, while other patrons join in a game of group soccer ball juggling. Mamita's rents lounge chairs and umbrellas and offers beachside drink and meal service, with fish, shrimp, tacos, and other Mexican specialties topping the menu.

Channeling 1950s Brazil, ★ **Canibal Royale** (48th Street at the beach, www .canibalroyal.com) offers a trendy tri-level spot to sit by the beach, swim in the pool, and imbibe. Guests must buy food and drinks to use the facilities, but the menu, designed by a chef from Nobu Miami, is much better than your typical local beach club fare. Refreshing juices, buckets of beer, and mixed cocktails ensure that there's a delicious beverage for every palate.

The exclusive **Coco Maya Beach Club** (14th Street at the beach, www.coco mayabeachclub.net), next to the Blue Parrot Hotel, is the preferred daytime hang-out for stylish beachgoers showing off their new bathing suits, new boobs, or new gym results. It's a great place to sunbathe, listen to lounge music, and feel cool. At night, a DJ spins popular music in front of a dance floor and lounge area, and a movie projector plays old Mexican classics.

Lounging at the Canibal Royale beach club

Family-friendly **Kool Beach Club** (28th Street at the beach, www.koolbeachclub.com.mx), just north of the ROYAL Resort, is popular with day-trippers, cruise passengers, and downtown Playa beachgoers. There are lounge chairs and beach umbrellas for rent, plus a kids' pool, a restaurant serving seafood and Mexican food, and, of course, cold beer right on the beach. Active folks can play beach volleyball and soccer, ride WaveRunners, or go parasailing, banana-boat riding, kiteboarding, or body surfing. Massage service is provided on the beach or in a shady *cabaña*.

Located in Playa's original downtown, **Zenzi Beach Club** (10th Street and the beach, www.zenzi-playa.com) offers stylish sun beds, shades, lounge chairs, and other amenities. The club has a full kitchen and bar and stays open from 8 AM to 2 AM most nights.

Indigo Beach Club (14th Street at the beach, www.indigobeach.com.mx) offers a popular breakfast for 150 pesos to start your day lounging above its perfect white sand beach. At dinner, it hosts different theme-night celebrations Wednesday through Sunday, themed to Mexican fiestas, jazz, rock and reggae.

Press Your Luck

Though far from being a casino destination, the Playa del Carmen does offer one opportunity for tourists with an itch to gamble.

If you're in Playa del Carmen, drop by the back room at **Tequila Barrel** (Quinta between 10th and 12th Streets, www.tequilabarrel.com) for a quick fix. This sports betting lounge offers bets on games around the world, using Las Vegas odds. Watch on the dozens of TVs or head to the beach, then come back to see if you won.

Shopping & Services

While Playa's streets are overflowing with shops, and your hotel concierge can always point you in the right direction for a quick sundry and supply run, a few stops present something unique and atypical. In short, they're pure Playa del Carmen.

If you're looking for a specific tequila, or just to learn something, **Casa Tequila—La Tequilaria** (Quinta between Fourth and Sixth Streets; Quinta at 14th Street) offers one-liter bottles ranging from $7 to $250. Most can be purchased by the shot, making for a fun sampling experiment. Souvenir bottles and flasks are available.

Despite today's dominance of digital downloads and streaming music services, **Casita de la Musica** (Quinta between Avenue Juárez and Second Street) may be the only place you'll be able to easily find the latest Latin and international tracks you've been hearing during your trip. They sell local and international music, including merengue, salsa, Cuban, Mayan, pop, mariachi, and lounge music.

★ **Jellyfish Lamp Shop** (Fourth Street at Quinta, www.jellyfish.com.mx) spills onto the sidewalk, showcasing the tropical lanterns seen adorning many restaurants and bars. They're made from coconuts or similarly shaped gourds adorned with jewels, whimsical designs, and streamers that make them look like

Find original Mexican art and handicrafts, like these embroidered candles made of dried orange peels turned inside out, at La Catrina. Chip Rankin

jellyfish, with their dangling tentacles. They range from baseball-sized lanterns selling for a few dollars to basketball-sized works of art selling for more than $100.

Original works of art made by hand in Mexico also spill into the street from the small **La Catrina** (14th Street between Quinta and 10th Avenue). Proprietor Ariadne Gamas creates many of the heart-shaped works herself and curates popular items from local artists and workers. Expect to find traditional Mexican handicrafts with modern twists and surprises, such as photos of graffiti poetry from around Mexico on small canvases and images of Frida Kahlo wearing a Daft Punk t-shirt.

The only shops dedicated to rewarding the little ones you left at home (or with a sitter at the hotel), **Caribbean Puzzles** (storefronts and kiosks roughly every five blocks along Quinta) offers unique, brightly colored wooden puzzles and other fun stuff for the kiddos. Most of the stock is of the educational variety—nothing makes loud noises or goes fast—and much of it derives from local culture and geography.

Six blocks straight back from the ferry dock, the local **Marsan Market** (30th Avenue at South First Street) has fresh meats and fish, fishing supplies, clothing, shoes, fresh fruits, and a wide variety of items found at a typical Mexican market. It's a good place for picking up a unique gift item or just strolling around to sample the local color.

A popular regional chain, **Roger's Boots** (Second Street between Quinta and 10th Avenue) offers handmade leather boots starting at around $100. Custom boots are also available, if you're going to be around a while. They also sell leather bags, belts, fancy belt buckles, hats, holsters, and rifle cases.

Although this may seem like an average little **Flower Shop** (Avenue Juárez between 20th and 25th Streets), it may hold the key to an unforgettable evening,

Cuban Cigars: Don't Get Ripped Off

Courtesy of SeePlaya

Locally rolled cigars are available in downtown Playa.

For many travelers, the question of where to find authentic Cuban cigars comes up at least once during their trip to the Riviera Maya. A little information can go a long way toward losing your hard-earned pesos on fake Cohibas on Playa del Carmen's Quinta Aveninda.

COUNTERFEITS ABOUND

First, be aware that the majority of so-called "Cuban" cigars you'll see in Playa are counterfeit, even those sold in cigar stores. If you see a Cohiba sitting in a jar next to a cash register it is almost certainly fake. The scam here is that the store owners know that visiting Americans will pay high prices for authentic Cubans, so they re-label secondhand cigars (factory rejects) or cheaper brands.

DON'T buy so-called "Cuban" cigars from any shop or vendor unless the box has a holographic sticker of authenticity attached. The Cuban government now places a hologram on genuine boxes (or the three and five packs) of legitimate Cuban cigars. Even the Montecristos at the high-end resorts usually don't have these holograms, and most are just pretty good looking fakes.

WHERE TO FIND AUTHENTIC CUBAN CIGARS

What's a tourist to do? The best source for authentic Cuban cigars is, believe it or not, the Walmart tobacco shop on the corner of 30th Avenue and Eighth Street. You can be assured that not only are they authentic, they are likely the cheapest source in town (you can purchase budget-priced booze while you are there, as well).

La Casa del Habano on Quinta between 26th and 28th Streets (www.lacasadelhabanoplayadelcarmen.com), is also a reputable source for authentic Cubans cigars and offers a good local alternative if you are opposed to "big box" stores. If you choose to stay at a resort, many of them carry a limited number of brands in their store. Some do have authentic Cubans, but be sure to look for the hologram label.

BRINGING CIGARS HOME

It is illegal for U.S. citizens to bring Cuban cigars into the U.S. or even to purchase and consume them in Mexico. We do not condone the illegal importing of Cuban products to the U.S., and if you do choose to purchase Cuban cigars, it would be wise to smoke them while in Playa.

That said, many U.S. citizens carry cigars back with them in their luggage. Less than ten percent of travelers arriving in the U.S. are randomly selected to have their luggage inspected, so the odds are in your favor. Some U.S. citizens have been known to ship unlabeled Cuban cigars back home via an international courier. Be aware that this will be very expensive, and there is a good chance that if you ship labeled cigars they will be confiscated.

Surprise your date with a fresh tropical bouquet. Prices are about half of what you'd expect to pay back home.

Looking for that permanent reminder of a temporary feeling? **Screamink Tattoos** (10th Street at Quinta, www.screaminktattooshop.com) offers tribal tattoos, Mayan designs, and custom jobs. T-shirts and piercings are also available.

Casa Partagas (Quinta at 14th Street) is a good spot to purchase real Cuban cigars. Ask the staff for an explanation of how to spot the fakes. T-shirts, smoking accessories, and gifts are also sold.

Fitness & Spa Services

Founded by veteran Californian holistic health practitioner Sharon Sedgwick, the modern ★ **Spa Itzá** (Calle Corazon/14th Street, near Quinta, on the Calle Corazon pedestrian walk, www.spaitza.com) takes a traditional approach to body treatments, accenting its services with ancient Mayan healing principles.

Located at the ROYAL Resort, ★ **SPAzul** (Constituyentes between First Avenue and the beach, www.realresorts.com) is open to the public and offers a fantastic *temazcal*, sweat lodge, a great whirlpool room, plunge pools, and therapy rooms.

THE ROYAL Resort offers a touch of luxury with the temazcal experience. ROYAL Resort Playa del Carmen

Temazcal

The word *temazcal* means "bath house" in the Nahuatl language of the ancient Aztecs, and the centuries-old *temazcal* sweat-lodge ceremony hasn't changed much over the years. The ritual, performed by a shaman or trained healer, is designed to serve both spiritual and medical purposes. Native women were known to give birth inside the dark, warm environment of the *temazcal*, thus making the transition from the womb more gradual. The sweat-lodge ceremony takes place in a stone or adobe hut, dug into the earth and forming a dome large enough for about a dozen participants. Before entering the *temazcal*, all those who will participate reflect on the four cardinal points and are cleansed with incense. Volcanic stones are heated in a wood fire, carried into the *temazcal*, and placed in the center of the floor.

Each participant sits behind a clay pot full of water, and the door is closed and sealed, making the inside completely dark and very hot. The leader pours water onto the rocks, creating steam that fills the *temazcal* and helps partakers liberate their minds, bodies, and souls. Ancient chants are repeated, songs are sung, and participants are led through a cleansing ritual. In some versions, regional fruits are passed around to be tasted and rubbed on the skin. Modern-day participants generally wear their bathing suits and can splash water on themselves to regulate their breathing and prevent overheating.

Many people have visions and even see an animal or other creature rising from the glowing rocks. The ceremony leader can help interpret whatever you may see. At the end of the ceremony, it is customary to run to the ocean and bathe in the shallows, letting the cool water wash away the sweat and complete the renewal process. Next, a soothing herbal tea helps lock in the benefits reaped during the ceremony. It's a wonderfully spiritual experience that can leave you energized and refreshed for hours afterward.

Places in the Riviera Maya with *temazcal* facilities include Maroma Resort & Spa, Punta Maroma (see chapter 6); ROYAL Playa del Carmen; Tulum Dreams/ Resort & Spa, Tulum; Viceroy Riviera Maya, Playa Xcalacoco (see chapter 6); and Ana y José Charming Hotel & Spa, south of Tulum (see chapter 5).

Affordable spa treatments are offered at **Magic Hands** (Quinta between 10th and 12th, Quinta between Sixth and Eighth Avenues), amidst candlelight and relaxing music. Pedicures and manicures are also offered in this relaxed setting.

Perched upon the rooftop of the Soho Playa Hotel, ★ **Yoga by the Sea** (Tenth Avenue at 24th Street, www.morethanyoga.com) instructors Arielle Thomas Newman and Ellen de Jonge offer daily Hatha yoga classes, yoga retreats, specialized programs, and meditation and relaxation techniques. They have special yoga programs for couples, divers, and golfers.

Authentic Bikram yoga classes are offered every day of the week at **Bikram Yoga Riviera Maya** (Quinta between 40th and 42nd, bikramyogarivieramaya.com).

Modern and upscale, **The Gym** (First Avenue between Constituyentes and

Keep up with your "hot yoga" routine.

16th Street, www.thegymplaya.com) offers top-of-the-line weight and cardio vascular equipment, fitness classes, and personal training.

Evolve Gym (24 Street, between Quinta and 10th Avenue) has top-of-the line machines, tons of weights, and some great classes. They offer pilates, yoga, spinning, and cardio kick boxing instruction.

15 Luxurious Resorts & Spas for Indulgent Travelers

1. Viceroy Riviera Maya spa resort (Punta Bete)
2. Fairmont Mayakobá spa resort (Punta Bete)
3. Banyan Tree Mayakobá spa resort (Punta Bete)
4. Coqui Coqui Spa Hotel (Tulum)
5. El Dorado Royale—A Spa Resort by Karisma (Playa Secreto)
6. Hotel Esencia (Xpu-Ha)
7. Hotel Villa Rolandi Thalasso Spa (Isla Mujeres)
8. The Beloved Hotel spa (Playa Mujeres)
9. Live Aqua Cancún resort and spa (Cancún)
10. Maroma Resort & Spa (Punta Maroma)
11. Mezzanine hotel (Tulum)
12. Occidental Royal Hideaway spa resort (Playacar)
13. Zoëtry Paraiso de la Bonita (Bahia Petempich near Puerto Morelos)
14. Rosewood Mayakobá spa resort (Punta Bete)
15. ROYAL Resort Playa del Carmen SPAzul (Playa del Carmen)

The Riviera Maya: A Land of Business Opportunity

by Brenda Alfaro

Great business opportunities abound in the Riviera Maya, and with careful consideration and planning, foreigners can invest successfully in this growth. Doing business in Mexico is not for the faint of heart, however. It requires moxie and experienced advice to be successful. Having a local on your side is always a plus, especially in Latin America, where polite business relationships guide you through the maze of paperwork, labor relationships, and license requirements. Patience is also a must-have virtue to survive the relaxing *mañana* Latin style.

Where do you start to create a business in Mexico? Well, not with the "slick talker and aggressive salesperson" attitude. First, look for someone who has been successful in a quiet way, who obviously has learned the ropes and has created the business and official relationships that have kept her in business.

Second, before stepping into the business community with a substantial investment, research and understand the legal system and labor relationships in Mexico. This is easily done on the Internet. Mexico laws are based on the Napoleonic Code, similar to the laws of France or Louisiana in the United States. Labor relationships are based on the "employee is always right" philosophy. Mexican employees know their rights and use them effectively—as do the lawyers representing them.

Third, understand the importance of a Mexican notary, a powerful appointed position in Mexico. Notaries create most of the official legal documents in Mexico, including establishment of corporations, buy-sell agreements, and real estate transactions. No transaction or legal agreement is considered legal in Mexico unless it has been officially registered. All parties to an agreement must sign it in front of a notary, and that agreement must be registered in the municipality's official records.

Fourth, before completing a business transaction, seek the advice of a person who is completely independent of the parties involved in the transaction and one you trust to translate the agreements to you accurately. I am always amazed when I hear that someone is using a lawyer or notary who was recommended by those who stand to benefit from the transaction, such as a seller or a real estate agent. A good rule of thumb is "If you would not do this in your country, you should not do it here."

48 Hours
in Playa del Carmen

If your time is limited, pick a hotel on the beach in downtown Playa del Carmen. Mosquito Beach, Playa Maya, or Fusion Hotel would all be good options. No need to go all-inclusive, since you won't be spending much time at the hotel anyway. Drop your bags in your room and head straight for the beach.

Head north along the waterfront to the Canibal Royal beach club on the edge of town. Order a bucket of ice-cold Coronas, fresh ceviche, and a whole fried fish. Vacation has arrived.

Spend the afternoon enjoying the sunshine and fresh air, taking frequent

Fifth, contract an accountant to keep you current with your tax filings and license requirements. Be careful whom you contract, and seek the advice of those who have experience here.

Sixth, avoid all lawsuits and labor board actions. Swallow your pride or anger and settle with an employee who is leaving or involved in a legal situation. In the end, it will save you money and stress and allow you to focus on your business at hand rather than revenge or a compelling desire to "win." If you do end up needing a lawyer, find one who actually knows the law and has strong legal contacts.

Seventh, be polite and patient—always! Mexican people are intelligent and are part of a formal, polite society. Do not underestimate their abilities or insult them. Stop, listen, and think before you answer or react. Directness is not a business asset in Mexico. Talk, smile, and never argue or raise your voice. If you do, the costs will be great.

Eighth, follow the rules. It is so much easier when you are always in compliance, which means no extra favors need to be made to run your business. Remember, the person who receives a favor will be out of power in a few months or years, and the new official will expect the same or more—so why begin? And get your FM3, our resident work visa. Don't risk deportation.

Ninth, treat your employees with respect, learn the labor laws, and use employee contracts. Talk with business owners in your field and understand your employee base. Call for references before hiring someone. Identify the "professional labor board employees" who move from business to business, collecting labor settlements. Look prospective employees in the eye—if they do not look back or seem distrustful, do not hire them. Trust your instincts.

Tenth, enjoy the experience. When your patience begins to wear thin, escape to the beach to relax, recharge, and remember why you chose to live and work in this paradise in the first place.

Brenda Long Alfaro and her Mayan husband, Jorge Luis Alfaro Mérida, are successful restaurateurs in Playa del Carmen. They own Ajua Weddings, which offers custom-designed weddings and event services on the Riviera Maya.

dips in the ocean and applying sunscreen each time you order another round of drinks. Later that evening, head to Quinta (Fifth Avenue) just in time for Magic Hour—the enchanting hour before sunset, when the air cools down, the bars start to bustle, and the parade of vacationers makes its way through town.

Pick a restaurant along Quinta for a leisurely meal, then enjoy Playa's version of a pub crawl, with a stop at any bar that strikes your fancy. Consider swinging on the barstools at Pez Vela, placing a bet at the sports book at Tequila Barrel or checking out the rooftop lounge at La Santanera.

For late-night excitement, head to Coco Bongo and secure a spot upstairs near the DJ booth—the perfect vantage point to watch the action on the stage—and on the dance floor.

The marines and local police make a presence on the beach.

Start your second day at Ah Cacao for coffee and pastries. Stock up on snacks for a day of fun in the sun. You've got two choices for your day today. For zip-lining, jungle tours, and Mayan-style water sports, head to the Xplor eco-adventure park where you'll spend several hours in the trees and on the sand. For a softer sense of adventure, take an expedition with Alltournative Tours and visit a traditional Mayan village, swim in a freshwater lagoon, and maybe even meet a friendly monkey.

For your final night in Playa del Carmen, consider lobster at the Blue Lobster or Big Lobster downtown, or walk to Yaxche Restaurant on the north end of Fifth Avenue to sample authentic Mayan cuisine with a contemporary twist. Keep the evening going at the beachfront bar at the Fusion Hotel and witness the fire dancer show.

Ready for more? The Blue Parrot just up the beach is open until 4 AM, with one of the town's largest thatched-roof bars, swinging barstools, and tables in the sand surrounding a dance floor that's always filled with happy revelers. Want to sample more of Playa's nightlife? Take a stroll along the *Zona Doce*, the 12th Street strip, and find dance clubs, lounge bars, student bars, and more, all within a few city blocks.

On your final vacation morning, have breakfast on Fifth Avenue, then hit up the souvenir shops close to the town square. If time permits, enjoy one more visit to the beach for a final swim in the Caribbean.

Where Do Jellyfish Lamps Come From?

Uniquely Playa del Carmen, these gourd lanterns are sold at shops and featured in restaurants and bars throughout downtown Playa. Carved from local gourds and jicaras, they're often adorned with tendrils of natural materials like seeds and shells and sometimes inset with stained glass panes and marbles.

Local artisans and entrepreneurs are responsible for the manufacturing of these lanterns, which by necessity are all made by hand. The proprietors of The Jellyfish Lamp shop have gone as far as to implement a rigorous training and certification program for local artisans.

Through their program, Mayan workers received training for a four-year period before earning the designation of Master Crafter. Starting out, they make the hanging tendrils that fall from the bottom of the lamp. From there, artisans focus on one of three specialties: designing, cutting and encrusting stain glass, or polishing and finishing the gourds themselves. Four workshops are located throughout the Riviera Maya, including one in Playa del Carmen.

Guests who don't want to be responsible for toting a lantern back home, can also order them online from the Jellyfish Lamp shop (www.jellyfish.com.mx).

Extend Your Stay

If you're lucky enough to have more than a couple weeks to spend in the Riviera Maya, you'll have the chance to explore well beyond the traditional tourist attractions.

KOHUNLICH—These Mayan ruins are located near the border with Belize. Since the location is quite remote, the site is in excellent condition, and it's worth the trip.

BACALAR—This ice-blue freshwater lagoon is one of the main attractions in the Mayan Coast. It can be done as a day trip from the southern Riviera Maya, but if you're able to spend several days, there are plenty of other nearby sites to explore.

MERIDA—The capital city of Yucatan state is a wonderful place to learn more about Mayan culture and experience the slow pace of a modern Mexican city with deep roots in the past.

HAVANA, CUBA—There are regular flights from Cancún to Havana. Package deals, including airfare and hotel, are available for less than $350 and can be booked at local travel agencies around Playa del Carmen and even many hotel tour desks. If you're an American, it's recommended that you purchase your package in cash and remember that your credit cards and debit cards will be useless once you arrive in Havana.

PLAYA DEL CARMEN

2

The Riviera Maya

SOUTH OF PLAYA DEL CARMEN

TRAVELERS VENTURING FARTHER SOUTH of Playa del Carmen will find a striking variety of options for lodging and recreation, and the farther south you go, the more remote, unspoiled, and adventurous things become. A stone's throw from Playa del Carmen, Playacar is home to nearly a dozen all-inclusive mega-resorts, where travelers from around the world visit to play golf, lie on the beach, and be pampered in every way possible. The beachfront towns of Puerto Aventuras and Akumal beckon scuba divers and fishing enthusiasts with excellent conditions year-round, while the abundant *cenotes*, hidden beaches, eco-adventure parks, and Mayan ruins provide venturesome travelers with the kind of vacation experiences that turn postcards home into exotic tales of intrigue and exploration.

Many of the hotels and resorts south of Playa are all-inclusives, with vast campuses featuring luxurious accommodations, multiple dining options, on-site nightlife, spas, recreational activities, and everything else guests need to spend a week of fun in the sun without ever getting into a car. Other lodging options in this area include local inns; eco-conscious *cabañas* with an emphasis on nature, rather than luxury; and low-cost hut-like properties fashioned from native materials and devoted to students, traditionalists, and other budget-conscious travelers who want to experience Riviera Maya's splendor, much as the locals have been doing for hundreds of years.

PLAYACAR

Just south of Playa del Carmen, off Highway 307, at km 285, the large-scale, gated resort community of Playacar surrounds the ancient Mayan ruins of Xaman-Ha and is composed of resort hotels, condos, private residences, shopping plazas,

LEFT: Be sure to bargain when shopping for local goods. Brian E. Miller Photography/www.lomimonk.com

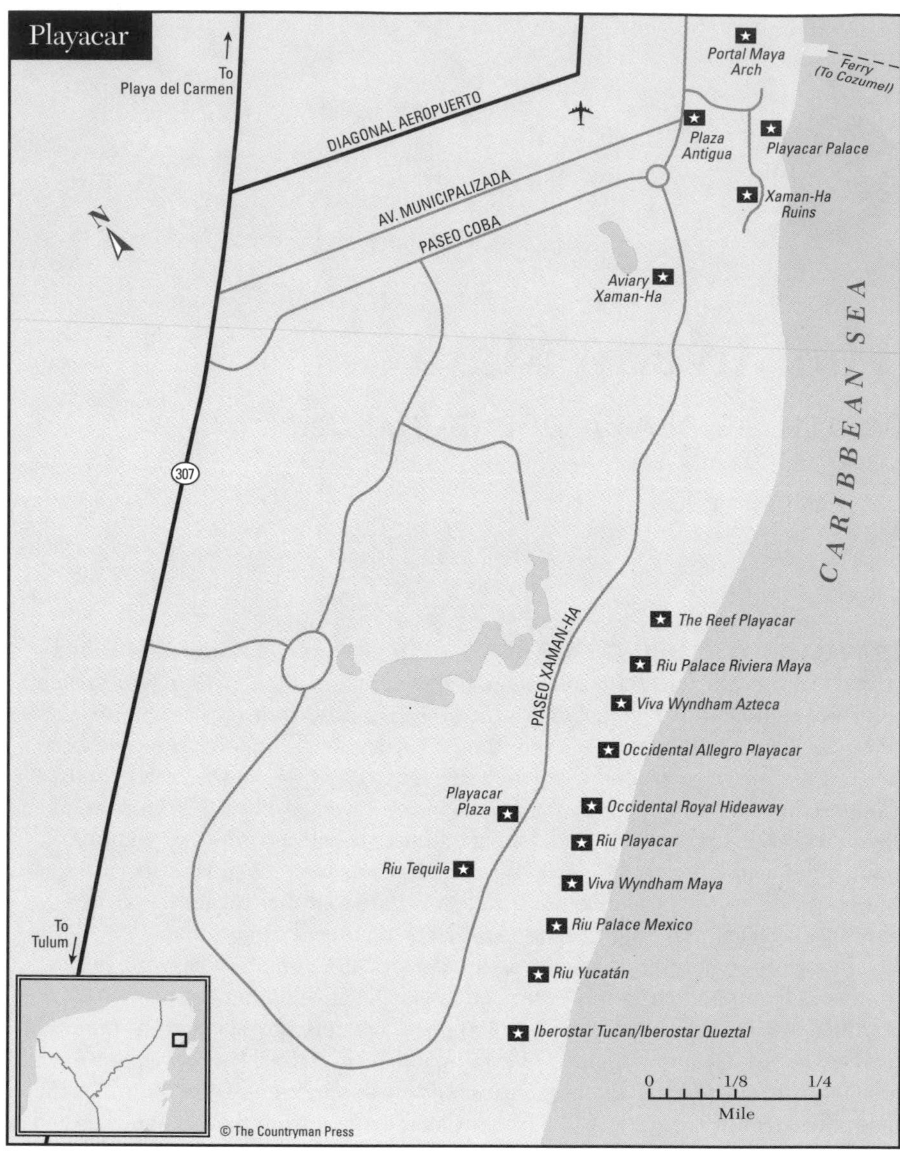

restaurants, a golf course, activities centers, and one of the most pristine stretches of beach in the whole Riviera Maya.

The creation of Playacar was the single most important event in the development of large-scale tourism in the Riviera Maya. Before that, travelers were content with small, locally owned hotels, relatively few services, and European plan (no meals included) rates. Aside from a few standouts, accommodations were generally simple affairs, with basic amenities and very few luxuries but a strong feeling of tradition and harmony with the surroundings. Strict density restrictions in Playa del Carmen made the town less than ideal for large resort development, and had allowed the town to grow slowly and organically, unlike the rampant development seen in Cancún.

In the early 1990s, though, things started to change. Mexico's real estate conglomerate Grupo Situr purchased a huge plot of barren beachfront land just south of Avenida Juárez and christened it Playacar, a term deemed more marketable and English-friendly than the name of the town itself. Since it was out of the jurisdiction of the development restrictions, the Riviera Maya had its first opportunity to build international-class hotels, which needed a larger scale and higher volume of guests to turn a profit.

Today, there are more than a dozen large resorts owned by international corporations and averaging some three hundred rooms each. Unlike the small inns and guest houses of years past, these resorts offer a vast array of services and luxuries, including imported linens, efficient air-conditioning, abundant hot water, water-sports centers, on-site scuba training, dry-cleaning service, Jacuzzi tubs, tennis courts, swimming pools, and kids' clubs. Most are operated as all-inclusives, where guests pay one price that includes accommodations plus all meals, drinks, and activities. Many hotels have on-site gourmet restaurants, multiple bars, and even amphitheaters and nightclubs.

The area has become a playground for tourists from the United States, Canada, and Europe. It is an extremely popular wedding and honeymoon destination, and the resorts are quite adept at catering to vacationing couples with welcome amenities (fruit baskets, chilled champagne, flowers), special dinner reservations, and couples' spa treatments. Other common Playacar visitors are families and budget travelers with flexible schedules, who compare prices weekly, waiting for a bargain. Frequently, these travelers will choose their resort based on what special offers are available and tend to be less loyal to the brands or specific hotel properties. Others have had a good experience at one of the resorts and become avid ambassadors for it, claiming that its services and amenities are unbeatable. These travelers wouldn't dream of staying anywhere else and pride themselves on returning year after year, sometimes bringing gifts for their favorite bartenders and waiters.

The main road through the complex, Xaman-Ha Avenue, is made of cobblestone and is lined with manicured tropical plants and an occasional actual Mayan ruin, lending a timeless quality to the otherwise modern resort community. The road parallels the beachfront and splits Playacar into two sides. Phase I, along the water, features a nearly solid line of hotels, though they are mostly low-rise buildings of two or three stories surrounded by tropical vegetation, so the area does not feel overdeveloped or crowded. Phase II, on the other side of the avenue, includes the golf course, hundreds of vacation villas and private homes, and several hotels that are not directly on the beach. These hotels shuttle guests to a beach club, so even though their rooms don't front the beach, their guests are still able to have a beach vacation. Craft stores, restaurants, bars, and tour agencies are housed in various shopping plazas along Xaman-Ha and at Plaza Marina, near the ferry dock. Most guests, however, either take their meals on-site at their all-inclusive resorts or venture into the neighboring town of Playa del Carmen to experience the abundant dining options offered along Quinta Avenida and throughout town. Shopping, nightlife, and other tourist attractions can be found in Playa as well.

During the day, the beach bustles with activity. Some guests stroll along the water, play volleyball, sail, kayak, windsurf, swim, Jet Ski, and enjoy the plethora

Hotel Choices: All-Inclusive or European Plan

Courtesy of SeePlaya

One of the first decisions travelers need to make when planning their trip is whether to stay in an all-inclusive (AI) or European Plan (EP) hotel. AI resorts generally include all food and drinks consumed on-site, plus a variety of non-motorized watersports, activity programs, and fitness centers. Some even include premium alcohol, gourmet a la carte meals, stocked minibars, and other amenities. European Plan (EP) hotels frequently have their own restaurants and bars also, but guests have to pay for any meals or drinks that they have.

The Riviera Maya has a growing number of all-inclusive resorts, practically pioneering the concept in Mexico. Most of the large-scale full-service beachfront resorts are operated as AIs, while the smaller independently run hotels along the beach and near Playa del Carmen's Quinta Avenida are operated on an EP basis.

Overall, the decision on whether to choose for an AI or an EP is up to the traveler. There are positives and negatives to both choices.

AI RESORTS ARE GENERALLY GOOD IF:

You don't want to do much planning. AIs are generally higher priced than hotels because you are getting all the meals, activities, and alcohol. However, the food and activity choices can get tiresome, and some guests complain that mixed drinks are watered down, though this is certainly not always the case.

EP HOTELS ARE GENERALLY GOOD IF:

You are a little more adventuresome. You will pay less on average but will need to make arrangements for food, activities, and alcohol yourself. Since you'll likely be spending more time away from the hotel, you will get a more authentic Mexican experience.

Now let's get into the details.

FOOD

Obviously, meals are included at AIs, while they are extra for those staying in hotels. AIs generally have limited choices, and, unless you go for the very expensive resorts, the quality of the food can range from poor to very good. Most AIs have a main dining room where meals are served buffet-style and a small selection of a la carte restaurants on-site available for little or no extra charge. Reservations are usually required for the a la carte restaurants and can be difficult to get if the resort is busy. It is not unusual for guests at AIs to report that they get tired of the food choices by the end of their stay.

On the other hand, most Playa hotels have limited menus, meaning you'll either have to go grocery shopping at the local super market or eat out at the surrounding restaurants. The quality and prices of the restaurants varies widely, but exploring the town looking for a good place to eat can also be a lot of fun.

DRINKS

AIs include unlimited drinks, including water, juices, sodas, beer, and mixed drinks, which is one of their main selling points. This is unfortunately not always as good of a deal as it sounds. In Mexico, the same brands of liquor are available in different "grades," where each grade carries a different level of alcohol. The liquor you find in the AIs is generally of the lowest grade, and some guests report that drinks sometimes taste watered down.

If you stay at an EP hotel, you will generally purchase your drinks at local bars, restaurants, or from the in-room minibar. The prices for liquor differ by location, but you are generally assured of quality. If you really want to save money, take a trip over to Walmart and stock up on the cheapest liquor in town.

ACTIVITIES

Most AIs have a variety of activities tailored to their clientele: Sports, exercise classes, dance classes, arts and crafts, pool games, and team sports are common offerings. It is less common for EP hotels to have these options.

One problem with AI-sponsored activities is that these resorts tend to draw a very diverse crowd. Visitors are encouraged to research their resort fully, since you will generally spend most of your time there and you will likely end up socializing with other guests.

BRINGING THE FAMILY?

Although parents should always know where their children are, the setup of an AI resort, with their kids' clubs and activity programs, may allow parents to give children more freedom than they would get in a hotel that has a lot of casual traffic. This can be a big plus for AIs when parents and children are interested in doing different activities. Again, parents should never get too lax with their children's safety while on vacation.

CONVENIENCE

Many people like the convenience of not having to carry money to pay for meals and activities. This is a nice perk of AIs.

ROOMS

There is a wide range of room quality at both AI resorts and EP hotels. If having a very nice room is important, you should make sure you do your research carefully. Don't make the mistake of thinking that an AI will automatically be nicer than a nearby EP hotel; the quality of both varies greatly.

COST

Although many believe AIs are cheaper than EP hotels, this may vary depending on the vacationer and what kinds of activities they do while on vacation. Travelers who spend most of their time at the resort and partake in the free activities will probably find that an all-inclusive is the more economical choice. Vacationers who plan to take several tours and spend a lot of time outside the resort will probably find that an EP hotel is the lower-cost alternative.

Still unsure? Here's a helpful rule of thumb: If you have read this far, it means you like to do your research and enjoy learning about new things and should almost certainly stay at an EP hotel.

of activities, while others seek respite in a lounge chair or hammock and read and snooze to the warm breezes. To the north of Playacar is the town of Playa del Carmen, reachable by bicycle (loaners available at most hotels) or a short taxi ride. To the south is a mile-long stretch of deserted beach decorated with massive boulders, which starts at the Gala Resort and ends at the Xcaret resort and ecopark.

Guests at Playacar resorts can spend an entire week without leaving the complex and have all their needs and whims catered to. Others, however, like to visit Playa del Carmen in the evening to go shopping, stroll the tourist plazas, try some local foods, and enjoy the nightlife.

Checking In

Best places to stay in and around Playacar

It can be a bit difficult to differentiate the all-inclusive resorts of Playacar. For the most part, the hotels share a common beach, which is just about perfect anywhere along the stretch. The hotels themselves are large-scale affairs, with comparable pools, gyms, restaurants, bars, and activities programs. Nearly all the rooms offer good air-conditioning, plenty of hot water, comfortable bedding, private balconies, minibars, and standard amenities. Most have bicycles for guest use, which makes the couple-mile trip into Playa del Carmen a breeze. The main considerations and differentiating factors are the size of the resort, whether or not it's adults-only, whether it's on the beach or the golf course, and your budget. Rates range from $100 per person per night up to $250. As the price goes up, generally, the rooms are larger, the grounds better maintained, food and beverage quality is higher, and the vibe is more exclusive.

Adjacent to the Cozumel ferry dock and the Playa del Carmen town plaza, the chic **Playacar Palace** (north end of Paseo Xaman-Ha, www.palaceresorts.com) is a good spot for travelers seeking the luxury of Playacar but with ready access to downtown Playa. Playacar's original flagship resort, the structure was first large hotel built around Playa and was completely renovated in 2005.

Luxury and all-inclusives don't always go together. But at the adults-only, 13-acre, 200-room ★ **Occidental Royal Hideaway** (Paseo Xaman-Ha, www.royalhideaway.com), the two meld like piña coladas and sunset—which, by the way, are included in the rate. The lavish property has meandering rivers, waterfalls, tropical gardens, six pools (three reserved for quiet relaxation), and several restaurants and bars. Men are required to wear long pants, closed-toe shoes, and collared shirts for dinner.

Spanish-owned ★ **Riu Hotels and**

You can step off the sidewalk inspect this small Mayan structure, located across the street from Playacar Palace. Chip Rankin

10 Adults-Only Resorts for a Kid-Free Getaway

1. Hard Rock Hotel Riviera Maya (Puerto Aventuras)
2. El Dorado Royale—A Spa Resort by Karisma (Playa Secreto)
3. Excellence Playa Mujeres resort (Playa Mujeres)
4. Iberostar Grand Hotel Paraíso resort (Playa Paraíso)
5. Viceroy Riviera Maya (Punta Bete)
6. Mahékal Beach Resort (Playa del Carmen)
7. Occidental Royal Hideaway spa resort (Playacar)
8. Hotel Reina Roja (Playa del Carmen)
9. ROYAL Resort Playa del Carmen (Playa del Carmen)
10. Temptation Resort Cancún (Cancún)

Resorts (Paseo Xaman-Ha, www.riu.com) has six all-inclusive properties on Playacar's southern end. Guests staying at one hotel can enjoy the facilities at the others, including the nightclub, which is located at the party-friendly **Riu Tequila** (well, that makes sense!). The resorts include the upscale **Riu Palace Mexico** and **Riu Palace Riviera Maya**, hacienda-style **Yucatán**, budget-friendly **Riu Playacar**, and the **Riu Lupita**, set in the middle of the golf course back from the beach.

On the south side of Playa del Carmen, the all-inclusive **Iberostar Resort Complex** (Paseo Xaman-Ha, www.iberostar.com) includes the **Tucan** and **Quetzal** resorts, each with 350 rooms. The resort is a sun-worshipers mecca, with a great rock-free beachfront, multiple pools, and outdoor Jacuzzis.

The all-inclusive **Viva Wyndham Resorts** (Paseo Xaman-Ha, www.vivaresorts.com) include the smaller Mexican colonial-style, 234-room, kid-friendly **Azteca** and the more contemporary 400-room **Maya**. Guests may choose to dine at any of the seven restaurants at the two resorts, although several require reservations.

Home rental powerhouse **Airbnb** (www.airbnb.com) usually has more than 1,000 condos, homes, apartments, and private rooms available for rent in Playa del Carmen and Playacar alone. Vacation rental websites **VRBO** (www.vrbo.com) and **Home Away** (www.homeaway.com) each have more than 150 condos and villas listed in Playacar alone, including locations on the beach, on the golf course, and around the development. Both websites lists all of properties and amenities to help you select one that may suit you.

XCARET TO PAAMUL

South of Xcaret, visitors get their first glimpse of the wild side of the Riviera Maya. No longer will you see souvenir stands, gas stations, and convenience stores every few miles. Here a thick jungle canopy has kept tourism development at bay, while palm trees, unexplored Mayan ruins, and tiny traditional villages dot the landscape. To visit this part of the Yucatán, travelers either take a shuttle bus from the airport or rent a car so they can go where they choose. Public bus service is spotty and will

Xcaret offers a sense of the Mayan past. Riviera Maya Destination Marketing Office

Mi Casa es Su Casa—Vacation Home Rentals

For years, shrewd travelers to Mexico have chosen private condos and homes over hotels. As the popularity of these vacation rentals has soared internationally and development in Riviera Maya has multiplied, there are more options than ever.

Private rentals can often accommodate larger groups at a lower overall price, and they feature kitchens and amenities allowing guests to dine in, and greater degrees of privacy than hotels.

As with hotels, quality and pricing levels range from budget to deluxe. You'll want to see as many photos of the actual unit you'll be staying in, have a clear idea of its exact location, and review a full list of amenities and restrictions.

Most rental services offer private accommodations designed for vacation rental. However, the popularity of Airbnb has also introduced and popularized the concept of renting private rooms in shared homes. These are generally cheaper options and appeal to younger travelers (and homeowners or renters) who are on a tighter budget or are seeking to get to know local residents.

Airbnb (Airbnb.com) has more than local 1,000 rental listings, including private homes, condos, apartments, and shared rooms where guests stay with the owner. Terms and conditions vary from listing to listing.

HomeAway (www.HomeAway.com) has done much to popularize the private vacation home–rental concept in recent years, and the website has more than 2,000 private rental listings across the state of Quintana Roo.

VRBO (www.VRBO.com), or Vacation Rental by Owner, is owned by HomeAway but has a separate listing service that also features more than 2,000 private rental listings across the region. Many listings are exclusive, so you'll want to check HomeAway and VRBO for the most thorough selection.

Playa Beach Rentals (www.PlayaBeachRentals.com) is a small, local outfit specializing in rentals and property management. They manage between 20 and 30 properties through their offices, and reservations are booked directly through their listing service.

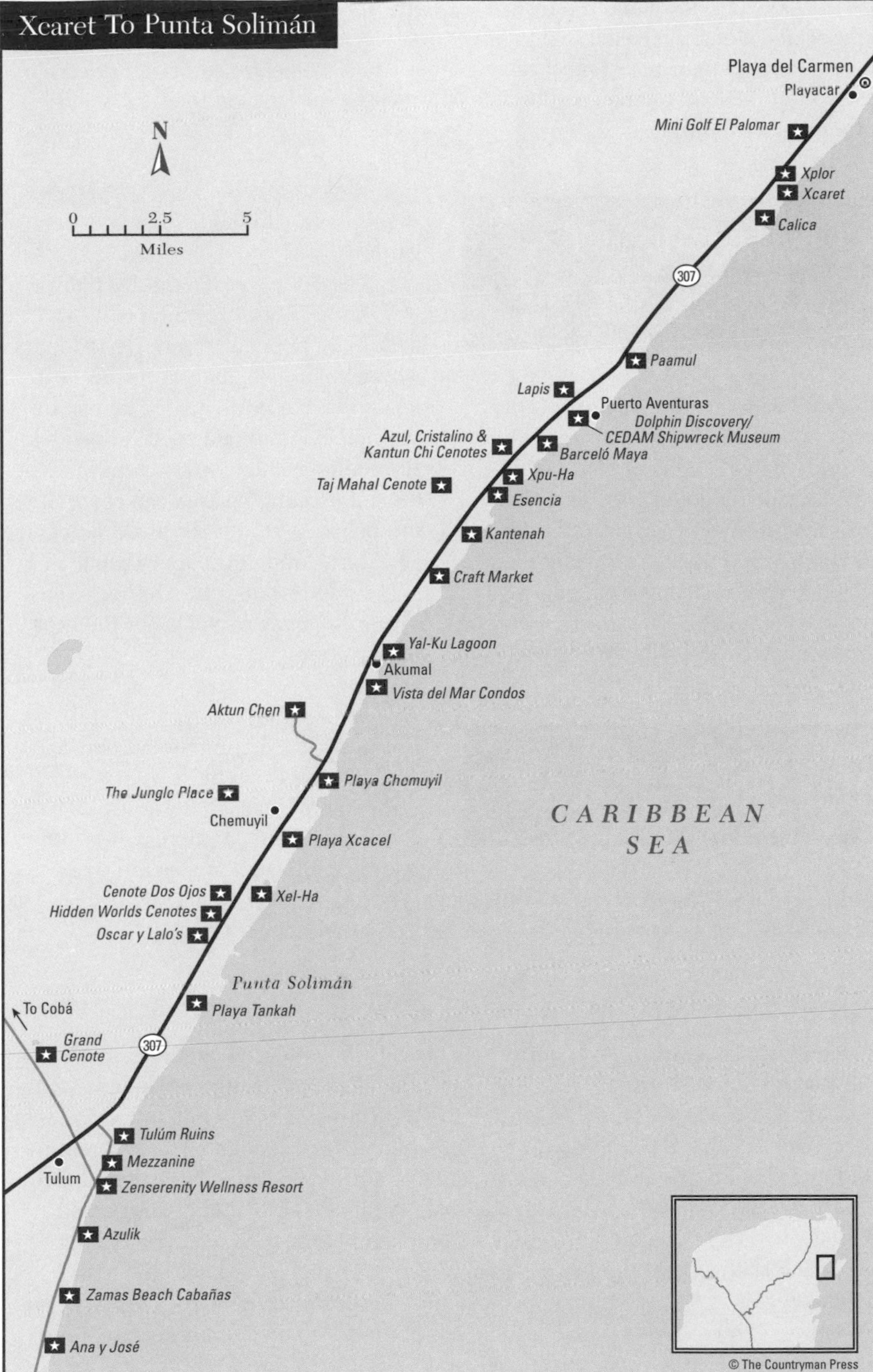
Xcaret To Punta Solimán
N
0
2.5
5
Miles
Playa del Carmen
Playacar
Mini Golf El Palomar
Xplor
Xcaret
Calica
307
Paamul
Lapis
Puerto Aventuras
Dolphin Discovery/
CEDAM Shipwreck Museum
Azul, Cristalino &
Kantun Chi Cenotes
Barceló Maya
Xpu-Ha
Taj Mahal Cenote
Esencia
Kantenah
Craft Market
Yal-Ku Lagoon
Akumal
Vista del Mar Condos
Aktun Chen
Playa Chomuyil
The Jungle Place
Chemuyil
Playa Xcacel
CARIBBEAN
SEA
Cenote Dos Ojos
Xel-Ha
Hidden Worlds Cenotes
Oscar y Lalo's
Punta Solimán
To Cobá
Playa Tankah
Grand
Cenote
307
Tulúm Ruins
Mezzanine
Tulum
Zenserenity Wellness Resort
Azulik
Zamas Beach Cabañas
Ana y José
© The Countryman Press

let travelers off only along the main road, while most of the hotels and attractions are located along the beach several miles away. Tourists either take their meals on-property at their resort or, if staying at an EP (European plan) hotel or condo, stop off at the supermarket in Playa del Carmen to stock up on foodstuffs and other essential supplies.

Checking In

Best places to stay in and around Xcaret to Paamul

Located adjacent to the Xcaret ecology park, the 769-room ★ **Occidental Grand Xcaret** (Highway 307, km 282, www.occidentalhotels.com) is a wondrous, all-inclusive playground catering to families and travelers looking for a lot of activities. Rooms at the massive resort are housed in low-rise buildings surrounded by five free-form swimming pools, winding rivers, and tropical gardens.

The RV haven **Paamul** (Highway 307, km 273, www.paamul.com) is gaining in popularity with day-trippers who come to see the sea turtles nest, go snorkeling or diving, or lounge on the beach. The main road is lined with RV shelters, some of which have been there for years. Visitors can camp on the beach or stay at the small hotel, and there are a few super-casual beachside restaurants. The rocky beach along this shallow bay is not the best for swimming.

Attractions

Formerly just a commercial port and dock for the Cozumel car ferry, the **Calica** port facility (Highway 307, km 280) is becoming a popular stop-off point for international cruise ships and includes a commercial plaza with shops, restaurants, and souvenir stands. **Transcaribe** (transcaribemex.com) operates the Cozumel car ferry.

PUERTO AVENTURAS (Highway 307, km 269)

The exclusive resort town of Puerto Aventuras is the only true sheltered marina in the Riviera Maya. It was also the first major development south of Cancún, though it hasn't had the rapid growth seen in Playa del Carmen. If you talk to the locals, they'll tell you this is by design, to retain the small-town feel and exclusive nature of the resort. But it's also likely a byproduct of a gated community designed with expatriates and relocating Mexican nationals in mind. Hurricane Emily passed directly over the marina in 2005, sinking boats, beaching others, and wreaking havoc across town, but thousands of palm trees were replanted, and the area quickly regained its pre-storm appeal. In fact, encouraged the town's recovery and resilience, condo sales boomed and the community's challenge became keeping its small-town luster. The global recession that followed the 2008 financial crisis cooled that growth, but Puerto Aventuras has regained modest popularity with foreign buyers and well off Mexican nationals fleeing Mexico City.

Visitors enter through a large security gate just off Highway 307. The road

Puerto Aventuras is built around a central lagoon filled with dolphins.

winds down to the beach and ends at the 250-slip marina, packed with fishing boats, dive boats, sailboats, and pleasure yachts. The marina channels wind through an open-air pedestrian plaza, lined with restaurants, shops, bars, pharmacies, Internet cafés, and a few grocery/convenience stores. A Dolphin Discovery location is built into the marina, and visitors can stroll the plaza while watching the dolphins cavort, swim, and even jump out of the water. Given how pleasantly landscaped and maintained everything is, it's surprising how few places there are to stay. There is a nine-hole golf course, a museum, a crafts market, tennis courts, and a beautiful beach where the reef is close to shore.

Checking In

Best places to stay in and around Puerto Aventuras

Originally designed to be a Mexican hacienda with a contemporary flair, the 1,264-room **Hard Rock Hotel Riviera Maya** (Highway 307, km 270, www.hrhrivieramaya.com) is an all-inclusive resort occupying 85 tropical acres along the beach. The resort features an exclusive adults-only section, featuring an added degree of swank. Built around a natural ocean inlet, the resort is ideal for protected-water snorkeling, swimming, and sunbathing. The hotel has turned the dial up a few notches since it was renovated and changed its name from Aventura Spa Palace. It now features heavier event programming, including concerts with internationally celebrated pop and rock celebrities. While it can be expected to draw a younger, often single, crowd many guests are still vacationing couples celebrating a honeymoon, anniversary, or other special occasion. Expect this to evolve somewhat as Hard Rock's marketing takes hold.

Adjacent to the white sandy beach

Hurricane Emily: An Unwelcome Guest

What it's like to be at a resort hotel when a hurricane hits

At 5 PM on July 17, 2005, management at the Moon Palace announced an immediate termination of alcohol sales and room service, instructing guests to stay indoors until further notice. Earlier in the day, the staff had lashed down all the outdoor furniture and plucked all the coconuts from their trees. The guests, many from the northern United States, Canada, and Europe, were complete strangers to tropical weather and immediately lost any romantic notions of hurricane parties or the amusing thrill of riding out a storm. It was an ominous sign of what was to come, as the largest Atlantic hurricane ever recorded in the month of July was bearing down on the Riviera Maya.

Just after midnight, Hurricane Emily, a category 4 storm, ripped across the southern tip of Cozumel Island, enveloping the Punta Sur lighthouse in the eerie calm of the eye. The hammocks at the Reggae Shack swung wildly until the wooden poles supporting them collapsed in a heap, followed by the *palapa* roof of the bar. Up the east side of the island, angry waves licked at the walls of Mezcalito's restaurant as wind-driven rain lashed into the kitchen. A 160 mph gust of wind tore at the roof, pulling it apart bit by bit and spitting it into the ocean. Hundreds of trees along Rafael Melgar Boulevard, the main road along the western beachfront, fell, almost in unison, as the storm continued east. At 1 AM the clock tower in the town square clanged a single time, but the howling wind and distant sirens made it impossible for anyone to hear it.

As the eye moved across the Cozumel channel, the normally ubiquitous ferry boats were nowhere to be seen. The angry storm stirred up massive waves as it traced a path for Puerto Aventuras, hungry for the luxury yachts docked at the marina. Waves crashed over the bulkhead, flooding into shops, restaurants, and hotels. The roof of the Copacabana (now Catalonia Royal Tulum) hotel came crashing down, exposing the lobby to the full force of the storm. Luckily, all the guests were huddled in the relative safety of the hotel's ballroom. A huge metal navigational buoy broke free from its anchor and barreled toward shore, beaching itself in front of the Riu Palace in Playacar. Concrete and wooden utility poles across the region snapped like twigs while billboards along Highway 307 advertising XX Beer and Xcaret Park were crumpled like paper in a fist.

Thousands of people hunkered down in shelters from Cancún to Tulum. Several hundred sought refuge in the convention center at the Mayan Palace, thousands more crowded into the Playa del Carmen municipal gym, and some six hundred others waited and prayed from inside the concrete walls of a bordello on the outskirts of town. Locals and visitors in Cancún rode out the storm together in the tiny rooms of an elementary school. When one room flooded, the group had to brave the elements and run to another. Shortly thereafter, the door to that room was torn from its hinges.

The eye passed right by Paamul, rumbling the mobile homes and testing their window seals with driving rain. Palm trees were gouged from the ground, and rain-soaked sand whipped into the trailers, sounding like thousands of BBs being shot into beer cans.

As the night wore on, bloggers tapped away on computer keyboards in sheltered Internet cafés, updating Internet users around the world of the storm's progress.

Their missives grew less frequent as power lines fell and connection became impossible. A key Tel-Mex cell phone tower swayed in the wind, then bent and fell, cutting off yet another mode of communication.

It was still drizzling when dawn broke, but the heavy winds were gone and the furious sea had calmed. Locals and visitors alike crept from their shelters and spilled into the streets to survey the damage. Along Quinta Avenida in Playa, many shops suffered from broken glass and ruined merchandise. Water was nearly waist deep along Constituyentes. Many homes in the humble residential area north of the tourist zone had collapsed and lay in ruin, and distraught locals sat on the beach and on the street, numb from shock and unsure of where to go. Swimming pools were filled with sand and debris, street signs littered the streets, the beaches were full of trash, *palapas* were torn down, and uprooted or stripped trees outnumbered healthy ones.

The National Guard arrived early to begin clearing the streets and cleaning up the heavily touristy areas, including Quinta. There were widespread power outages, but some stores were open, selling food, water, and other supplies. Hotel guests and staff worked side by side to clear broken glass, sweep out flood waters, and repair damages.

It quickly became apparent that things were not nearly as bad as they could have been. Though powerful, the storm was compact and fast moving, so it did not cause as much damage as it could have. Cozumel, Puerto Aventuras, and Akumal were the hardest hit, with thousands of trees downed and many roofs torn off and buildings flooded. The beach in Playa Paraíso was badly eroded, but in Tankah, just down the coast, there seemed to be more sand than before. Two gas stations lost their roofs and were in shambles, but no fires had broken out. Local farms suffered greatly, with the summer's corn, papaya, and citrus crops enduring major losses.

It was clear that the Riviera Maya had learned the hard lessons since being caught severely underprepared for Hurricane Gilbert in 1988. The large-scale evacuation effort had worked. A convoy of 500 buses had moved 60,000 tourists to safety in less than 12 hours. Some hotels in the Riviera Maya sent guests to sister properties in Cancún, while others were sent to shelters in Vallodolid, Mérida, and elsewhere. Hundreds of petrochemical workers were evacuated from rigs and oil platforms in the storm's path.

The storm claimed the lives of four people in Jamaica, and two men working on oil rig evacuations were killed when their helicopter crashed in the Gulf of Mexico. A German dive instructor living in Playacar also died when he was electrocuted as he prepared his home for the storm. Miraculously, no other major injuries or deaths were reported.

The airports in Cancún and Cozumel opened the day after the storm, and hotels and restaurants opened as quickly as they could. Some were back in business in days, while others took weeks or even months before they were ready again. The people of the Riviera Maya kept their faith, helping each other make it through the hard times. New palm trees were planted, *palapas* were constructed, signs replaced, homes built, and lives repaired. No doubt Hurricane Emily was strong, but she was no match for the determination, the will, and the community spirit of the Riviera Maya.

and the commercial marina, the luxurious **Omni Puerto Aventuras Hotel Beach Resort** (Highway 307, km 269, www.omnihotels.com) is placed at the center of activity in town. Despite offering just 30 rooms, the amenities would seem appropriate for a hotel five times its size.

On a beach south of the marina and 1 mile from Puerto Aventuras' main plaza, the very upscale ★ **Casa del Agua** (Highway 307, km 268, www.casadelagua.com) has four rooms right on a perfect, quiet beach in a residential area. Formerly a private residence, the house is contemporary Mexican, with handcrafted furniture, colorful Mexican textiles, and original artwork throughout. A good option for guests seeking simplicity, luxury, romance, and privacy.

Upscale and family-friendly, the 324-room, all-inclusive **Catalonia Riviera Maya** (Avenue Xcacel, Lot 1, off Highway 307, near km 271, www.hoteles-catalonia.com) gives guests a taste of the Mexican Caribbean while still providing high-end resort luxuries.

Local Flavors

Taste of the town—restaurants, cafés, bars, bistros, etc.

Most restaurants in Puerto Aventuras are located around the central marina plaza, overlooking the Dolphin Discovery waterway, and most have small interior dining rooms and patios with shaded tables. All in close proximity, it's easy to walk from one to the next, checking to see what looks good. Prices are a bit higher than in other areas of the region due to the resorts' exclusive nature and lower volume of visitors.

Notable options include **Dos Chiles**, offering good Mexican food, shrimp, fajitas, and tacos in a casual outdoor eatery, and **The Pub**, a popular sports bar surrounded by shade trees and serving inexpensive breakfast, pizzas, fresh fish, tacos, enchiladas, and shepherd's pie. Open for breakfast, lunch, and dinner, the pricier **Ristorante Massimo** specializes in Italian food including beef lasagna, pizzas, pastas, and a good selection of ice cream and desserts. Aventura Gelato offers an array of Italian ices, sorbets, and gelatos.

Attractions & Activities

Aventuras's attractions are also found around the marina. The small **CEDAM Shipwreck Museum**, operated by the Club de Exploraciones y Deportes Acuáticos de México (Water Sports & Exploration Club), which is responsible for locating and protecting the region's wrecks. Founded in 1959 by Pablo Bush Romero, it displays many artifacts recovered from shipwrecks in Mexico and around the world, revealing how they were excavated and how materials were recovered and restored. Free to the public (donations accepted).

More tactile guests can interact with the dolphins at **Dolphin Discovery** (www.dolphindiscovery.com), and there are several different packages, offering everything from simple contact to being propelled through the water by two dolphins.

Nobody can resist a kiss from a dolphin. Delphinius & the Wilkerson Family

20 Romantic Spots for Couples

1. Viceroy Riveria Maya resort (Punta Bete)
2. Azulik clothing-optional hotel (Tulum)
3. Excellence Playa Mujeres resort (Playa Mujeres)
4. Hotel Esencia resort (Xpu-Ha)
5. Fairmont Mayakobá resort (Punta Bete)
6. Hotel Lunata (Playa del Carmen)
7. John Gray's Place restaurant & bar (Puerto Morelos)
8. La Casa del Agua restaurant (Playa del Carmen)
9. La Habichuela restaurant (downtown Cancún)
10. Le Reve Hotel & Spa (Punta Bete)
11. Live Aqua Cancún resort (Cancún)
12. Mahékal Beach Resort (Playa del Carmen)
13. Mayan Beach Garden hotel (Mahahual)
14. Mosquito Beach Hotel (Playa del Carmen)
15. Occidental Royal Hideway resort (Playacar)
16. Hotel Reina Roja (Playa del Carmen)
17. ROYAL Resort Playa del Carmen (Playa del Carmen)
18. The Glass Bar restaurant & bar (Playa del Carmen)
19. Ula Gula restaurant & bar (Playa del Carmen)
20. Villa Las Brisas bed and breakfast (Isla Mujeres)

Live Like a Celebrity for a Week

If hotels and condos aren't your thing and you want to experience the Riviera Maya with first-class luxury and privacy, consider renting a beach house for your visit. Akumal Villas (www.akumal-villas.com) manages a collection of some of the finest private rental homes and villas in the area, with properties in Puerto Aventuras, Akumal, Jade Bay, South Akumal, Soliman Bay, and Tankah. These homes have one to six bedrooms and feature swimming pools, hammocks, full kitchens, purified water, safes, balconies, satellite TV, and other amenities. Full-time maids, caretakers, and on-call chefs and massage therapists are also provided.

The well-respected **Riviera Maya Parasail Adventures** (www.rivieramaya parasail.com) offers activities for vacationers seeking a bit of adventure, including dry parasailing, in which tandem and solo riders take off from the back of a boat and soar high above the water.

XPU-HA (Highway 307, km 264)

Several different access roads lead from Highway 307 to Xpu-Ha beach, making for fun exploration of the various areas. The picturesque beach is very low-key, with a wide bay, coconut palms, and a shallow reef, making it a good spot for snorkeling. To find the best spots, walk to the north near the Xpu-Ha Palace Resort, where the water is calm and the access is easier. The beach to the south is not as sandy, with some rocks, vegetation, and seaweed. There are a few small family-run restaurants serving fresh fish and cold drinks on the beach, one renting snorkeling equipment and WaveRunners. For overnight stays, there are several major resorts and a handful of *cabañas* and villas for rent. On the west side of the highway, across from the Xpu-Ha turnoff, are a pair of small but swimmable *cenotes*.

Checking In

Best places to stay in and around Xpu-Ha

A unique resort built on 50 secluded beachfront acres, ★ **Hotel Esencia** (Highway 307, km 264, www.hotel esencia.com) has hosted many celebrities and is more an opulent private residence than hotel. Once the home of an Italian duchess, it has 29 luxurious rooms and ultra-cool Italian-Mexican decor. The property has large breezy terraces, an idyllic beachfront, high ceilings, an organic spa, a fitness center, and an on-site *cenote*. Rooms feature premium bedding and liquor (including full-size bottles).

Private guesthouse ★ **Al Cielo Hotel** (Highway 307, km 264.5, www .alcielohotel.com) has four rooms built right on the beach, with easy access to the water. There's a small beach club and a gourmet restaurant specializing in fresh seafood and meat. An on-site spa offers shiatsu, Reiki, reflexology, and face and skin treatments.

The **Barcelo Maya Resort**

Complex (Highway 307, km 265, direct entrance from the highway, www.barcelo.com) offers more than two thousand rooms in five different hotels (**Tropical, Beach, Caribe, Colonial, Maya Palace Deluxe**). They're very popular for group trips, corporate incentive travel, family reunions, weddings, honeymoons, and other occasions. The complex's scale makes it a great place for first-time Riviera Maya travelers who would feel most comfortable surrounded by similar vacationers, rather than submersing themselves in the local culture.

The all-inclusive, 144-room **Bel Air Collection Xpu-Ha Riviera Maya** (Highway 307, km 265, www.belairxpuha.com) offers beachfront accommodations to families and couples who refuse to travel without their pets.

Local Flavors

Taste of the town—restaurants, cafés, bars, bistros, etc.

On the grounds of the Al Cielo hotel, the casually upscale beachfront ★ **Restaurante al Cielo** (Highway 307, km 264.5, www.alcielohotel.com) has a *palapa* roof and several tables right next to the sand. The internationally trained chef prepares shrimp, seafood paella, Angus beef, duck, quail, and lamb. No credit cards.

Run by a former Four Seasons chef, ★ **Sal y Fuego** (www.hotelesencia.com) at Hotel Esencia specializes in seafood. Many signature dishes at this upscale restaurant use organic ingredients native to the area.

The small family-owned **La Playa** has several tables in the shade or right on the beach.

The beach *cabanas* at Hotel Esencia are perfectly designed.

KANTENAH

A small sign on Highway 307 at km 262 points the way to Kantenah beach, which is a couple miles down a washboard road. There are many coconut trees and a quiet bay with a shallow reef for snorkeling. Near the beach, there is a large handicrafts market with better prices than in Cancún or even Playa del Carmen, and there's another one on the highway, at km 259.5, with a large assortment of pots, rugs, and blankets.

Checking In

Best places to stay in and around Kantenah

The adults-only, 133-room, all-inclusive **El Dorado Seaside Suites** (9 Highway 307, km 262, www.karismahotels.com) is a popular destination for honeymooners, couples, and even families seeking to experience the Riviera Maya's less populated areas without sacrificing first-class service, comfort, and convenience. Three restaurants serve Asian, Mexican, and seafood specialties (and no buffets), and several bars are sprinkled throughout the property. El Dorado Guests can pay a day-use fee to visit the clothing-optional Hidden Beach hotel next door.

The 414-room, all-inclusive, family-friendly **Grand Palladium Kantenah Resort & Spa** (Highway 307, km 260, www.palladiumhotelgroup.com) features Mayan-inspired architecture, suitable to its natural surroundings. A staff biologist monitors the hotel's impact on the environment and advises on ways to preserve native flora and fauna. As a result, there are many trees, tropical gardens, and native animals on the property. A half-mile stretch of open beach is perfect for jogging, sunbathing, and sun-worshipping.

The 42-room, all-inclusive, clothing-optional and upscale **Hidden Beach Resort** (Highway 307, km 262, www.hiddenbeachresort.com) boasts a pool, hot tub, and beach *cabañas*. Guests can enjoy nude dining, sunbathing, and ocean swimming (though it's mostly rocky). The hotel's gourmet restaurant serves three meals per day, either in the shaded dining room or alfresco, next to the pool. There is a swim-up bar, where bartenders (clothed, for the most part) are happy to mix up special drinks. At night, guests head to the on-site mini-discotheque for nude salsa lessons, dance music, and socializing. This is not a swingers resort and doesn't allow public displays of anything not allowed at a clothed hotel. Singles welcome.

AKUMAL (Highway 307, km 255)

Five separate highway exits lead to this marina town, whose name translates into "Place of the Turtles." It is known as a family-friendly resort area with calm and shallow coves, dozens of nearby dive sites, superior sportfishing, pleasant pedestrian plazas, quality restaurants, lively bars, and a variety of accommodations options. The area consists of three separate bays: Half Moon, Akumal, and Aventuras. The late author John D. McDonald wrote several of the books in his famous Travis McGee series of boat bum/private detective novels while lounging on these beaches.

The area is still a nesting ground for sea turtles, and they are now closely protected by the government and privately funded preservation organizations. Visitors can take guided tours to see the turtle nests and, if the timing is right, see the turtles lay their eggs or watch the hatchlings return to the water. An information center at the main entrance can book tours, provide directions, and reserve accommodations ranging from simple hotel rooms to large private villas. There are several grocery stores, an Internet café, a dive center, a kiteboarding office, and handicrafts available near the main entrance. There's free parking in a safe lot just before the gate if you're just visiting for the day. The best beach within a short walking distance is just beyond the dive shop.

Checking In

Best places to stay in and around Akumal

Accommodations at the sprawling beachfront ★ **Vista del Mar Condos & Hotel** (Half Moon Bay, www.akumalinfo.com) range from a basic hotel room to a three-room condo at the water's edge that's darn near luxurious.

With 241 rooms and a broad white-sand beach, the all-inclusive **Akumal Beach Resort** (Highway 307, km 255, www.akumalbeachresort.com) is ideal for families and couples seeking casual and comfortable surroundings without superfluous luxuries.

Open since the early 1990s, the family-friendly, all-inclusive **Gran Bahia Principe** (Highway 307, km 250, www.bahia-principe.es) is a massive upscale complex (more than two thousand rooms) that includes the **Tulum, Akumal,** and **Coba** resorts and a central plaza with resort shops, tour desk, and most popular nightlife attractions. The more upscale, modern, and adults-only **Sian Ka'an** sits in the middle of the new 27-hole, Robert Trent Jones, II–designed **Bahia Principe** golf course.

Set upon Yalku Lagoon, the nine-room **Posada Que Onda** (on Caleta Yalku street, north of Half Moon Bay) offers charming and affordable accommodations, with a large pool and the beach a ten-minute walk away. The onsite Italian restaurant serves seafood and homemade pasta under a large *palapa* roof.

Local Flavors

Taste of the town—restaurants, cafés, bars, bistros, etc.

Just inside the main entry gate to Akumal, you'll find a cluster of restaurants and shops. ★ **Turtle Bay Café** (www.turtlebaycafe.com) offers a little of everything in a small, homey building with a large *palapa* out front. With several ceiling fans, it's often one of the cooler spots in town and is frequented by local ex-pats and villa owners.

The ultracasual and delightfully rustic beach bar ★ **La Buena Vida** (on the beach of Half Moon Bay, www.akumalinfo.com) has chair swings, a long happy hour, good music, and an upstairs indoor dining room with a nice view of the beach and serves seafood, burgers, and steaks. Treehouse seating 20 feet in the air is accessible via ladders, and waiters will even climb up carrying traysful of drinks.

The casual **La Lunita Restaurant** (at La Tortuga Condos on the beachfront a half mile south of the marina, Half Moon Bay, www.lalunita-akumal.com) serves international and Mexican dishes for breakfast and dinner.

CHEMUYIL (Highway 307, km 249)

Not really a touristy town, the dusty beachfront village of Chemuyil hosts many of the service workers for nearby Akumal and other developments. It has a gated entry, and the guards are not necessarily welcoming of foreign adventure-seekers, but if you can't get enough of the Riviera Maya beaches and you won't be content until you see them all, you should be able to talk your way in and make your way to the beach for a look.

The beach itself is relatively clean, and the water is very calm and shallow since the reef comes all the way to the surface and acts as a breakwater keeping out the waves. A couple of private campsites and some basic hotels accommodate the few backpackers, naturalists, and escape artists who find their way here, and there's a handful of beachside restaurants and bars.

A waiter delivers drinks to one of the elevated tables at La Buena Vida.

Checking In

Best place to stay in Chemuyil

Although there have been plans for a luxury retreat in the area, nothing has been built. You can typically find at least 15 private homes or vacation rentals in Chemuyil listed on either VRBO (www.vrbo.com) or Airbnb (www.airbnb.com).

Attractions

Known in the native Mayan language as kuxi k'aax, the ★ **Jungle Place** (East of Highway 307, km 248; just inland from Chemuyil, www.thejungleplace.com) is a sanctuary for the endangered spider monkey who were rescued from the illegal pet trade, poaching, and habitat desctruction. "Monkey Tours" are available to see the monkeys' home and the care these unique animals receive—animals that would be unable to care for themselves back in the wild. Tours are very limited and must be scheduled in advance. A minimum $80 donation per person is required for each tour, and all funds raised go directly to the care and feeding of the monkeys.

Get a Job and Stay a While

Though it's not always easy to make the transition from tourist to local, it is possible. With a bit of determination and luck, you can find a job and live in paradise. The Mexican government requires that all foreign workers have an FM3 visa, which your employer must obtain for you. Fluency in Spanish is required, though exceptions are sometimes made. And don't expect to make anything near what you could earn back home: Minimum wage in Mexico is about $10 per day, and most jobs available to foreigners generally pay around $1,000 per month. Depending on the job, sales commission, bonuses, room and board, and other perks can help sweeten the pot. The cost of living can be much less, but only if you plan on living like a local. If you're looking for a permanent vacation and expecting to work during the day and then party at tourist clubs every night, you'll probably need additional financial resources.

XCACEL (Highway 307, km 247; between Chemuyil and Xel-Ha)

A popular nesting ground for loggerhead and green turtles, Xcacel has very few services and no electricity. The area is a nature preserve with skunks, snakes, and other protected animals, plus a combination of beaches, *cenotes*, mangroves, and jungle terrain. The turtles are most common in the warmer part of the year, from May to October. If visiting during this time, it's very important to avoid the nests and not bother any of the turtles. A *cenote* large enough to swim in is on the southern end of the beach (walk to the right, as you're facing the ocean). A small path leads from the beach to the *cenote*; look for a small, wooden sign. To the north, the reef comes close to the beach, making it a good spot for snorkeling. A primitive camping facility offers a place to pitch a tent.

PUNTA SOLIMAN

(Highway 307, km 240)

A restful beach good for jogging, sunbathing, and shell collecting, Soliman, as the locals call it, is the kind of place where you feel compelled to arrange your Corona bottles and lime on the table and take a picture with the sundown in the background. In fact, this beach has become famous for being featured in a popular series of Corona beer commercials.

Top 10 Jobs for Foreigners

- Entrepreneur
- Bartender
- English teacher
- Hotel activities staff/animation (all-inclusives)
- Hotel front desk, guest services, concierge, or tour guide
- Real estate sales
- Restaurant host/hostess
- Scuba instructor
- Time-share representative/sales
- Waiter/waitress

Building a Life, an Ecosystem and Floating Islands

The incredible tale of one man, two floating islands, and 300,000 recycled plastic bottles

After Hurricane Emily ended a unique chapter in the history of Puerto Aventuras in July 2005, a new chapter in floating-debris lifestyles was launched near Isla Mujeres.

The story began in 1998, when British ex-pat, artist, and musician Richy Sowa (or "Reishee," as the locals call him) moved to the Riviera Maya with a dream of living a life of relaxation and simplicity based around recycling and low-impact survival. He started collecting empty water bottles and loading them into fishing nets, which were arranged in a spiral pattern to create an artificial island, which he cast adrift in Puerto Aventuras. He planted mangroves and fruit trees, added some ten tons of sand, and built a house from discarded wood, bamboo, and thatched palm.

The island, sometimes called Bottle Island, reached the size of half a basketball court and could be maneuvered around the marina with an outboard boat motor attached to one end. Built on a foundation of more than 250,000 plastic bottles that he collected, it had a solar cooker (with reflectors laid out in a spiral) and a self-composting toilet and was home to several cats, dogs, and sometimes ducks. Richy's island was featured on *Ripley's Believe It or Not!* in 2000.

Local Flavors

Taste of the town— restaurants, cafés, bars, bistros, etc.

Set right along the highway directly across the street from the Soliman Bay entrance, **Oscar y Lalo's** (Highway 307, km 241, www.oscarandlalo.com) serves delicious fresh seafood, including great ceviche and fish fillets. The best thing on the menu is the fried whole fish, large enough for two.

TANKAH (Highway 307, km 237; between Xel-Ha and Tulum)

Tankah is a small bay that was once an important ceremonial site for the ancient Mayans, and there are minor ruins in the area, though they are still being explored by archaeologists and are not open to the public. The main road parallels the beach and is home to several guesthouses and inns, and one of the largest is Casa Cenote, which is between the beach and a large freshwater lagoon called Manatee Cenote, rumored to have a manatee living in it (though not even the locals have seen one in recent years). The *cenote* has a channel that leads underground, below the road and the hotel, and ends 100 feet offshore from the beach. Only experienced cave divers should do the swim, however.

Checking In

Best places to stay in Tankah

The tiny **Blue Sky Resort** (Highway 307, km 237, on the beach, just past the *cenote* in Tankah, www.blueskyhotel.com.mx) has nine

His self-stated, long-term goal for the project was to "use the waste from this world as a foundation to create a tranquil piece of paradise and sail around the earth on a floating island with the message of love and faith."

When Hurricane Emily hit in 2005, Richy and his animal friends took shelter on the mainland. When morning dawned, his island lay in ruins, ripped apart and beached on the sand. Despite the total destruction of the island's surface, the mangrove roots held much of the fishing nets and bottles together.

In late 2007, he began construction of a second island in a bay on Isla Mujeres, once again building on a foundation of plastic bottles. This time he grouped them together in vegetable sacks. At last count, the island contains about 100,000 plastic bottles, which Sowa continues to expand.

Joyxee Island opened for tours in 2008, charging visitors 50 pesos to come aboard and inspect his ingenuity, which produced an island home that boasts three beaches, a house, two ponds, a solar-powered waterfall and river, a wave-powered washing machine, solar panels, and even air-conditioning in the bedroom should the need arise.

Richey doesn't maintain anything as formal as a website—much less a phone number—so the best strategy is to ask around, show up, and see if he's there.

modern rooms and a small pool in the courtyard, right by the beach. An on site restaurant serves a varied international menu and is open to the public.

A charming collection of casitas, Casa Cenote (www.casacenote.com) sits on the beach between the calm waters of Tankah Bay and Manatee Cenote. The rooms are along the beach and have terra-cotta tile floors, local artwork, and ceiling fans; some also have air-conditioning. The main hotel has a small restaurant and bar with a *palapa* roof and grill and several plastic tables on the beach.

TULUM (Highway 307, km 230)

The dusty but incredibly fast-growing town of Tulum lies about 80 miles south of the Cancún airport. The Riviera Maya officially ends where Highway 307 intersects the road to Cobá, and just north of there is the turnoff to the Tulum ruins. Turn west at the crossroads, and the town of Cobá, a picturesque lagoon, and the Mayan ruins of the same name are about an hour away. Go south and you'll be in the Mayan Coast, also called the Sun Coast (see chapter 7), where the road bypasses Laguna Bacalar as it skirts the Sian Ka'an biosphere and heads toward Kohunlich and on to Chetumal, and eventually to the beach town of Xcalak and the border with Belize.

Many of the resorts do not have power-line electricity and rely on solar power or generators to keep the lights on and the beer cold. It is common for rooms not to have electric light and for hotel staff to light candles along the walkway, and even in the rooms. Guests at these hotels are encouraged to bring flashlights, mosquito repellent, and nature guides and to leave their mobile phones, laptop computers, and urban mindset behind.

Take your bathing suit if you visit Tulum. Dr. John Anderson

Buses depart for Tulum from Playa del Carmen from the bus station near the town square every hour and cost $5. A *colectivo* shuttle van departs Playa from Second Street between 15th and 20th Avenues and will drop passengers off anywhere along the way between Playa and Tulum for $5, even along the main road. The van fits eight people and departs as soon as it is full, from 7 AM–8 PM.

There are two bus stations on Tulum Avenue, across the street from each other on the southern edge of town, between Alfa and Jupiter Streets. Buses depart hourly for Playa del Carmen, Cancún, Mérida, Chetumal, Bacalar, and other towns in the region.

Checking In

Best places to stay in and around Tulum

Notable hotels and guesthouses can be found on the beachfront to the north and south of Tulum, as well within the *pueblo*, or downtown area, of Tulum itself.

Just a stone's throw from the Tulum ruins, the Thai and Mediterranean-influenced beachfront hotel, restaurant, and lounge ★ **Mezzanine** (1 mile north of the crossroads from Tulum, www.mezzanine.com.mx) oozes with style, with provocative decor and deep-rooted romantic appeal. A smallish *cenote*-like plunge pool and a cozy bar and lounge front its four hotel rooms. At night, tiki torches and red and orange candles bathe the entire pool deck and dining room in a sensual

VIDAS—Helping Pets and People in the Riviera Maya

A group of volunteer animal lovers called International Veterinarians Dedicated to Animal Health (VIDAS) travels each year to the Riviera Maya, providing education and free veterinary care in an effort to fight pet overpopulation, which leads to starvation, disease, and other health problems. They work with local communities to improve the lives of pets and the people who love them. Their first trip, in 2002, involved two vets and six students and resulted in the sterilization of 100 cats and dogs over five days in Playa del Carmen. Since then, more than 5,000 animals have been sterilized and vaccinated throughout the Yucatan peninsula.

If you'd like to help the group by sponsoring a pet, making a contribution, or otherwise participating, log on to www.vidas.org.

amber glow. The bar has become a trendy spot for traveling hipsters and locals alike. Every Friday, visiting DJs from Europe and around the world spin house- and chill-out music for as many as 250 people.

The ten trendy *cabañas* at **Om Tulum Hotel Cabanas & Lounge** (6 miles south of the Tulum crossroads, www.tulum-playa.com) front a picture-perfect white sand beach. Guests and visitors gather at the lounge, open nightly until 2 AM, to listen to chill-out music, enjoy cocktails, and make new friends. Rooms have electricity until 1 AM and free Internet service. Rooms can be reserved online, but all local charges are cash only.

Though it bills itself as "not a luxury hotel," ★ **Casa de las Olas** (southern limits of Tulum, www.casadelasolas.com) comes pretty close in a city where a hotel is typically judged for its vista, beach quality, and connection to the environment. The hotel's five richly appointed rooms offer a serene and sensory escape from the everyday. The hotel is proud not to publish its address or exact location online, only noting that it lies close to the stunning Sian Ka'an Biosphere Reserve south of Tulum. Upon making reservations, guests receive specific location instructions. While it's somewhat remote, the hotel remains accessible to Tulum. Their secret is worth keeping.

La Vita è Bella (on the Tulum beachfront, 1½ miles north of the turn-off to Tulum pueblo, www.lavitaebellatulum.com) is composed of ten villas strung along the beach, quite luxurious given the Tulum's casual atmosphere. The hotel offers in-room massage service, and an on-site restaurant serves Italian and Mexican food.

With clean, smooth beaches and an environmentally sustainable aesthetic, **Ahau Tulum** (Tulum beach road, km 7.8, www.ahautulum.com) is a solid representation of modern Tulum, with style meeting eco-minded substance. Most featuring high, triangular Polynesian-style thatched roofs, the charming and rustic rooms all include romantic, yet functional, mosquito netting. The hotel offers yoga classes and kite and paddle surfing lessons.

Zenserenity Wellness Resort (www.zenserenityresorts.com) enjoys a prime setting at the center of Tulum's coastal hotel zone, although it is curiously one of the few lacking its own direct beach access. As the only local large-scale property, it can appear a bit garish, but if you overlook the size and slightly corporate feel, it's an amazing hotel that truly offers a complete getaway. Small villas house 96 rooms, featuring rain showers, Italian linens, and butler service. It offers three gourmet restaurants and a lavish day spa featuring a Mayan *temazcal* sweat lodge, meditation classes, and other treatments. The hotel facilities themselves have undergone several owners and concepts, including Blue Tulum and a gay resort named Adonis. Due to a rocky waterfront and aggressive waves, ocean access is offered at the nearby beach club.

Located one block off the main strip in Tulum pueblo, the small and stylish **Hotel Latino** (Andromeda Street at Colonia Centro, www.hotellatinotulum.com) has a facade vaguely reminiscent of Hotel Deseo hotel in Playa del Carmen. There is a small pool, and rates include free bicycle rental.

The center of low-budget info and activity for Tulum pueblo, **The Weary Traveler Hostel** (Tulum Avenue between Jupiter and Acuario Streets, tulum.wearytravelerhostel.com) has a nice shaded courtyard and snack bar, a common refrigerator, and acceptable rooms with bunk beds. The hostel offers discounted tours, gear rental, traveler camaraderie, and is known as a good place to party with other backpackers.

Uno AstroLodge Tulum (on the Tulum beachfront, near Punta Piedra beach, www.unoastrolodge.com) is all about spiritual healing, global positivity, and energy balance. Rooms have a New Age vibe and there's a small kitchen for guest use. When not lounging on the perfect beach, guests can enjoy a variety of therapeutic treatments, including a full-body massage accompanied with Egyptian harp music, Reiki, yoga classes, and a moonlight temazcal ceremony.

More bohemian beachfront venues can be found south of Tulum pueblo on the Punta Allen road. The adults-only, gay-friendly, clothing-optional resort **Azulik** (a half mile south of Tulum pueblo, www.azulik.com) features 15 beachside huts made from local hardwoods. Each sports a waterfront deck, private bathroom with hot water, and wooden bathtub situated smack in the middle of the room. Candles and matches are provided as no room has electricity. The beach right behind the hotel is rocky with many sea fans that wash in with the tide, but there are sandy access points good for swimming a short walk away. Despite its devil-may-care attitude about clothing and personal relationships, this is not a swingers' hotel. Rather it's just a laid-back eco-lodge designed to let people connect with nature.

The 22 rooms at ★ **Zahra** (1 mile south of Tulum, www.zahra.com.mx) have thatched roofs, but with ceiling fans, electric lights, hot water, in-room spa services, room service, and wireless Internet access, they're not entirely rustic. There are beaches on two sides of the hotel and many palm trees. An on-site restaurant, often showcasing live music, serves traditional Mayan and Mexican food.

Situated on a small, quiet beach, **Zamas Beach Cabañas** (3 miles south of Tulum, www.zamas.com) takes its name from the Mayan word for "sunrise" and has 15 *palapa* bungalows. Wind- and solar-generated power stays on until late at night. An open-air restaurant features Mayan-inspired dishes, Mexican specialties, wood-oven pizza, and fresh seafood, including lobster.

A rustic beach *cabana* at Azulik in Tulum

With a self-styled jungle-chic vibe, **La Zebra Beachfront Cabanas & Cantina** (3.7 miles south of Tulum, www.lazebratulum.com) seems a landmark of an imagined and storied 1980s Tulum—even though there was nothing like it in Tulum's hippie heyday. Its owners, the same Aussies who own the slick Mezzanine Hotel up the beach, say it's understated. Nevertheless, premium bed linens, ceiling fans, large beds, hole-free mosquito nets, wireless Internet access, and local artwork ensure an air of casual luxury. The nine *cabañas* are staffed by a group of sisters who delight guests with their hearty Mexican cooking and drinks at the on-site cantina. Outdoor pit-roasts are featured on the giant charcoal grill each Sunday. Guests and visitors are invited.

Past the simple hotels and Mayan-style huts of the main Tulum hotel zone, where the road is encroached by palm trees and brush, the upscale day spa and seven-room ★ **Coqui Coqui Spa Hotel** (5 miles south of Tulum, www.coquicoquispa.com) offers guests a true escape without sacrificing comfort or style. The home, known locally as the Xtabay Estate, offers a lifestyle designed to enhance the harmony between body, mind, and soul. Guests can reserve a single room or the entire home, decorated with Mexican artifacts, handmade furnishings, tapestries, and a variety of European and Asian accents. The owners have launched Coqui Coqui Perfumes, reportedly based on ancient Mayan formulas, available for purchase on site and at other locations throughout the Yucatan peninsula.

The 14-room **Ana y José Charming Hotel & Spa** (5 miles south of Tulum, www.anayjose.com) offers clean, comfortable, and well-designed rooms. Its beach club has developed a reputation for having a party scene and frequently has day-tripping revelers from Playa del Carmen and beyond, which can add to the excitement in an otherwise fairly remote spot. Electricity stays on 24 hours.

Nearby, the ten serene beachfront casitas of **Shambala Petit Hotel** (www.shambalapetithotel.com) serve as a haven for couples and close friends seeking to disconnect with their regular lives and reconnect with each other, nature, and themselves. The hotel offers traditional Mayan-style rooms with *palapa* roofs and mosquito nets, plus yoga classes, Thai massage, scuba trips, wedding planning, and a pristine beach.

Local Flavors

Taste of the town—restaurants, cafés, bars, bistros, etc.

Open for dinner only Wednesday through Sunday, ★ **Hartwood** (Jungle side of the beach highway, www.hartwoodtulum.com) is an open-air, expat-owned establishment that eschews electricity. All cooking is powered naturally and Hardwood's limited supply of electricity use is provided by solar panels. But the scene itself is rustically hip. The farm-to-table concept features a constantly evolving menu that reflects the local meats and produce available on the given week.

The seaside dining at ★ **Mezzanine** (1 mile north of the crossroads from Tulum, www.mezzanine.com.mx), in the hotel of the same name, features stunning views and tasty Thai and Asian fusion dishes. Plus it's a good place for a cocktail.

La Coqueta (Tulum Avenue and Coba Avenue) delights locals and visitors with traditional Mexican food in Downtown Tulum. Expect live music, a casual atmosphere, good food served quickly, and a friendly environment—everything you would expect from a flirt!

Traditional local fare is served up with some culinary style at the popular **El Tábano** (Tulum at Boca Paila, www.eltabanorestaurant.com). Seemingly squirreled away in the jungle growth, the rustic restaurant evidences some legit modern foodie skill.

Il Giardino (Satelite Avenue at Sagitario Street) serves moderately priced Italian food, including lasagna, pasta, and fresh fish, in a tropical garden setting.

Meanwhile, staking its figurative flag in the ground, **El Pequeno Buenos Aires** or the **Buenos Aires Grill** (Tulum Avenue at Calle Beta) claims to be the only steakhouse south of Puerto Aventuras. It serves moderately priced Angus beef, grilled lobster, shrimp, fish, and vegetarian food.

A popular local spot, **El Camello Jr.** (Tulum and Luna Sur) offers up fresh local seafood at a steal in a no frills market setting.

Find fresh vegetarian and vegan dishes at the coffee shop **Element Fusion Restaurant** (Centauro Sur, www.elementfusion.wordpress.com) every day from 8:30 AM–10:30 PM. The menu features fresh salads, seafood, wraps, noodles, and curries.

If you're spending the day at the beach, most of the featured lodging options also have great little beachfront cafes. It's hard to go wrong with tacos or fresh seafood with your toes in the sand.

How Green Was My Getaway?

Evaluating Ecological and Sustainable Marketing Claims

Around 2006, it suddenly became stylish for hotels and tourism businesses to be environmentally sensitive. Terms like *green, sustainability, carbon offsets*, and *eco-friendly* began to appear with increasing frequency.

Once companies saw marketing advantages in being environmentally and culturally conscious, the claims came fast and furious. Many are genuine. Many are superficial. And many lay in between.

No hotel or company on Earth has perfected its sustainability programs, so a business making a genuine effort today, and seeking to improve it, represents progress.

If you're booking a trip and want to stay in sustainable properties, it can be hard to determine just how valid a company's marketing might be. Here are a few rules of thumb that should help you determine if the marketing claims are sincere.

Seek specific details. If a hotel or business is actively making an effort to engage in true sustainability programs, they'll be glad to be specific about their efforts. You'll often see them articulated on their website. If not, sending an email asking about specific examples can usually reveal what you want to know.

Make sure they aren't just focused on your sacrifice. If green programs are based on your willingness to make a sacrifice, then that business isn't doing very much. All hotels want you to limit the number of items you send through their laundry and to reduce your consumption of their energy and resources. It costs them less. And while it's great that they may want to educate you about recycling once you return home, that doesn't take much effort on their part. If they aren't actively engaging in daily practices and programs themselves, then their marketing claims are hardly genuine.

It's not all about LEED certification. In the U.S., a LEED-certified (Leadership in Energy and Environmental Design) building shows the builder's observation of environment principles. But LEED is an American program and is often unrecognized overseas. Even with certification, ongoing operations involving energy conservation, recycling, use of environmentally safe cleaning agents, and buying food and resources from local producers can have a much larger impact.

Be forgiving with smaller, established "ecological" hotels. Although all the above points hold true, the term "ecological" has been in use for a long time in Latin American and the Caribbean, signifying a smaller, rustic, low-impact property. Some hotels of this type continue to use the term without intentionally making any new specific efforts towards sustainability. Often, it's the context of the word that changed on them. But even without specific programs, these smaller hotels have a similarly small environmental footprint and their overall negative impacts are typically much smaller than the concrete box resorts found along the beach.

Spa

Beachfront ★ Maya Spa (adjacent to the Azulik hotel, www.maya-spa.com) offers daily yoga classes, lucid dreaming courses, and a *temazcal*, a Mayan-style sweat lodge. Local shamans perform traditional Mayan treatments, and local healers use native plants and herbs to perform various healing ceremonies. Other services include body wraps, Reiki, aesthetic treatments, Mayan massage, and flotation-chamber therapy.

BOCA PAILA, SIAN KA'AN & PUNTA ALLEN

Very few travelers will ever have the chance to visit a place as remote—and as starkly beautiful—as the Sian Ka'an biosphere reserve in their entire lives. Meaning "gift from the sky" or "the sky's beginning" (depending on which translation you believe), Sian Ka'an was officially designated a nature reserve in 1986. It spans more than 1.25 million acres, 10 percent of the land in the state of Quintana Roo, and it is an official UNESCO World Heritage site. Don't expect to find picnic tables, public bathrooms, concession stands, or beach bars—this is not a nature park like Xcaret or Xel-Ha. This land is remote and does not have any of the facilities or services that one sometimes associates with a "park." Once Sian Ka'an became a federal reserve, all development was frozen, and all activities are strictly regulated in order to protect the wild diversity of flora, fauna, and geography encompassed in the reserve. There are more than three hundred species of birds (including herons, ibis, roseate spoonbills, and parrots), one hundred types of mammals (such as wild cats, monkeys, coatimundis, and deer), and such land features as barrier reefs, mangrove swamps, lagoons, marshes, and tropical forests. There are also more than 25 Mayan relics, small native villages, and ruins of abandoned ranches, hotels, restaurants, and homes.

The goal of the reserve is to provide a place where nature can thrive on its own, without the negative impacts that come with the presence of humans and the development that always seems to follow. A portion of the biosphere is completely restricted, but much of it is open to exploration, as long as visitors follow the reserve's strict rules of low- or no-impact adventuring. A rocky and sometimes sandy road passes through the area, and vehicles may not depart from the path. There is no inland fishing or scuba diving, though snorkeling is allowed since it has less impact on the reefs. A handful of fishing lodges and rustic hotels operate in the reserve, though they must provide their own water and electricity since there are no utilities in the area.

There is a $3-per-person fee to enter the park, and all travelers must check in at the visitors center. Jeeps and four-wheel-drive vehicles are recommended, as the road is heavily rutted, rocky, and sometimes muddy. Taking a regular rental sedan on the road makes for slow going and may violate your renter's agreement, nullifying any sort of insurance you may have purchased, so it's best to check in advance. There are plenty of picturesque and totally deserted beaches where you can stop for a bit of beachcombing, picture-taking, and stretching. Unfortunately, since the beach is not tended to, like at the resorts, years of washed-up trash remains at the high-tide mark, making a silent yet very compelling case for the need for more awareness of garbage-dumping in the world's oceans.

20 Eco-Friendly Spots for Eco-Conscious Travelers

1. Aktun Chen nature park (near Akumal)
2. Cesiak Centro Ecologico tour (Boca Paila)
3. Alltournative Expeditions (Playa del Carmen)
4. Viceroy Riviera Maya (Punte Bete)
5. Caverna de los Murcielagos *cenote* (Hidden Worlds Cenotes near Tulum)
6. Chankanaab Park (Cozumel)
7. EcoColors excursions (Cancún and throughout the region)
8. Friends of Sian Ka'an Tour (Sian Ka'an)
9. Garrafon Park (Isla Mujeres)
10. Hotel Bucaneros (Isla Mujeres)
11. Yalahau Cenote (Isla Holbox)
12. Azulik clothing-optional hotel (Tulum)
13. Hotelito Casa Las Tortugas (Isla Holbox)
14. Hotel Laguna Bacalar (Laguna Bacalar)
15. Island of the Birds excursion (Isla Holbox)
16. Maya Spa (Tulum)
17. Crococun Crocodile Farm & Zoo (Puerto Morelos)
18. The Explorean Kohunlich by Fiesta Americana jungle retreat (Kohunlich, near Belize)
19. The Jungle Place lodge (Chemuyil)
20. VEA Excursions (Sian Ka'an)

At the southern end of the road, you'll reach the tiny village of Punta Allen. And no, some gringo named Allen doesn't own the town. The name comes from the Mayan word *allin*, which means "crocodile." The village is home to 600 inhabitants, said to originate from 90 original families. There are a handful of lodges, a couple of restaurants, a bar, and a general store called Tienda Socorro, where travelers can purchase basic supplies.

With mangrove swamps, shallow lagoons, and a barrier reef that comes quite close to the beach, this region is a favorite for birdwatchers, anglers, and shell collectors. Crocodiles and manatees also make their home here, which adds to the excitement and improves your chance for a once-in-a-lifetime natural encounter. Jimmy Buffett fans will recognize this area as the setting for the singer's novel *A Salty Piece of Land*, which chronicles an American expatriate cowboy who sails with his horse to the fictitious island of Punta Margarita (sound familiar?) in Ascension Bay and becomes a fishing guide.

Speaking of fishing, the shallow flats, coves, and tiny coastal islands of Sian Ka'an, Punta Allen, and Ascension Bay offer some of the best fly- and light-tackle fishing in the world. Popular catches include barracuda, bonefish, and the coveted permit, which range from 2 to 20 pounds. Many of the lodges host fly-tying sessions for anglers who want to tie their own flies. If you're not familiar with fly-fishing techniques, local guides can teach you how to do it. If that's not your thing, you can fish in many of the same spots using light tackle. Most fish are caught by

7 Active Ideas for Adventurous Travelers

Bike rentals (Akumal, Playa del Carmen)

Bikram Yoga Riviera Maya (Playa del Carmen)

Horseback riding (Cozumel, Isla Holbox, Paamul, and south of Playa del Carmen)

Ikarus Kiteboarding (Playa del Carmen)

Selvatica park (Puerto Morelos)

Xplor park (Xcaret)

YucaTreks Far Out Adventures (Playa del Carmen and throughout the region)

sight-casting, where the guide or the angler stands on the boat and searches the water for signs of fish, and then makes pinpoint casts to land the fish. At other times, anglers will wade into the waist-deep water and cast into the schools.

The author bringing in the catch of the day

Getting There

Take Highway 307, the main highway along the Riviera Maya, south from Playa del Carmen to the town of Tulum, about 45 minutes away. At the main Cobá crossroads, one stoplight past the turnoff to the Tulum ruins, turn east and follow the paved road a couple of miles to the end, and then turn right, to the south, and parallel the beach. After passing the Tulum beach hotel zone, you'll cross a usually empty guard post marking the unofficial beginning of the Sian Ka'an biosphere reserve. Three miles later, you'll come to an arch across the road and the official, always-manned biosphere entrance. All vehicles must stop to be logged in and pay a $2-per-person fee to enter. Once inside the park, follow the road along the beach for another 10 miles (about 45 minutes' worth of bumping up and down), and you will reach Boca Paila, marked by twin bridges (one wooden, one concrete, built in 2005) over the lagoon. Twenty miles into the trip, you'll come across a small, unmarked Mayan temple partially hidden in the scrub brush next to the road, on the west side of the road. Several miles later, the road ends at the town of Punta Allen. Once you've left Tulum, the next gas station is in Punta Allen, which is 40 miles and about an hour and a half away (in good conditions), so don't leave without filling up.

Colectivo shuttle service is available from Tulum to Punta Allen, departing from a garage on Highway 307, two blocks north of the Weary Traveler. It leaves daily at 2 PM.

Checking In

Best places to stay in and around Boca Paila, Sian Ka'an & Punta Allen

Accommodations are eco-friendly "lodges," which means they are simple, with few luxuries and no air-conditioning, bathtubs, orswimming pools. Travelers in these parts tend to be nature enthusiasts, backpacking adventurers, serious anglers, and others who are comfortable in tents, wooden *cabañas*, and other no-frills accommodations. For the hearty few that are up to the task, staying the night in the biosphere can reveal wondrous parts of the jungle that are rarely seen by others. The hotels in the area offer shuttle service from Cancún or the Riviera Maya, with advance notice required. Credit cards are not accepted, except for advance reservations in some cases, so plan ahead.

Just when you think you can't take the bumpy road through Sian Ka'an anymore, you arrive at **Pesca Maya** (3 miles north of Punta Allen, www.pescamaya.com) on Mexico's Ascension Bay. The lodge is built on the land of the Chenchomac (Mayan for "land of the foxes") ranch, a former coconut plantation. It has a large, well-built *palapa* restaurant and bar, which serves as the library, fly-tying station, and social center.

Ascension Bay Bonefish Club (on the edge of Ascension Bay, Punta Allen, www.ascensionbay.com) hosts only six anglers per week, in a small house built right on the beach. All-inclusive packages run Friday to Friday and include transfers from Cancún, lodging, meals, and six days with a private fishing boat and guide.

Eco-friendly lodge **Cesiak** (2 miles north of the Boca Paila bridge on the road from Tulum to Punta Allen, www.cesiak.org) is located on a 15-acre beachfront ranch that housed an upscale resort until 1982. Opened in 2000, Cesiak's eco-conscious rooms are housed in tents on wooden platforms and have terraces, hardwood furniture, and great views.

The rustic **Casa Cuzan** (on the southern edge of Punta Allen, www.flyfishmx.com) offers 12 fan-cooled, thatch-roofed cabañas, a restaurant (think lobster, fish, Mexican/Mayan cuisine), and great access to the area's best fishing spots.

Activities & Tours

Housed at the Cesiak eco-lodge camp in Boca Paila (see Lodging), **Cesiak Centro Ecologico** (www.cesiak.org) offers an all-day Sian Ka'an tour and a sunset bird-watching tour; both include visits to a Mayan ruin and boat-tours.

Led by a bilingual guide, the ★ **Friends of Sian Ka'an Tour** (www.amigosdesiankaan.org) takes guests on a driving tour through the reserve, a boat trip through the mangroves, and a visit to a freshwater spring.

If you have only one day to visit Sian Ka'an but want to fit in as much as possible, try **VEA Jeep Safari** (www.jeep-safari.com), which includes a Jeep ride to the biosphere entrance, a boat tour to see dolphins, swimming, snorkeling, bird-watching, and beachcombing.

3

The Riviera Maya

NORTH OF PLAYA DEL CARMEN

ALSO EXTENDING NORTH OF PLAYA DEL CARMEN, the Riviera Maya is dotted by more exclusive destination resorts, such as those in the grandiose and exotically modern Mayakobá development, and the growing town of Puerto Morelos, which today is much like Playa was way back in 1990.

PUNTA BETE REGION

Marked by the large wood-and-stone entrance of the Mayakobá megadevelopment, Punta Bete is just 4 miles north of Playa del Carmen, at km 296–298, making it popular for visitors who want to stay somewhere out of the way but still be close to the action of town. Each fall, Mayakobá's El Cameleón Golf Course hosts the OHL Golf Classic, the only official PGA Tour event held outside of the U.S., which adds to the development's prestige and reputation.

Checking In

Best places to stay in and around the Punta Bete Region

This area is dominated by the 1,600-acre master planned luxury resort development **Mayakobá** (Highway 307, km 297, www.mayakoba.com), whose name is translated roughly into "Village of Water" in Mayan. The complex features a mile-long white sand beach, the 18-hole, Greg Norman–designed El Cameleón Golf Course, and three exclusive resorts, each with its own custom spa. Each hotel presents a distinct design and luxurious atmosphere. All Mayakobá guests and residents are encouraged to travel between the three

LEFT: Arrivals to Viceroy Riviera Maya's stylish palapa-covered reception are greeted by name and offered a tasty refreshing juice drink. Viceroy Riviera Maya

20 Stylish Spots for Trendsetters

1. Canibal Royal Beach Club (Playa del Carmen)
2. Diablito Cha Cha Cha lounge (Playa del Carmen)
3. La Santanera bar and lounge (Playa del Carmen)
4. Hotel Deseo and Deseo Bar (Playa del Carmen)
5. In Fashion Boutique Hotel (Playa del Carmen)
6. Kartabar (Playa del Carmen)
7. Almirante Pech restaurant and bar (Playa del Carman)
8. Live Aqua Cancún resort (Cancún)
9. Mamita's Beach Club (Playa del Carmen)
10. Mandala Bar (Playa del Carmen)
11. Viceroy Riviera Maya resort (Punta Bete)
12. Mezzanine hotel (Tulum)
13. Acanto Boutique Condo Hotel (Playa del Carmen)
14. Plank restaurant (Playa del Carmen)
15. Mosquito Beach Hotel (Playa del Carmen)
16. Hotel Reina Roja (Playa del Carmen)
17. Fairmont Mayakobá resort (Punta Bete)
18. Hotel La Semilla (Playa del Carmen)
19. Palazzo nightclub (Playa del Carmen)
20. Dolores YucaBar (Playa del Carmen)

resorts via a series of pristine jungle-lined waterways and sample a wider variety of spa and dining options.

To build the resort and the waterways, the developer collapsed the land's limestone crust in strategic spots throughout the property, creating the basins for the lakes and canals, as well as producing the limestone material that comprises most of Mayakobá buildings. Although the resorts all have private beach access and limited beachfront accommodations, most of the development rests in the jungle behind a natural mangrove buffer. These natural jungle reserves were preserved to maintain the natural defenses that originally made the Riviera Maya resilient to hurricanes but have been stripped out with development up and down the coast.

Situated at the very heart of the development is the warm and family-friendly, 401-room ★ **Fairmont Mayakobá** (www.fairmont.com), which features a grand, home-style Mexican décor, highlighted by dark woods, light stone, and a palette of gold, soft reds, and oranges throughout. The cool, comfortably elegant, open-air lobby overlooks a stunning lagoon a story below. A wide and arching bridge crosses over the far side of the lagoon, connecting to a green island concealing many of the resort's amenities.

The canals winding through the Fairmont sit lower than most of the resort itself, revealing rocky and porous limestone walls, topped off by thick and lush jungle vegetation. The effect is sublime, offering both a direct con-

The main building at the Fairmont Mayakoba overlooks a picturesque sunken lagoon.
Fairmont Mayakoba

nection to nature and an uncommonly exposed, but still pristine, visual.

The resort itself sits on expansive grounds, allowing for dense vegetation between many structures. Open-air motorized shuttles whisk guests from the lobby to their rooms, the resort's three pools, the fitness center, or the private beach and adjacent beachfront restaurant.

Guestrooms offer very private marble bathrooms with a rain shower and a bathtub beneath a large window that is shielded from public view. Rooms come with all the luxurious modern amenities you would expect from the Fairmont, including ample pillows, high-thread-count sheets, plush bathrobes, and slippers.

In addition to a large family swimming pool, a more serene adult pool, beach diversions, and golf prospects at the adjacent El Cameleón, the Fairmont offers a 40-minute boat ride through Mayakobá's canal system. The shaded motor launch takes riders beyond the resort's grounds into the untouched and natural habitat that surrounds it. It's a fun, captivating, and intimate exchange with nature. And the wildlife around you makes the trip unpredictable as well.

The Fairmont is the one Mayakobá resort that primarily operates on the European plan. Some all-inclusive packages are available, but you must specifically select these packages to receive the extras, which are limited to select hotel restaurants and facilities. There are several excellent restaurants and bars on-site, which are not included in any all-inclusive offers. If you want to experience all of the Fairmont's dining options, plan to pay for those meals in addition to your stay.

Nearby, the 107-room **Banyan Tree Mayakobá** (www.banyantree.com/en) has a stark modern Asian-meets-Mayan motif and aspires to connect guests to the elements. The hotel and most of the villas are set back, inland from the beach, along a series of canals and waterways winding through the hotel and connecting it to the larger resort. All rooms are stand-alone villas, each complete with a private garden, pool, and outdoor bathtub.

The unusual 128-room **Rosewood Mayakobá** (www.rosewoodmayakoba.com) features a very modern design that contrasts with its natural setting. It maintains its jungle ties through the use of local materials, integration of tropical flourishes, and the easy proximity it provides to Mayakobá's network of canals. Rooms on and near the beach tend to be crowded together, while accommodations farther back, especially the adults-only island suites, are almost entirely secluded.

Small and very upscale, ★ **Viceroy Riviera Maya** (Highway 307, km 294, Playa Xcalacoco, just south of Punta Bete, www.viceroyhotelsandresorts.com) is one of the more likely places to spot a vacationing celebrity or business tycoon. It dispenses with the grandeur of Mayakobá, offering a small, private, and intimate experience that would be difficult to replicate at any other hotel or resort in the region. Far from pretentious, the lush resort strives to provide a warm and sophisticated environment that harmonizes with nature. A thatched palm pavilion at the hotel entrance passes as the lobby, and the 41 villas are housed in freestanding modernized versions of Mayan-style huts scattered along a winding sand trail that leads from the powdery white beach to the jungle. The villas and furnishings are made from local stones and hardwoods and feature all modern amenities and comforts, plus a few big extras like large private plunge pools, private outdoor moon showers, and soap carved for you personally as you check in.

Most villas are set back in the jungle, and entrances are designed to carefully conceal all views of the private outdoor space. A few select villas are situated near the pool, offering clear views of the beach, and providing outside views of these villas' outdoor pool areas in return. Most hotel guests are couples, straight and sometimes gay, and children are permitted only when the entire resort is rented out for a private event.

Each room at the luxurious Viceroy Riviera Maya is a standalone jungle bungalow with a private plunge pool, moon shower, and grand thatched roof. Viceroy Riviera Maya

Wondering along the Viceroy's winding pathways you'll come across one of the region's most sought-after spas, several outdoor living rooms comprised of colonial furniture arranged in a jungle clearing, a large and undulating infinity pool, a beachside restaurant, a modern fitness center, and more.

With a barefoot-chic décor, the stylish 25-room boutique **Le Reve Hotel & Spa** (www.hotellereve.com) mixes modern design elements with tropical flourishes. The restaurant showcases an evolving, chef-prepared menu utilizing many fresh ingredients, local products, and international flavors. There is a fitness center onsite and yoga classes are available on the beach. Packages are available for those who wish to rent the entire hotel for private celebrations, including weddings, retreats, and family reunions.

The 128-room, adults-only **Blue Diamond Riviera Maya** (Highway 307, km 298, www.bluediamond-rivieramaya.com) sits squarely in the ultra-luxury, all-inclusive category. Formerly the Mandarin Oriental Riviera Maya, the hotel was remodeled in 2012 with thoroughly modern architecture showcasing smooth lines and cool colors. Interiors utilize native hardwoods, stone, and other local accents.

PLAYA DEL SECRETO & PLAYA PARAÍSO (Highway 307, km 308–312)

Playa del Secreto and Playa Paraíso combine to form one of the largest stretches of mostly undeveloped beach remaining in the area. Several spots along the shoreline are frequented by sea turtles, which lay their eggs in the balmy summer months. The area is dominated by the massive Iberostar resort complex, which includes five separate but connected all-inclusive resorts, a convention center, and an 18-hole golf course.

Checking In

Best places to stay in Playa del Secreto, Playa Paraíso & Punta Maroma

The 432-room, all-inclusive, adults-only **El Dorado Royale—A Spa Resort by Karisma** (Highway 307, km 312, Playa Paraíso, www.karismahotels.com) bills itself as "laid-back luxury," and it seems to be an appropriate description for a resort best known for its in-room hot tubs and patio hammocks. Spanning 450 acres of prime beachfront land, the hotel has a mile-long beach (called Punta Brava) marked by white sand, a few rocks, and hundreds of palm trees. The on-site European day spa offers a variety of traditional European and regional Mayan treatments.

Five resorts share amenities at this massive all-inclusive ★ **Iberostar Playa Paraíso Complex** (Highway 307, km 309, www.iberostar.com), with more than 1,900 rooms in Iberostar's **Paraíso Beach, del Mar, Lindo, and Maya** hotels. Varied architectural themes are exhibited across the resorts, with rooms varying in price, décor, and amenities. Guests at all properties are encouraged to visit the shared beach, which is almost a mile long, and to visit select pools, restaurants, and bars located throughout the property. Also on site, the Iberostar Playa Paraíso Golf Club features 18 holes of golf designed by P. B. Dye, son of renowned course designer Pete Dye. In addition to the facilities offered at each individual

Playa Xcalacoco

Some small Mayan ruins and a coconut grove mark the small, secluded beach of Xcalacoco, which is just south of Punta Bete. There are a couple of *palapa* restaurants that serve seafood and Mexican dishes, and campers can set up their temporary home at the Xcalacoco campsite, which has solar power and public showers.

The Iberostar complex is one of the area's largest—and nicest—resorts. Iberostar Resorts

hotel, a central shopping and entertainment center contains a nightclub, a sports bar, spa, and a variety of stores. Guests of the most luxurious and adults-only **Iberostar Grand Hotel Paraíso** have access to all complex features, but also enjoy a level of privacy and luxury not found in the other hotels.

Home to what may be the largest and most impressive entryway of any hotel in the Riviera Maya, the aptly named **Mayan Palace Riviera Maya** (Highway 307, km 310, Playa Paraíso, www.mayanpalace.com.mx) is equally inspiring once inside. With such a grand entrance, it's a bit surprising that the resort has only 336 rooms. Though the architecture may be inspired by the traditional Mayan building style, with thatched-palm roofs, low-rise buildings, and heavy use of local materials, the standards of luxury are significantly higher than even the Mayan gods could have imagined. The beach is beautiful but rocky, so be prepared to pick your way through the rough terrain if you want to go swimming. There is the on-site, 18-hole Jack Nicklaus golf course El Manglar, tennis courts, and kids' club, which provides complimentary childcare in a fun environment. Since the property is so large, some guests complain about the walking distances from one attraction to another, but the landscaping and the natural beauty seem to keep most happy.

PUNTA MAROMA

Six miles south of Playa Paraíso, quiet Punta Maroma has the kind of sugar-sand beach that's so often featured on postcards and full-screen digital desktops. The beach, more than 100 feet wide in many parts, is bordered by coconut palms and sea oats, and there are very few rocks and light waves, making it a great place for swimming and snorkeling. There are a few upscale resorts, villas, and private homes, but it has an uncrowded, timeless, and faraway feel to it, making it an ideal spot for a tropical escape.

Top 10 See-and-Be-Seen Hotels of the Riviera Maya Area

Viceroy Riviera Maya, Punta Bete. Pretend you don't recognize the celebrities across the bar at this understated luxury resort (see this chapter).

Fairmont Mayakobá, Punta Bete. Rub elbows with the elite floating on the canals of this lush tropical resort (see this chapter).

Live Aqua Cancún. Cancún's one and only lounge hotel, with 24-hour DJ and unlimited top-shelf tequilas (see chapter 7).

Hotel Deseo, Playa del Carmen. Up the unmarked stairs, it's the hip hangout for the Playa glitterati (see chapter 4).

Hotel Esencia, Xpu-Ha. The former estate of an Italian duchess can be yours, for a price (see chapter 5).

Belmond Maroma Resort & Spa, Punta Maroma. If it's good enough for Tom Cruise, you'll probably enjoy it also (see this chapter).

Mezzanine Hotel, north of Tulum pueblo. Swanky digs, topless beaches, and DJ parties in the shadow of the Tulum ruins (see chapter 5)

Hotel Reina Roja, Playa del Carmen. The crimson queen brings shades of Amsterdam's Red Light District to downtown Playa (see chapter 5).

Zoëtry Paraiso de la Bonita Resort & Thalasso Spa, north of Puerto Morelos. With a $3,000-a-night penthouse, you never know who you might bump into at the swim-up bar (see this chapter).

Playa Palms at the Blue Parrot, Playa del Carmen. With an open-air dance floor and fire dancers at your back door, you can't go wrong (see chapter 4).

Recognized as one of the top hotels in the world, the 65-room ★ Belmond Maroma Resort & Spa (Highway 307, km 305; enter through the Venta Club entrance, www.maromahotel.com) deserves its stellar reputation, with repeat guests making up a large percentage of the monthly reservations. The resort occupies some 25 acres of land, giving it an uncluttered and private feeling hard to find in the region. Unlike many Riviera Maya resorts, the Belmond is not the kind of place where visitors hang out in their cutoffs and tank tops, swilling margaritas and playing volleyball in the pool. Guests are much more subdued, and there is even a dress code at the restaurant for dinner. Don't get the feeling that it's stuffy, though. It's definitely still relaxed, just upscale.

The resort is closed for upgrades each August. The four-bedroom Villa Pisces has its own private pool and feels much more like a beach house than part of a hotel.

A lavish resort complex on 71 acres of pristine beach just south of

Celebrity Guests at Maroma Resort

Tim Allen • Tony Blair • Tom Cruise • Claire Danes • Danny DeVito • Cameron Diaz • Matt Dillon • Minnie Driver • Farrah Fawcett • Enrique Iglesias • Brad Paisley • Sean Penn • Robert Plant • Prince Charles • Sharon Stone

Maroma's Lomi-Lomi Massage

The Lomi-Lomi massage is one of the oldest and most powerful forms of healing. It works gently yet deeply into the muscles with continuous, flowing strokes, offering a complete nurturing of the body and gifting the recipient with a deep sense of relaxation and wellbeing. This flowing massage allows for a very close bond between the energy and bodies of therapist and client, as the therapist uses long and slow movements and a very loving touch to relax you to the inner core, helping you to let go of old beliefs, patterns, and behaviors. Some people cry, others laugh, and others have a near out-of-body experience as they descend into a very deep state of relaxation.

Playa Maroma, the 285-room ★ **Secrets Maroma Beach** (Highway 307, km 298, www.secretsresorts.com) is adults-only and all-inclusive and appeals to active couples wanting to experience a broad range of recreational options while submerged in the comforts of a high-end resort. The architecture is a combination of Mediterranean and colonial Mexican, with graceful arches, tile work, and tropical plants throughout. Guests are welcomed into the lobby with a glass of champagne and a chilled towel before they descend a grand staircase to the pool deck area. This is a popular spot for weddings and honeymoons, and it offers an on-site wedding planner.

PUERTO MORELOS (Highway 307, km 320; 20 miles north of Playa del Carmen)

If you want to know what Playa del Carmen was like 20 years ago, just take a look at modern-day Puerto Morelos, the official northern edge of the Riviera Maya. The quiet town square ringed by a few restaurants and shops, the natural beach, the encroaching jungle—it's almost exactly how Playa used to be. The road from the highway to town is a straight shot on a clean, modern road through 2 miles of scrub brush and mangrove swampland before ending at the town square. Most of the development is within a mile of the square, which has a couple of beachside restaurants, several open-air sidewalk restaurants, a couple of Internet cafés, a coffee/pastry shop, and a few souvenir stores, pharmacies, money exchange offices, and dive shops. Along the beach you'll see a leaning lighthouse and a fishing pier where the boats dock when they're not pulled up onto the beach. Less than a half mile offshore is the barrier reef, and you can see the waves breaking where the coral meets the surface, which indicates a great spot for snorkeling when the seas are calm. The roads leading north and south from town are dusty and unpaved, but they lead to some of the nicest natural beaches in the area. To the north are a collection of rental homes and small hotels, plus a couple of recently developed large-scale resorts. To the south, the road curves behind an Army base and then a shipping and industrial area before meeting the beach again near the entrance to a laid-back budget hotel and a clothing-optional "lifestyle" resort.

A gambling-boat operator had petitioned to operate a casino boat from the port to take travelers to international waters, but the petition was denied, and the area retains its calming and relaxed feeling. A ferry transfers vehicles from Puerto Morelos to Cozumel.

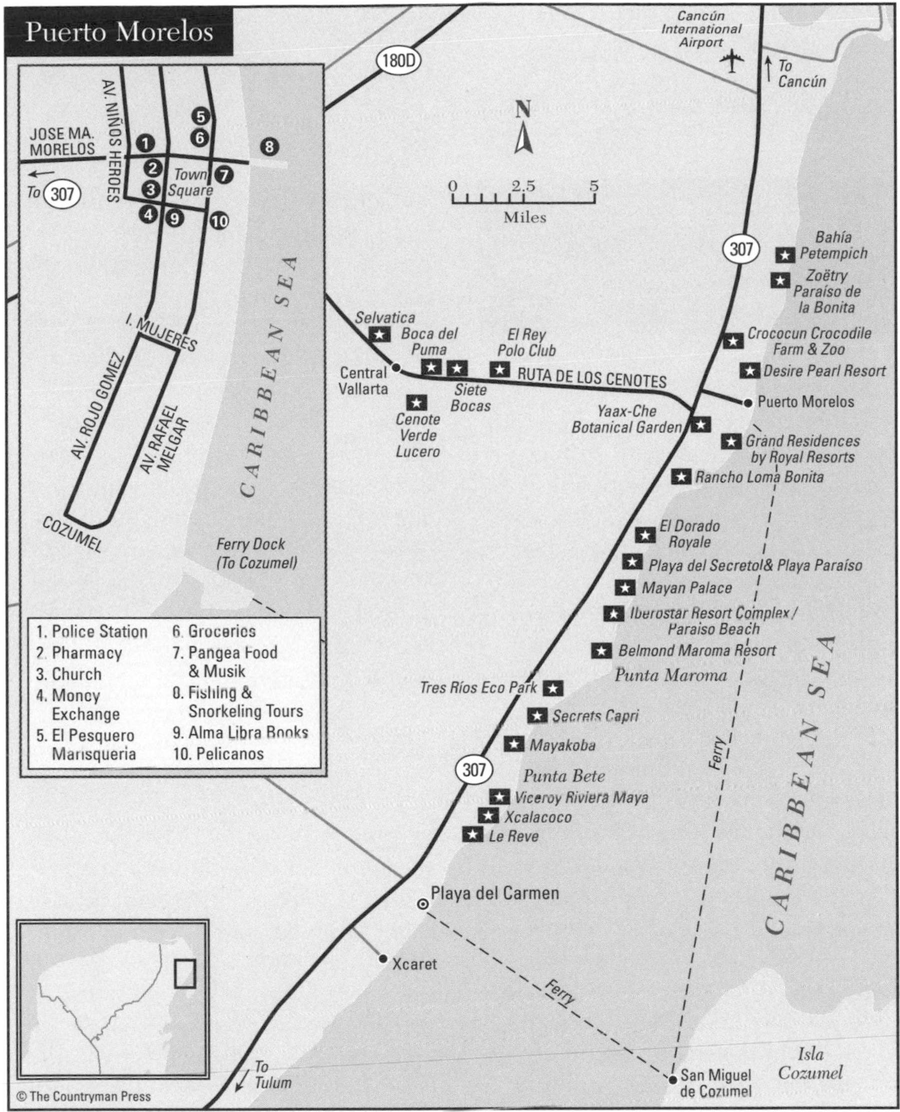

Getting There

Puerto Morelos is located at the midpoint between Cancún and Playa del Carmen. The turnoff from Highway 307 was marked with just a speed bump only a few years ago, but now it's a busy intersection with a raised highway, a traffic light, turning lanes, several shops, and even a road sign. Another road, just north of the Crococun Zoo, leads to the north end of town and the Secrets Excellence and Paradisus hotels. From there the road winds and turns as you head south, passing by private homes and small family-run hotels. After a few miles, the road ends at the town square. There are frequent buses from the Cancún and Playa del Carmen bus stations that will drop you off at the crossroads, and from there it's a 2-mile hike to town or a $3 taxi ride. A new bus station was built in 2008 on Highway 307, just south of the main crossroads, next to the 7-Eleven convenience store, with regular departures to Tulum, Playa del Carmen, and Cancún. Though it may not be generally encouraged, it's also fairly easy to hitch a ride along the road that leads to town. Since the road basically goes to only one place, it's a pretty fair bet that anyone headed down that road is going somewhere close to where you are.

Checking In

Best places to stay in and around Puerto Merelos

Bahia Petempich

With fewer than 100 rooms and suites, the very high-end, all-suite ★ **Zoëtry Paraiso de la Bonita Resort & Thalasso Spa** (Highway 307, km 330, www.zoetryresorts.com/paraiso) has 1,100-square-foot standard rooms with ocean views. The service is impeccable, and the staff does an excellent job of making guests feel special. The architecture and decor are unusual, with a combination of African, Asian, Balinese, Caribbean, European, and Mayan inspirations. The beach is raked clean, but the tides are full of seaweed, making swimming less than pleasant.

The Feng Shui–friendly **Azul Beach Hotel by Karisma** (Highway 307, km 330, www.karismahotels.com) is an up-market, family-friendly, all-inclusive boutique resort located just a few miles north of Puerto Morelos, past the gated entrance to Bahia Petempich, on an idyllic beach. The lobby has marble floors and minimalist decor, with lots of whites and blues, and calming music playing in the background. The 148-room hotel welcomes families and even has an activities program for kids. Unlike many all-inclusives, the hotel features gourmet menu options and the bars serve premium liquors. The new VASSA Spa offers spa, beauty and hydrotherapy treatments, and a fitness center.

If you venture into the original **Desire Resort and Spa** (Highway 307, km 326, www.desireresorts.com) or the more recently opened **Desire Pearl Resort** (Highway 307, km 323; northern end of Puerto Morelos, www.desireresorts.com) you'll quickly see that neither is for the prudish. In fact, if you're not a swinger or at least open to the swinger lifestyle, you're best off choosing another place to spend your vacation. If, however, you're into that kind of thing, these stylishly done resorts deserve a serious look. Desire is known in the "lifestyle" circles as one of the best hotel destinations around for swingers who enjoy traveling to the tropics to meet others, have fun, and cast away their inhibitions, assuming they had any to begin with.

Technically, the 88-room Desire Pearl Resort is located in Puerto Morelos proper. It was the Ceiba del Mar Resort until it was acquired in early 2012 and converted into a kissing cousin property of the original 110-room Desire Resort. The same atmosphere and amenities pervade at both properties.

The resorts accept only adult couples. Billed as "clothing optional," the all-inclusive hotels cater much more to the sexually liberated set than the run-of-the-mill nudist or "naturist." Public displays of affection, even extreme affection, are allowed and, in some designated areas, encouraged. And even though there's a strict "no means no" policy, it's clear that there are lots of yeses going on.

There is a great beach at the original hotel site, and the local officials look the other way (literally), allowing guests to be on the beach in the buff, though it's generally frowned upon in most other areas in the Riviera Maya. There

Puerto Morelos's infamous leaning lighthouse still adds local color despite the presence of its larger modern replacement.
Chip Rankin

are two pools and a huge Jacuzzi with room for 30 people (I'm sure you could fit more if you tried), which seems to be the center of attraction most days. Next to the dance bar there is a "play room" where most of the sexual activity takes place.

Puerto Morelos Proper

On a northern beach between Bahia Petempich and the town square, the simple and inexpensive **Hotel Ojo de Agua** (Highway 307, km 321, Avenue Javier Rojo Gómez at the beach, www.ojo-de-agua.com) serves as somewhat of a home base for local beachfront activity. The hotel's 36 rooms, decorated in contemporary Mexican style, have air-conditioning or a fan and a kitchenette.

Located south of Puerto Morelos' town square, **Grand Residences by Royal Resorts** (El Cid Boulevard, www.grandresidencesrivieracancun.com) offers 103 spacious luxury suites along the beach and around a large swimming pool.

South of Puerto Morelos

Rancho Sak Ol (Highway 307, km 318, southern end of Puerto Morelos, past the Army base and shipping facility, www.ranchosakol.com), formerly known as Rancho Libertad, offers an alternative to the large, corporate-owned hotels for travelers seeking simplicity and serenity over luxury and indulgence. Fourteen minimalist rooms feature suspended beds, air-conditioning (downstairs units), and purified drinking water and face a rocky yet calm and natural beach that is practically deserted—a good spot for more hotels. You can look to the north and see a half-sunken barge that has been there for years.

Local Flavors

Taste of the town—restaurants, cafés, bars, bistros, etc.

This casual beachfront **Ojo de Agua Restaurant & Bar** (Avenue Javier Rojo Gómez; on a northern beach near Excellence Riviera hotel, www.ojo-de-agua.com) offers a daily breakfast buffet, fresh seafood, and Mexican dishes.

In the town square, the second-story, air-conditioned **La Casa del Pescador** (north side of the town square) offers fresh lobster, *chiles rellenos*, hogfish in butter, grouper, and other seafood dishes, plus grilled steak and chicken. Waiters are longtime local residents who can give you advice on tours and activities.

The most prominent restaurant near the town square, **Pelicanos** (southeast corner), is also the largest, offering a selection of Mexican and American breakfasts for less than $5, and for lunch and dinner, it's seafood or nothing. Try the fried whole fish, the shrimp ceviche, or the grilled shrimp, and you can't go wrong.

Also on the beach on your left side when facing the pier, with the road into Morelos behind you, **Pangea Food and Musik** (Jose Maria Morelos and Rafael

4 Spots to Show (or See) Some Skin

It's generally accepted for women to be topless on many beaches across the Riviera Maya, but there are several places in the region where both men and women are encouraged to reduce their tanlines a bit more.

Azulik hotel (Tulum). Even though it's adults-only, there's no funny business at this rustic, clothing-optional beachfront hotel.

Desire Resort & Spa and Desire Pearl Resort (Puerto Morelos). Pretty much anything goes at this fairly wild, couples-only swingers resort for the "lifestyle" set.

Hidden Beach Resort (Kantenah). Singles and couples are welcome at this upscale, clothing-optional resort, known for its more traditional (and definitely non-swinging) position on PDA.

Temptation Resort Cancún (Cancún). A topless pool, sexy shows, and heavily flirtatious undertones tease travelers at this stylish, adults-only resort.

Melgar Streets) offers traditional Mexican and seafood dishes in an open atmosphere. Dancers and musicians perform most nights.

Even though it's not on the beach, **El Pesquero Marisqueria** (half a block north of the town square on Rafael Melgar Street) keeps drawing repeat visitors for its freshly caught and prepared seafood, friendly staff, and lively atmosphere.

Traditional Mexican dishes are the specialty of **Dona Triny's** (south side of the town square on Tulum Avenue between Rojo Gomez and Rafael Melga Streets).

Small and inexpensive, **Le Café D'Amancia** (southwest corner) serves sandwiches, fresh breads, cheesecake, fruit, espresso, cappuccino, and coffee.

Well known for its popular and now-shuttered location in Playa del Carmen, **John Gray's Kitchen** (Niños Heroes Avenue, north of the town square) is still going strong in uber-relaxed Morelos, serving up steaks, seafood, and Mexican fare. Even though this is likely one of the more upscale independent restaurants in Puerto Morelos, things remain flip-flop casual.

Offering a view of the luxury yachts docked at the marina, the casually elegant **La Marina** (on the Marina El Cid, www.elcid.com) serves lobster, fresh fish, and other seafood specialties.

Tours & Attractions

Part traditional polo field, part real estate development, **El Rey Polo Country Club** (8 miles down the Ruta de Cenotes Road in Puerto Morelos, www.poloincancun.com) hosts regular polo tournaments that are quite high in quality and draw players and spectators from around the country. The larger development encompasses 73 rustic home lots, clubhouse, dressing rooms, golf driving range, horse stables, and children's play area. It seems wildly out of place deep in the Mayan jungle, but is a curious

15 Party Spots for Tequila Drinkers, Mingling Singles, and the Party Crowd

1. Beer Bucket bar (Playa del Carmen)
2. Canibal Royal Beach Club (Playa del Carmen)
3. Casa Tequila—La Tequilaria store and shot bar (Playa del Carmen)
4. Coco Bongo nightclub (Cancún & Playa del Carmen)
5. Coco Maya Beach Club (Playa del Carmen)
6. Diablito Cha Cha Cha lounge (Playa del Carmen)
7. Hotel Deseo and Deseo Bar (Playa del Carmen)
8. Hotel Reina Roja and bar (Playa del Carmen)
9. Jimmy Buffett's Margaritaville Café (Cozumel)
10. Mamita's Beach Club (Playa del Carmen)
11. Mandala Bar (Playa del Carmen)
12. Mezzanine hotel (Tulum)
13. La Santanera bar (Playa del Carmen)
14. Señor Frog's bar (Cozumel & Playa del Carmen)
15. Palazzo nightclub (Playa del Carmen)

place to visit and ponder what may come if the region keeps growing so rapidly.

The largest new-and-used English bookstore in the Yucatan, **Alma Libra Books** (south side of the town square on Tulum Avenue between Rojo Gomez and Rafael Melga Streets, www.almalibrebooks.com) is a great place to dig up some new reading material and a good source for arranging local day trips and even vacation rentals.

The friendly folks at **Fishing & Snorkeling Tours** (northeast side of the town square, next to the beach) can arrange fishing and diving trips along the Puerto Morelos coastline, and, with their own fleet of shaded 25-foot boats and local guides, they can custom-create a trip that suits your fancy. It's preferred that you make your reservations the day before so the staff can get all the necessary equipment and supplies, though impromptu trips can be arranged as long as you're flexible.

Almost Heaven Adventures (one block north of the town square on Javier Rojo Gomez Avenue, www.almostheavenadventures.com) arranges diving, snorkeling, fishing, and jungle-tour excursions. They also manage a few private rentals in town.

Operating out of the Ojo de Agua hotel, **Puerto Morelos Adventure Tours** (Highway 307, km 321, Avenue Javier Rojo Gómez at the beach, www.ojo-de-agua.com) offers active tours in the area. Top trips include a two-hour snorkeling trip that includes lunch, beer, equipment, and a visit to a handicrafts market; an ATV tour that visits two *cenotes*, a Mayan village, and market; and a *cenote* and reef-snorkeling excursion, which includes visits to caves, *cenotes*, and a marine park.

The humble **Puerto Morelos Church** (west side of the town square) may not have any historical significance, but its Spanish-only services are open to visitors and it offers an authentic glimpse into life for locals.

★ **Selvatica** (Ruta de Cenotes, km 19, www.selvatica.com.mx) also runs adventure tours through a 300-acre nature preserve (see chapter 8).

4

Other Destinations Near Playa del Carmen

MEXICO'S ENTIRE CARIBBEAN COAST is marked by both popular and lesser known tourism destinations. Although the region known as the Riviera Maya is set smack in the middle of the coast, it doesn't technically include them all. The diving mecca of Isla Cozumel, the burgeoning resort city of Cancún, the bohemian island town of Isla Mujeres, the remote and authentic Isla Holbox, the unpopulated Isla Contoy, and the adventurous Mayan Coast all make noteworthy overnight side- or day-trip destinations.

Most travelers to the Riviera Maya arrive via Cancún, which is one of the world's most popular mega-resorts. The small islands to the north of Cancún offer an abundance of relaxation, sunshine, and pristine beaches without the crowds so often associated with area vacations. Cozumel, meanwhile, is a scuba diver's dream, where shore, wall, and night dives can all be done in a single day.

ISLA COZUMEL (11 miles from Playa del Carmen by boat)

Isla Cozumel was once considered the sacred home of Ix-Chel, the Mayan goddess of fertility and childbirth, and Mayan women from around Mesoamerica would travel to pay homage and pray for their unborn children. Several religious shrines have survived over the years and can still be visited today. Measuring 28 miles by 10 miles, Cozumel is only 5 percent developed and is mostly open land, ripe for exploration on Jeep, horseback, or moped. It's a mecca for scuba divers and snorkelers, who revel in the amazingly clear waters, easily accessible reefs, and first-class dive operators.

The ferry from Playa lands at the town square of San Miguel, the island's only town, on its western shore. From nearly every beach hotel on this side of the island, guests have a spectacular view of the sunset as it slowly dips into the

LEFT: The all-inclusive Live Aqua Cancún is one of the Cancún's most luxurious hotels resorts. Live Aqua Cancun

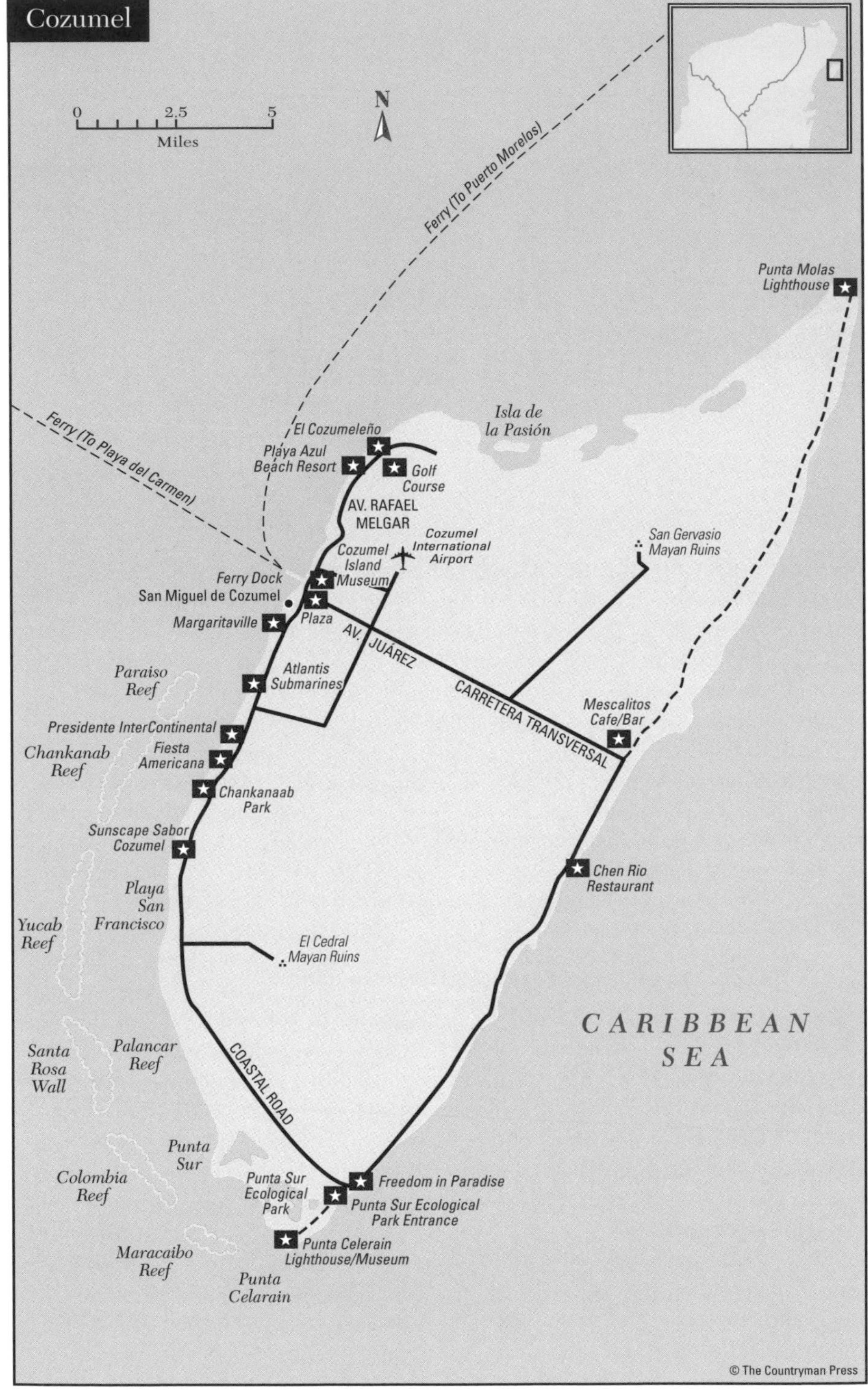
Cozumel
0
2.5
5
Miles
N
Ferry (To Puerto Morelos)
Punta Molas Lighthouse
Isla de la Pasión
Ferry (To Playa del Carmen)
El Cozumeleño
Playa Azul Beach Resort
Golf Course
AV. RAFAEL MELGAR
Cozumel International Airport
San Gervasio Mayan Ruins
Cozumel Island Museum
Ferry Dock
San Miguel de Cozumel
Plaza
Margaritaville
AV. JUÁREZ
Paraiso Reef
Atlantis Submarines
CARRETERA TRANSVERSAL
Mescalitos Cafe/Bar
Presidente InterContinental
Chankanab Reef
Fiesta Americana
Chankanaab Park
Sunscape Sabor Cozumel
Chen Rio Restaurant
Playa San Francisco
Yucab Reef
El Cedral Mayan Ruins
CARIBBEAN SEA
Santa Rosa Wall
Palancar Reef
COASTAL ROAD
Punta Sur
Colombia Reef
Punta Sur Ecological Park
Freedom in Paradise
Punta Sur Ecological Park Entrance
Punta Celerain Lighthouse/Museum
Maracaibo Reef
Punta Celarain
© The Countryman Press

Buy your ferry tickets in advance if you want, or just before you board.

Caribbean. Dozens of shops, restaurants, bars, and other attractions are within an easy walking distance of the ferry dock. A few hotels are downtown, and the rest are along the beaches to the north and south of the square. The eastern side of the island faces the open ocean, and the water is much rougher, with less reef and much less development. Visitors can drive around the south side of the island, hugging the shoreline almost the entire way. It's a great way to get away from the crowds and feel like a real explorer, though you are never more than 15 minutes away from a cold beer and tasty plate of food. A few Mayan ruins are run as federal parks, with information centers, gift shops, and certified multilingual guides.

Checking In

Best places to stay in and around Isla Cozumel

The all-inclusive 175-room dive resort ★ **Cozumel Palace** (southern hotel zone, km 2.5, www.palaceresorts.com) was extensively refurbished in 2005, sprucing up the pool, guest rooms, lobby, restaurants, and all common areas. Though right on the water, its shoreline is exposed reef, so a small beach was built up above the rocks. Snorkeling is excellent right at the hotel, with barracuda, parrot fish, colored coral, sea anemone, sea urchin, lobster, and other marine life.

At the southern end of the island, the casual 224-room ★ **Fiesta Americana Cozumel All Inclusive** (Southern Coastal Road, km 7.5, www.fiestaamericana.com) is popular with families, serious scuba divers, and other guests valuing ready access to the best

The Mexican navy on display just offshore from the Cozumel Palace

dive sites over proximity to downtown (20 minutes away by car). The hotel's beach club lies across the street from the main building. Refurbished in early 2014, the hotel's rooms have been completely updated and restaurants have been expanded to complement the new all-inclusive operation.

One of Cozumel's original hotels, the 251-room **El Cozumeleño** (northern hotel zone, km 4.5, Santa Pilar Beach, www.elcozumeleno.com) remains one of the most popular spots for families and others looking for affordable, all-inclusive beach vacations.

The **Sunscape Sabor Cozumel** (Coastal Highway Sur, km 12.9, www.sunscaperesorts.com/sabor) features family-friendly amenities. The nearby **Aura Cozumel Grand Resort** (www.auraresorts.com) has a loyal base of returning guests.

The 50-room, hacienda-style **Playa Azul Beach Resort** (northern hotel zone, km 4, San Juan Beach, www.playa-azul.com) offers its guests unlimited play at the Cozumel Country Club golf course, created by Nicklaus Design Group, just a few minutes away.

With comfortable modern rooms and facilities, the **Presidente InterContinental Cozumel Resort & Spa** (www.intercontinentalcozumel.com) places its focus on location. Situated on Cozumel's eastern shore, the hotel offers premium access to dive locations and sunset views.

Local Flavors

Taste of the town—restaurants, cafés, bars, bistros, etc.

Most of your meal options can be found downtown, on or within walking distance of the town square.

The popular ★ **Pasta Prima** (Melgar Avenue between 13th and 15th Streets, www.elcantilcondos.com) is beloved by anyone on Cozumel searching for an authentic Italian meal. Formerly located off the town square, the new restaurant is modern and comfortable, though it lacks some of its original and unexpected charm.

Facing the ferry dock on the west side of the town square, **Las Palmeras** (www.restaurantepalmeras.com) is fun spot to pass time waiting for the boat to Playa del Carmen. Famous for its fishbowl margaritas (served ice-cold, potent, and delicious), it offers breakfast, lunch, and dinner and has covered seating with open windows and walls, allowing in the ocean breezes.

Since 1945, inexpensive ★ **Casa Denis** (www.casadenis.com) has served some of the best food in town, especially fish, tacos, enchiladas, shrimp, and steak. They also have *sopes*, a traditional dish from Acapulco served on thick, soft corn tortillas with lettuce, cheese, refried beans, and meat toppings.

There are also several good choices when you leave downtown and explore the island. A great place for a lunchtime stop, ★ **Chen Rio Restaurant & Beach Bar** (7 miles up the coast on the island's east side) has a limited menu, with fried whole fish the main specialty, served by a rare beach on Cozumel's west coast with calm waters. No credit cards.

One of the fancier and pricier restaurants on the island, **Pepe's Grill** (one block south of the town square, www.pepescozumel.com/eng/) is the traditional spot for a first or last meal on Cozumel. The chef prepares tender steaks, fresh seafood, Mexican specialties, fresh salads, and pastas. It may be best known, however, for its Mayan coffee, containing *Xtabentun*, a local orange schnapps. Waiters make the after-dinner drinks tableside, and as they're prepared, the whole restaurant watches as the liquor is set aflame and poured into the coffee. The popular restaurant refreshed both its menu and its décor in 2013, bringing a more relaxed, upscale flavor to the already warm and friendly spot.

The casual outdoor café **Plaza Leza** (south side of town square) specializes in inexpensive fajitas and steak, and the smell from its grills will catch you as you walk by. After dinner, linger a while with a cup of coffee or a tropical drink and sidewalk parade. On Sunday nights, it's a great place to watch the music and festivities that take place at the plaza's gazebo.

Local favorite **Mezcalitos** (at the intersection of the cross-island road and the northern end of the road that goes along the eastern shoreline, www.mezcalitos.com) serves Mexican dishes and snacks and has a full bar. Everyone here is doing the same thing—cruising around the island—so it's easy to meet other travelers and pick up tips on hidden beaches and good places to go.

Bars & Nightlife

While restaurants welcome patrons to linger over drinks, most nightlife takes place in chain establishments located on Rafael Melgar Avenue between the town square and the cruise-ship dock.

Built on the water, ★ **Jimmy Buffet's Margaritaville Café** (Rafael Melgar Avenue by the cruise-ship dock, www.margaritaville.com) is a Parrothead paradise, with beachfront tiki bar, beach music (including plenty of Buffett hits), burgers, seafood, and an open-air dance floor. Patrons are passionate about their beach-bum hero and impromptu sing-alongs are commonplace.

With one atop the other, two Mexican mainstay tourist bars by the cruise-ship dock make bar-hopping easier than ever. Just take the escalator down from **Señor Frog's** (www.senorfrogs.com), and you're at **Carlos 'n Charlie's** (www.carlosand charlies.com). Frog's is more nightlife-oriented, with a stage, dancing waiters, and full-time party atmosphere, while Carlos 'n Charlie's is more of a restaurant, with a more subdued atmosphere until late at night, when it becomes a bar. Depending on the day and how many cruise ships are in town, these tourist havens can be packed or empty, raucous or tame. Both serve consistent Mexican food, seafood, and pasta.

Located away from downtown, the come-as-you-are daytime beach bar **Freedom in Paradise** (Southern Coastal Road at the southern tip of the island, www.bobmarleybar.com), has no electricity, doesn't accept credit cards, and is rather ramshackle, but it's a must-see waypoint for travelers circumnavigating the island.

BEACH CLUBS

Situated on Playa San Francisco, long considered Cozumel's best beach, ★ **San Francisco Beach Club** (Southern Coastal Road, km 15) is still its most popular. It's been the site of thousands of weddings and remains a favorite place for watersports, seafood, and cold beers.

At **Mr. Sancho's Beach Club** (Southern Coastal Road, km 13, www.mrsanchos.com), a lively beach club on a picture-perfect, white-sand beach south of town, visitors can swim, snorkel, ride ATVs or motorcycles into the jungle, or partake other playful activities. The beach is public property, but facilities have a fee.

The well-established **Playa Mia Grand Beach Park** (Southern Coastal Road, km 15.5, www.playamia.com) is like a tropical island recreation paradise. Visitors pass the day kayaking, sailing, parasailing, sunning, swimming, and applying sunblock. It's noted for its small zoo, floating climbing wall, and underwater replica Mayan relics submerged for snorkelers' enjoyment.

Attractions

Created in 1980 to protect the region's marine life and flora and fauna along the shoreline, ★ **Chankanaab Park** (Southern Coastal Road, km 9.5, www.cozumelparks.com/eng) is Cozumel's main beach and nature park. Crystal clear water, with more than 100 feet of visibility on most days, makes for excellent snorkeling and scuba diving, and the beach offers easy water access, slow currents, and exciting shore dives, where statues of Christ and the Virgin Mary beckon from the shallows. The park boasts a lush botanical garden, a reproduction of a Mayan village, and a dolphin and sea lion discovery lagoon.

★ **Punta Sur Lighthouse Park** (Southern Coastal Road, km 27, www.cozumelparks.com/eng), a 100-hectare ecology reserve and beach park, encompasses white-sand beaches, mangrove swamps, lagoons, and thick jungle.

Cozumel's primary Mayan site, the ★ **San Gervasio Mayan Ruins** (Cross-Island Road, km 7.5, www.cozumelparks.com/eng) were an important destination for Mayan women seeking to honor Ix-Chel, the goddess of fertility. The site, spanning a couple miles, has several different temples and small pyramids and is home to many tropical birds and iguanas (see chapter 9).

Way South: The Explorean Kohunlich

Set almost at the border of Belize, **The Explorean Kohunlich by Fiesta Americana** Ctra Chetumal Escarcega, km 5.65, Ruinas Kohunlich, www.explorean.com) is a remote all-inclusive jungle retreat for guests truly looking to escape and connect with nature. The low-rise hotel utilizes stone, thatched roofs, and native materials to blend with the jungle surroundings. It is located adjacent to the Kohunlich Mayan ruins, 30 miles from the Chetumal International Airport and approximately 200 miles from the Cancún airport. It emphasizes adventurous activities, with one excursion per day included in the rate, including jungle treks, hiking, Mayan ruin tours, kayaking at a nearby lagoon, cycling, rappelling, and bird-watching.

Meals are taken at the hotel restaurant, **La Palapa**, with a thatched-roof dining room and an open terrace, perched above the swimming pool and jungle canopy. The 40-room hotel features a modern take on jungle chic, with Mayan artifacts, handcrafted furnishings, and furnished terraces with sofas and hammocks where guests can sit and enjoy the natural landscape. Rooms don't have TVs or telephones, but do have air-conditioning, safes, and complimentary turndown service.

The hotel is popular with sophisticated and adventurous adults, who generally stay for a few days while touring Mayan ruins and eco-friendly tours. With no nightlife in the area, most guests retire fairly early after an evening of star-gazing and listening to the nighttime fauna.

★ **Cozumel Island Museum** (Rafael Melgar and Fourth Street, www.cozumelparks.com/eng) documents the island's story through a series of recreations, drawings, and artifacts. Displays range from Mayan days, 16th-century discoveries by Juan de Grijalva and Hernan Cortez, the pirate years, and the War of the Castes to the present day.

Rancho Buenavista (www.buenavistaranch.com) offers two-hour horseback tours through some of the island's most rugged and picturesque landscapes.

CANCÚN (45 miles north of Playa del Carmen)

Though officially too far north to be part of the Riviera Maya, many visitors choose to stay a night in Cancún for a taste of the world-class shopping, great restaurants, powdery beaches, and over-the-top nightlife. The hotel zone is about 14 miles long, with dozens of hotels and every tourist service imaginable. Once less commercial, Cancún's downtown area is quickly being built up and offers great local restaurants, many shops and nightspots, and a large bus station. The main tourist area is at the elbow of the 7-shaped tourist strip, near the convention center. Within a short walk, there are two malls, twenty restaurants, more than a dozen nightclubs and bars, pharmacies, cigar shops, grocery stores, souvenir shops, and—yes—even strip clubs. An 18-hole waterfront golf course is just a few minutes away, and there are even some impressive Mayan ruins just miles from the convention center.

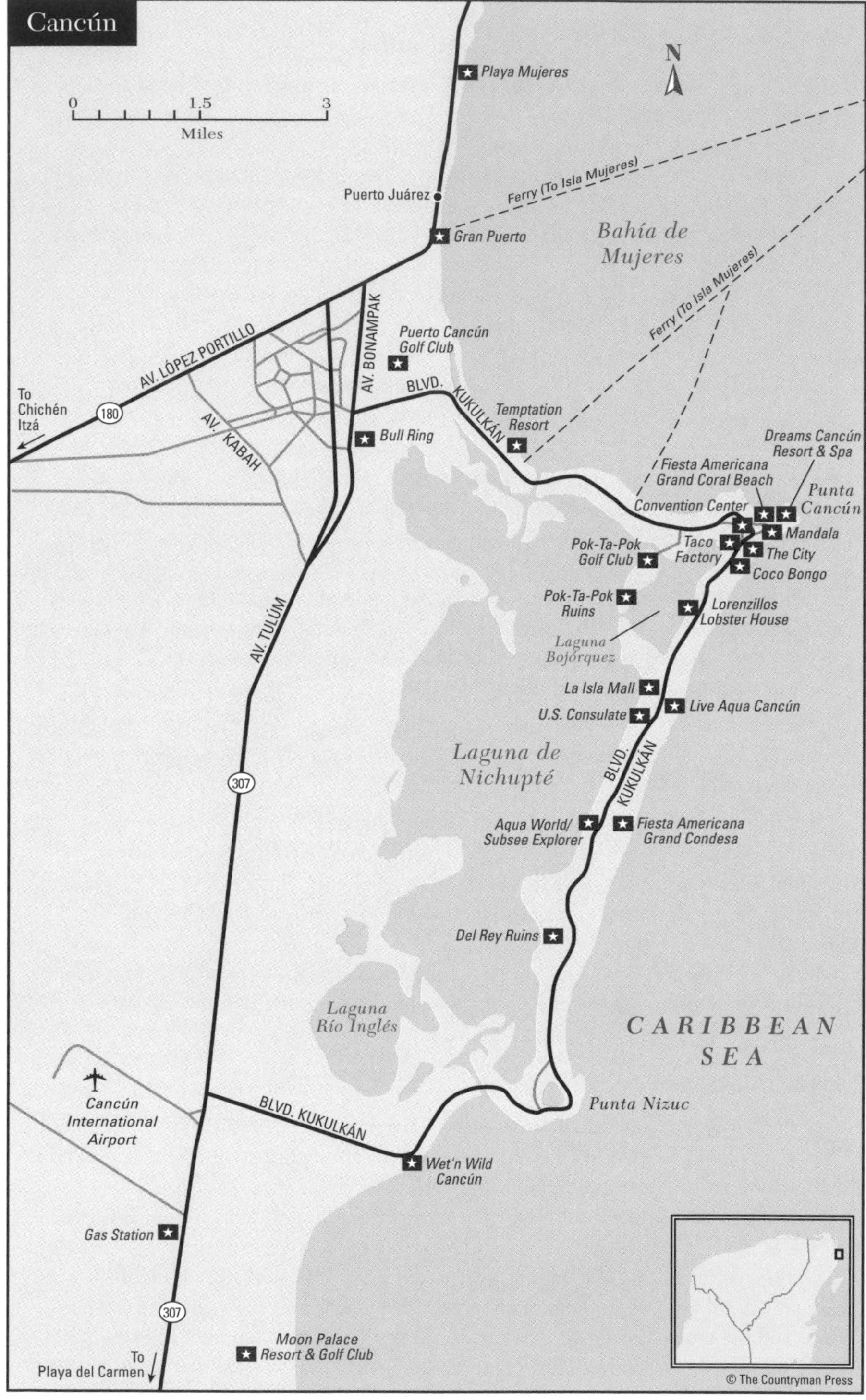
Cancún
0
1.5
3
Miles
N
Playa Mujeres
Puerto Juárez
Ferry (To Isla Mujeres)
Gran Puerto
Bahía de Mujeres
Ferry (To Isla Mujeres)
AV. LÓPEZ PORTILLO
AV. BONAMPAK
Puerto Cancún Golf Club
To Chichén Itzá
180
BLVD. KUKULKÁN
Temptation Resort
AV. KABAH
Bull Ring
Dreams Cancún Resort & Spa
Fiesta Americana Grand Coral Beach
Punta Cancún
Convention Center
Pok-Ta-Pok Golf Club
Taco Factory
Mandala
The City
Coco Bongo
Pok-Ta-Pok Ruins
Lorenzillos Lobster House
Laguna Bojórquez
AV. TULÚM
La Isla Mall
U.S. Consulate
Live Aqua Cancún
Laguna de Nichupté
BLVD. KUKULKÁN
307
Aqua World/ Subsee Explorer
Fiesta Americana Grand Condesa
Del Rey Ruins
Laguna Río Inglés
CARIBBEAN SEA
Cancún International Airport
Punta Nizuc
BLVD. KUKULKÁN
Wet'n Wild Cancún
Gas Station
307
Moon Palace Resort & Golf Club
To Playa del Carmen
© The Countryman Press

If you haven't been to Cancún in ten years, you may not recognize much of it. In late 2005, Hurricane Wilma battered the hotel zone with 150 mph winds, 25-foot waves, and an 11-foot storm surge when it stalled out over the city for nearly 12 hours. Beachfront resorts suffered major damage, and there was serious beach erosion. But not only were the hotels immediately rebuilt, they built things bigger, grander, and even more modern. Mexico's number-one tourist town reemerged with a larger beach and new hotel and condo towers dwarfing those that came before them.

Checking In

Best places to stay in and around Cancún

Most Cancún hotels (and all listed below) are located in the aptly named hotel zone. There are scores of resorts across different price categories that offer something to suit almost every type of traveler.

★ **Fiesta Americana Grand Coral Beach Resort & Spa** (Boulevard Kukulcán, km 9.5, www.fiestaamericana.com) sits on Cancún's most prime stretch of crystal white beach. It's so noteworthy that it bears repeating: This resort spills out onto an utterly spotless, perfect beach. With 602-rooms, it's regularly rated at the top of Mexico's resorts. It's modern, tropical, decadent.

Known for its near perfect location on the beach and in walking distance to the convention center and main tourism entertainment district, ★ **Dreams Cancún Resort & Spa** (Boulevard Kukulcán, km 10, Punta Cancún, www.dreamsresorts.com) has the best beach in this part of Cancún, hidden in a sheltered cove. There's no easy public access to the beach, making it especially safe and relaxing. Though all-inclusive, guests are not required to wear wristbands and instead sign all meals/drinks to their room. The staff goes out of their way to provide great service, even though tips are included in the room price.

For something a few miles removed from the central tourist area, ★ **Live Aqua Cancún** (Boulevard Kukulcán, km 13, www.liveaqua.com) is set on a perfect beach across from a new shopping center. Thoroughly contemporary in every way, the all-inclusive hotel showcases sensory touches such as aromatherapy kits in each room, 24-hour lounge music, and phosphorescent pillows at the beachside lounge. On-site restaurants feature celebrity chefs and have become the hip spots in town for the see-and-be-seen crowd. Guests, however, get preferential reservations. Other highlights include an upscale spa, a "garden of secrets" nature walk, wine and mezcal bar, and poolside lounge area with sun *cabañas*.

For those who complain that Cancún has no charm, the all-inclusive **Fiesta Americana Grand Condesa Cancún** (Boulevard Kukulcán, km 15.5, www.fiestaamericana.com) may change their mind. With the tallest *palapa* in all of Cancún, the resort evokes a grand imagination of a Mexican village. Inside, a slick mix of traditional Mexican hacienda décor is accented by local touches and modern upgrades. The lobby is cooled with ocean breezes, and the beach is composed of flourlike sand.

And for travelers who would gladly trade native charm for some good

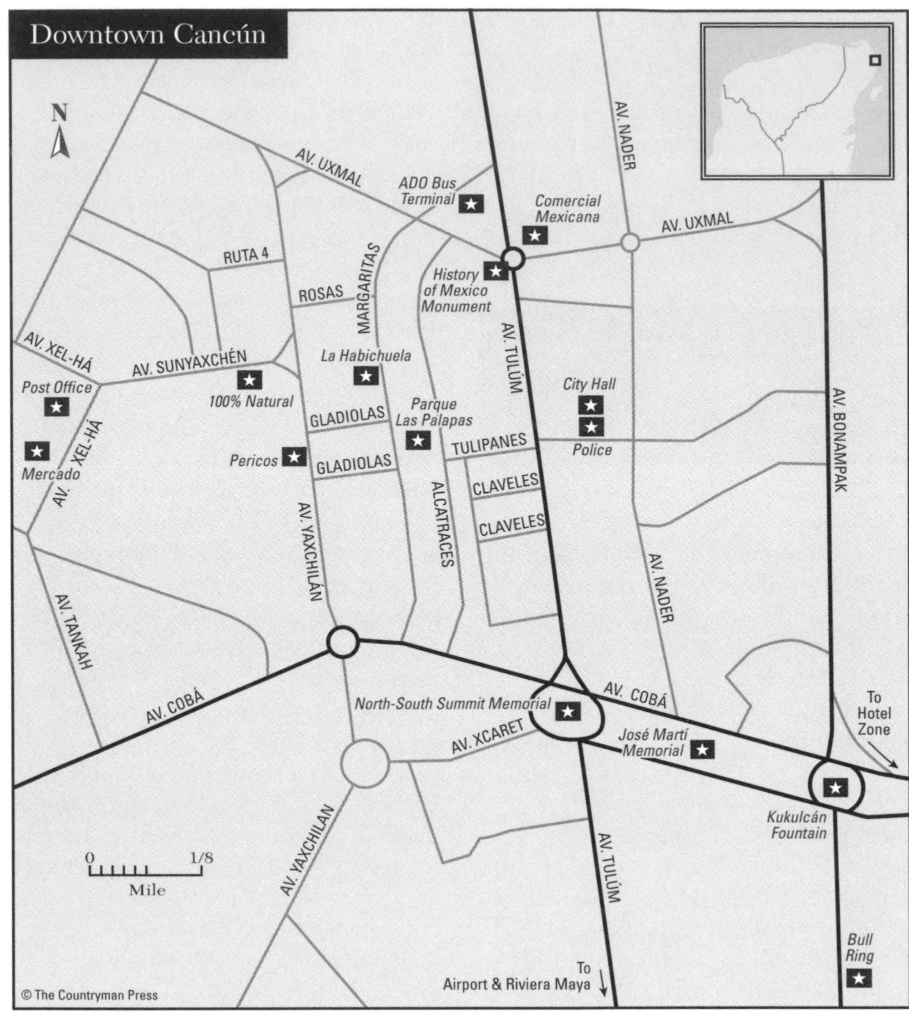

old-fashioned American hedonism, enter **Temptation Resort Cancún** (Boulevard Kukulcán km 3.5, www.temptationresorts.com). This resort is like a booze-fueled topless reality show, without the cameras. Though some nudity is allowed, it is not a "lifestyle" resort, meaning that sex in public is prohibited. In fact, though there's a sexy vibe throughout the complex, the all-inclusive resort somehow retains a touch of class and elegance, with upscale rooms and well-kept facilities. The hotel beach is powdery white with a waveless waterfront, though nude ocean swimming is strictly prohibited.

Although there's not a W Hotel Cancún (yet), you can find Starwood Hotels' swanky W offshoot **Aloft Cancún** (Boulevard Kukulcán, km 3.5, www.starwoodhotels.com) nestled against a revitalized Convention Center and shopping district. With sleek lines, bright accents, and playful designs, the hotel is exactly what you think it would be and fits in nicely with the bright blues, vivid pinks, and smooth white lines of Cancún's hotel zone.

Local Flavors

Taste of the town—restaurants, cafés, bars, bistros, etc.

Restaurants are plentiful in the hotel zone and on the main strips in downtown Cancún, making it easy to find options in or near your hotel. However, there are several destinations worth a special trip.

Though the indoor air-conditioned dining room at the original location in downtown Cancún of ★ **La Habichuela** (25 Margarita Street, www.lahabichuela.com) is quite pleasant and suitably upscale to impress any date, the true joy of this place in downtown Cancún is the back patio, where the trees, plants, Mayan replicas, and twinkling lights create a majestic setting for a long, slow meal. The specialty of the house at this restaurant is the Cocobichuela, featuring a coconut stuffed with lobster in a cream sauce. It has a unique flavor and goes great with ice-cold beer. Opt for a cab from the Hotel Zone to original, rather the newer, but less distinct, sunset location.

Although it's hardly an authentic cantina, ★ **Pericos** (Yaxchilán 61, in the downtown area of Cancún www.pericos.com.mx) throws a nightly fiesta that sure is fun. There are folkloric dancers, funny skits, conga lines, a live mariachi band, and even dancing masked little people. The menu features a selection of Mexican

The sprawling grounds of the all-inclusive Fiesta Americana Grand Condesa

Fiesta Americana Grand Condesa Cancun

standards, including fajitas, tacos, enchiladas, and grilled steak or shrimp.

Built on stilts over the water in the Nichupté lagoon, across the main road from the beach in the hotel zone, ★ **Lorenzillos Lobster House** (Boulevard Kukulcán, km 13, www.lorenzillos.com.mx) advertises its lobster all over town and lives up to its hype. It's like being on a luxury cruise ship in days gone by. Choose from tails or whole live lobster and pick your meal from the tank. It's a great place to watch the sunset, and at night you can see the city lights and the stars at the same time. The dining room fills up nearly every night, so go early or call ahead if you want one of the coveted waterside tables on the outer deck.

Right next door to Lorenzillos, The **Plantation House** (Boulevard Kukulcán, km 13) offers a more buttoned-up approach to seafood and the over-the-water dining. The waitstaff has a well-practiced Southern sense of service, and food, including grilled shrimp and lobster, is prepared fresh.

Enjoy a touristy take on Mexican food served by a lively wait staff at **Carlos 'n Charlies** (Boulevard Kukulcán, km 8.5, www.carlosandcharlies.com). Sure it's packaged, but the entertainment is nonstop and everyone stays engaged.

Find cheap, delicious tacos with great sauces and no frills at the always-busy **Taco Factory** (Fiesta Plaza at Boulevard Kukulcán, km 9, www.tacofactory.mx). The choice is inexpensive, delicious, and efficient.

Nightlife

One of the city's top nightspots sits across from the convention center. But to call ★ **Coco Bongo** (Boulevard Kukulcán, km 10.5, www.cocobongo.com.mx) a bar would be woefully inadequate—to even call it a nightclub is somewhat of a joke. It's more like an entertainment center where travelers congregate to celebrate life and get a bit crazy. There's often a line wrapping around the corner, but it moves fast, and you can start making friends before you even get inside. There you'll find a central bar area ringed by stadium-like seating, an upper deck with another bar and more seating, and an elevated stage, where most of the club's nonstop action happens. From celebrity impersonators and high-flying acrobats to live rock music, there's always something happening on stage or hanging from the rafters above the main bar. The atmosphere is very convivial, with a strong spirit of communal fun.

A sister club to Playa's own popular hotspot, ★ **Mandala** (Boulevard Kukulcán, km 9, www.mandalanightclub.com) sits next to Coco Bongo, but is entirely its opposite. The plush, vivid red interior is open to the street allowing all the world to see the bright lights and people dancing on the tables at this all-you-can-drink establishment. It's also ideally suited for mingling and making new friends.

Megaclub **The City Cancún** (Punta Cancún, Boulevard Kukulcán, km 10.5, www.thecitycancun.com) features a swanky Miami Beach–style *cabaña* bar and a massive indoor discotheque complete with laser light shows, smoke machines, and live performances. There are nine bars, big-name DJs, and a four-level dance floor. The whole place can accommodate more than four thousand partiers, making it one of the largest nightspots in all of Latin America.

The show at Coco Bongo lasts until sunrise.
Coco Bongo

PLAYA MUJERES

(9 miles north of Cancún)

Everything at the Playa Mujeres has been done big, by design. The master-planned resort welcomed its first guests in 2007, and even though it's near Cancún it's also isolated and feels like a separate destination.

Travelers who journey beyond Cancún's northern outskirts will find lush tropical landscaping framing a lavish grand entrance. Within the complex are two upscale luxury hotels, both with spas, an 18-hole Greg Norman–designed championship golf course, and an inland 176-slip marina. Both hotels are modern and elaborate, with a focus on luxury and comfort. People wanting to escape the world in style would find it easy to hide away for the week.

5 Standout Amenities at Moon Palace

When traveling south from Cancún in the direction of the Riviera Maya, Moon Palace (www.moonpalacecancun.com) is one of the first grand resorts you'll come across that has taken advantage of ample amounts of beachfront and has been built out, rather than up. Although it is still easy to head into Cancún's hotel zone or downtown for fun, dancing, and entertainment, the resort feels so isolated that it's natural to want to stay on the grounds. In addition to the normal all-inclusive attractions and benefits, Moon Place stands alone for several key factors.

1. **World-class entertainment.** The resort has hosted performances by the likes of Usher, Shakira, Enrique Iglesias, and Ricky Martin.

2. **Surfing simulator.** You can practice or compete against friends and family in the dual-wave, side-by-side Flowrider wave machine.

3. **Designer nightclub and bar.** Created by renowned French designer François Frossard, the new Noir nightclub and Sky Bar allow guests to unwind in style without leaving the resort.

4. **Pillow and aromatheraphy menu.** Choose from six pillow types and four aromatherapy scents in order to make your sleep experience sublime.

5. **Dedicated kids and teen clubs.** While kids can enjoy The Playroom, complete with special activities, games, and attractions broken out be age group, teenagers can retreat to Wired, where they can play video games, talk to their friends back home, and chill to DJ music.

Hurricane Wilma—Mexico's Costliest Natural Disaster Ever

Three months after Hurricane Emily tore through the Riviera Maya in July 2005, Tropical Storm Wilma formed in the Atlantic Basin, churning and sputtering for a few days without much strengthening or fanfare. On Wednesday, October 19, though, things changed quickly. Within 24 hours, the storm had developed into a massive category 5 hurricane, reaching a minimum central pressure of 882 millibars and sustained winds of 175 mph, making it the most intense hurricane on record in that part of the world. The U.S. State Department issued an urgent evacuation notice for all U.S. citizens in the region. By the morning of Thursday, October 20, the MTV Latin Music Video Awards in Xcaret had been canceled, and music performers and celebrities crowded the Cancún airport with thousands of tourists, all trying to get a flight back home. Meanwhile, the storm was poised offshore, forecast to veer to the east and spare the region, but not yet showing signs of the turn.

By late afternoon, winds from the outer bands of Hurricane Wilma began lashing the coast of Cancún and the Riviera Maya. Palm trees were bending and the waves were crashing, even though the storm was still 150 miles offshore. At dawn on Saturday, October 21, ten-foot waves were pounding into the seawall on the western shore of Cozumel, shooting sprays of water 30 feet into the air. The outer bands were tearing at the trees and rooftops, and some signs had already blown down. Up and down the Riviera Maya and Cancún, hotels prepared for the worst, and visitors and residents were bused to shelters while the military patrolled the streets, ensuring everyone had a place to ride out the storm. As the hurricane's eye neared the coast, the area braced for a direct hit, with landfall predicted to be somewhere between Playa del Carmen and Cancún.

At 10 AM on Friday, Cancún police reported the city's first death. A local woman was on her roof, cleaning debris, and a power line fell and electrocuted her. At 2 PM, the wall of the eye passed over the northern tip of Cozumel, while all across the region, the situation deteriorated rapidly. Gary Walten, an Akumal resident and owner of LocoGringo.com, was seeking shelter in his home while talking on the phone to CNN, which broadcast the conversation to the world. Wolf Blitzer asked him to hold his phone near the window so the audience could hear the sound. The noise was howling at a near-deafening volume, described by one survivor as "one thousand cats, screaming in pain." Water was washing across the main street through the Cancún hotel zone, and Quinta Avenida in downtown Playa del Carmen was a shallow river, with whitecaps cresting between storefronts. Most of the windows were boarded up; those that weren't were shattered. Cars were washing down the street in downtown Cancún and in the back streets of Playa and Puerto Morelos.

By sundown, the eye had stalled over the Cancún hotel zone, creating the worst-case scenario for the region, as the rainfall continued relentlessly. The wind created a 50-mile-long wall the strength of a force 2 tornado, and the storm surge inched higher and higher. Reports of an exploded gas tank and associated injuries made their way across the Internet, with readers praying for the safety of their loved ones, stranded in shelters across the area. Water was waist-deep along the

Cancún hotel zone and had completely washed out the road leading from Tulum to Punta Allen. Through the night, things only got worse. Witnesses in Playa del Carmen reported seeing 200-gallon water tanks, stoplights, plate glass, and even automobiles flying through the air. Water had washed completely over Kukulcán Boulevard in Cancún, connecting the ocean and the lagoon and making one solid sea of water.

At sunrise on Saturday, October 22, weary-eyed residents and tourists, many kept awake by the screeching winds and rising waters, peeked out the windows and were horrified by what they saw. The devastation was worse than anyone had imagined. Mexico's President Vincente Fox had already declared the entire region a disaster zone. To make matters worse, the storm was still stalled, meaning the misery would last at least another 12 hours. Nearly every hotel in Cancún had lost dozens, if not hundreds, of windows, while the ocean in Playa del Carmen had risen to meet Quinta Avenida, forming a sea of water 3 feet deep along the town's main tourist district. By 3 PM, the winds had receded to below hurricane strength for the first time in 24 hours, though the conditions were still too severe for anyone to leave the shelters. Food and water were running scarce, and reports of looters being arrested in Cancún did little to calm any fears. Across the entire region, waves of up to 25 feet continued to crash ashore, ripping apart everything in their path.

By Sunday, rumors of "total devastation" swept across the Internet, while Hurricane Wilma left the Yucatán and made a beeline for the Florida coast, where it went on to cause $11 billion in insured damages. Back in the Riviera Maya, thousands of travelers were stranded, with no way to get home. The Cancún airport was damaged, and some tourists paid up to $400 for a taxi to Mérida to catch a plane out. Tour operators scrambled to take care of their passengers and get them home. Some stranded survivors waited in line for two hours to use a payphone to tell loved ones that they were alright. Over the next week, the Mexican government passed out roofing materials for rebuilding houses and thousands of bottles of water and also cleared the streets. Generous locals prepared food for hungry tourists. Residents and visitors banded together to start cleaning up.

Within weeks, most of the damaged buildings had been cleared or were in the process of being rebuilt. The Capitan Lafitte, just north of Playa del Carmen, was declared a total loss. Cozumel's beachfront and Cancún's hotel zone took the brunt of the storm, with some hotels having to replace hundreds of windows and replace soft goods in all of their rooms. But over the following months, the beaches regained their natural splendor. Restaurants along Quinta in Playa put on fresh coats of paint and rebuilt their *palapas*. The large all-inclusive resorts along the Riviera Maya built back bigger and better than ever.

Thankfully, Hurricane Wilma claimed only five lives in all of Mexico. Once again, the region proved itself to be incredibly resilient, even in the face of great challenges. By 2006, the crowds were returning in droves, proving that the Riviera Maya is not only a destination full of history and stories of a splendid past, but also a world-class travel destination with unlimited drive for the future.

If you prefer finding the perfect beach for pure luxury, this is not your destination. The ocean beyond the resort is deeper than you'll typically find in the region, making for darker waters than some may expect. The beaches are kept clean, and while better than almost all U.S. beaches, they're more underwhelming that most beaches along the Mexican Caribbean.

Getting There

From Cancún's hotel zone, take Boulevard Kukulkan to downtown Cancún. Turn right onto Boulevard Bonampak, heading towards the ferry to Isla Mujeres. From downtown Cancún, continue 9 miles to the gated entrance to Playa Mujeres.

Checking In

Best places to stay in and around Playa Mujeres

Two resort hotels make up the accommodations within Playa Mujeres. The 450-room, all-inclusive **Excellence Playa Mujeres** (Prolongación Bonampak, Punta Sam, www.excellence-resorts.com) puts tropical grandeur and playful pomp on display in its ornate lobby with massive chandeliers and a promenade staircase leading down to the resort grounds. A modern, tropically chic pool and bar set the tone for this upscale, adults-only resort. Set right alongside the resort's seven winding pools, all ground floor rooms feature swim-up access, and some suites feature rooftop Jacuzzis.

With its crisp lobby showcasing many plush textures and shades of white, upscale boutiques, **The Beloved Hotel** (Prolongación Bonampak, Punta Sam, www.belovedhotels.com) makes no bones about its designer leanings. At The Beloved, originally known by its Spanish translation "La Amada," palm trees and local vegetation offset the bright white building and sands of the landscaped grounds. Honeymooners, couples, and guests docked at the adjacent La Amada Marina (www.laamadamarina.com) make use of the hotel's restaurants and bars.

ISLA MUJERES (15 miles north of Cancún, by boat)

Once a sacred pilgrimage site for Mayan natives, 5-mile-long Isla Mujeres is now a top spot for travelers seeking sunny days, pristine beaches, good food, tropical bars, yoga classes, and a casual lifestyle not found on the mainland. Spanish conquistador Francisco Hernandez de Cordoba named the island when he visited in 1517 looking for gold and other riches. He didn't find precious metals but did discover a large number of Mayan statuettes of women, once used in religious ceremonies. He named the spot Isla Mujeres, meaning "Island of the Women." Later visitors included pirates like Jean Lafitte, followed more recently by hippies and bohemians who used it as a place to get away from civilization and commune with nature. Today, the island's narrow roads are best explored in golf carts, which are available for rent by the hour or by the day. Draws include tranquil beaches, charming restaurants and bars, local shopping, snorkeling, fishing, and diving.

Parts of Isla Mujeres are still remote and unpopulated. Chip Rankin

Getting There

Sleek modern ferries depart every 30 minutes to Isla Mujeres from Gran Puerto (www.granpuerto.com.mx), located in the neighborhood of Puerto Juárez, and the nearby older port, which still officially goes by the name Puerto Juárez. Start times and evening schedules vary.

The shiny new port complex (complete with parking garage, convenience store, and McDonald's) is located 5 miles north of Cancún, while the older Puerto Juárez is just several blocks beyond it. Unless you want to indulge nostalgia for the old route, Gran Puerto offers the simpler bet.

And if you want a little local color on your trip, bypass the air-conditioned cabin, and head to the rooftop deck seating. Most days, once the boat gets going, you'll be treated to the sounds of a local musician covering tropical and popular classics—often in unintentionally entertaining ways. Be sure to have a few dollars (or 10 to 20 pesos) on hand for when they pass the hat.

Checking In

Best places to stay in and around Isla Mujeres

Accommodations options range from backpacker to boutique and offer several unique spots that make Isla Mujeres a unique stop for any budget.

Set on a perfect white sandy beach, the more elaborate ★ **Hotel Na Balam** (Calle Zazil-Ha, ★118, Playa Norte, www.nabalam.com) is adorned with Mayan décor, lush jungle foliage, and hammocks ideal for napping in the warm breeze. The hotel specializes in weddings, yoga retreats, and hosting other special groups.

Straight out of a trendy magazine photo shoot, the minimalist 12-room ★ **Hotel Secreto** (Punta Norte, www.hotelsecreto.com) overlooks a secluded cove of Halfmoon Beach and presents its guests with a sense of privacy and exclusivity that can be hard to find on the island. A great spot for a romantic hideaway, it regularly picks up visitors who found their original Isla accommodations more rustic than charming.

Hotel Secreto in Isla Mujeres is a hip getaway for couples. Chip Rankin

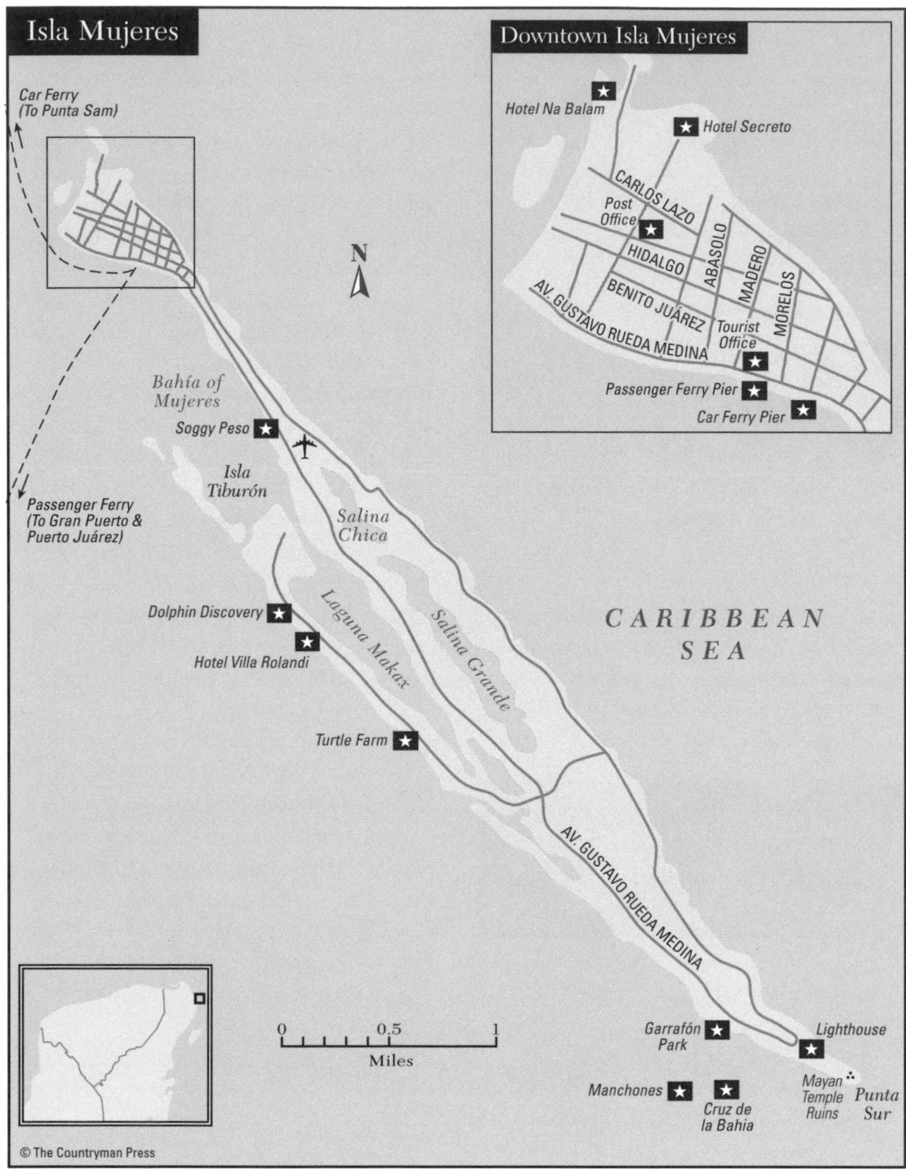

Although it's not a gay hotel, gay and lesbian travelers will find themselves welcomed without any eyes batted.

Ideal for budget travelers, the friendly ★ **Hotel Bucaneros** (downtown, www.bucaneros.com) exudes a genuinely local vibe. The inn's 16 rooms are simple, but attractive and clean, and some have air-conditioning. Restaurants and bars are within easy walking distance, and the beach is a 10-minute walk away.

Guests arrive to the opulent ★ **Hotel Villa Rolandi** (East Beach, www.villarolandi.com) via the "Cocoon I," a private luxury catamaran that picks them up in Cancún. Its sincere and insightful staff, opulent yet quirky rooms, elegant restaurant jutting over the sea, and private beach all ensure supreme satisfaction.

The six-room seaside bed and breakfast, **Villa la Bella** (2½ miles from Playa Norte, www.villalasbrisas.com), formerly known as Villa las Brisas, offers a relaxing respite from the hurried world, with no phones, TVs, or alarm clocks. From May to July, sea turtles nest on the hotel beach.

Exclusive and indulgent, ★ **Casa de los Sueños** (on the road to Garrafon, www.casasuenos.com) is more like a grand private villa than a hotel. It offers ten rooms and suites with ocean views, premium bedding, and unique décor.

Local Flavors

Taste of the town—restaurants, cafés, bars, bistros, etc.

Plenty of quality restaurants and cafes can be found in downtown Isla Chi-Chi & Charlie's (Playa Norte, www.chichisandcharliesislamujeres.com) serving inexpensive burgers, cocktails and sunset views; and the romantic ★ **Zazil Ha** (Calle Zazil-Ha, #118, Playa Norte, www.nabalam.com) at the Na Balam hotel, offering delicious vegetarian and regional specialties under a large *palapa* roof by the beach.

Removed from town and set on a dock behind the hotel of the same name, the gourmet restaurant **Casa Rolandi** (www.rolandi.com) at Hotel Villa Rolandi is known to draw the Cancún elite who boat over just for seafood, steak, shrimp, Mexican specialties, and an excellent wine list. The owners also have a more casual delicious outpost downtown, **Rolandi's Pizzeria** (Calle Hildalgo), which is very popular but doesn't offer the same romance or seaside views.

Bars & Nightlife

Popular with both locals and tourists, **Buho's** (Avenue Carlos Laza, Playa Norte, by the Maria del Mar hotel, www.cabanasdelmar.com) is Isla's de-facto happy-hour beach, offering cocktails made with tropical fruit and a playlist mixing reggae and American rock. Downtown's **La Adelita Tequileria** (Avenue Hidalgo) features a selection of 150 tequilas and often offers a 2-for-1 tequila special.

For some daytime drinking and a change of pace from downtown, head to the ★ **Soggy Peso Bar & Grill** (Avenue Rueda Medina, south of the

Buy Local for Local

Taking its individuality seriously, Isla Mujeres still frowns on international chains. Aside from a few small hotel groups, the only international brands permitted on island to date are the 7-Eleven convenience store and Grupo Anderson's Official Multi-Brand outlet, both across from the ferry dock. Even the Multi-Brand store is a concession to local policy. The corporation owning Carlos and Charlie's and Senor Frog's may sell official souvenirs, but it hasn't been allowed to use either brand name on its public signage nor open a restaurant or bar on island.

Isla Mujeres is just a short boat ride from Cancún, visible on the horizon. Chip Rankin

naval base on the bay side of the island, www.soggypeso.net). This ultra-casual Jimmy Buffett–friendly *palapa* bar is open from noon until around 8:30 PM, offering ceviche and other special treats. Marked only by a small handmade sign, it's hidden behind a house on the right, a few miles south of downtown. From downtown, you'll need a golf cart or a taxi, but finding it is part of the adventure.

Attractions

Set on the southeast tip of Isla Mujeres, **Garrafon Park** (Punta Sur, km 6, www.garrafon.com) marks Mexico's easternmost point. Each New Year's Day, locals flock to this spot to be the first of their countrymen to see the sun in the new year. With the Yucatán Peninsula's highest cliff, the park gets its name from the Spanish word for "canister," either because the site used to be a fuel depot or because the bay is shaped like a water bottle's curved neck, depending on whom you believe. It has several restaurants, souvenir shops, an ice cream parlor, a swimming pool, a protected snorkeling area, a sundeck, and a hammock area, and there is also a museum and

Texas Barbecued Ribs for Sunday Brunch at the Soggy Peso

If Sunday morning finds you on the island, swing by this hidden bar (www.soggypeso.net) for an amazing Bloody Mary and succulent barbecue lunch. Soggy Peso's owner, a former fine-dining proprietor from Austin, Texas, fires up his smoker every Saturday, smoking beef ribs for 24 hours for this weekly brunch. When they're done, juicy meat falls right off the bone, and visiting Texans routinely declare them "best ever!" The ribs sell out, so get there right at noon, and don't dawdle.

A typical beach restaurant in Isla Mujeres

an ancient Mayan lighthouse relic. Visitors can rent snorkeling equipment, clear-bottom kayaks, or Snuba or Sea Trek suits to experience the underwater realm.

ISLA HOLBOX

(105 miles northwest of Cancún)

Holbox (*hol-bosh*), a narrow island 7 miles off the Yucatán Peninsula's northern shore, is one of the region's lesser known and underappreciated destinations. It's also about to be discovered by that niche of American travelers who are actively looking for the next great authentic travel getaway.

Mayan for "black hole," Holbox's year-round population is less than two thousand, including descendants of the island's original eight families. Stories claim pirates settled it, using it as a hideout, mingling with the locals, and deciding to stay.

The island is a come-as-you-are hideaway for ultracasual vacationing. If the Riviera Maya is the land of *mañana* (tomorrow), then Holbox would be sometime next week. It's doubtful anyone has ever worn a tie here, unless it was a joke. Most locals don't even wear shoes, given the powdery sand roads. In fact, the mayor led an effort to pave the streets several years back, but locals voted it down.

Most visitors to the island come from Italy, Europe's Nordic and Scandinavian countries, or from Mexico itself. So aside from Spanish, you're more likely to hear Italian, Norwegian, Finnish, Swedish, and even Russian than English. Most Europeans come for the warmth, a low and reasonable cost, and proximity to nature, and they often stay for a couple of weeks.

Since the island faces the Gulf of Mexico, it doesn't have the turquoise water common in the Riviera Maya. It's blue, but has more of a greenish murky color. Some areas are clear enough for snorkeling. Due to currents and the island's location, thousands of shells wash on shore at each high tide. Complete with no cracks, many are highly prized by gatherers.

From November to January, the waves also wash heaps of seagrass onto the shores of most northern-facing beaches. The locals don't sweep it up because this grass is integral to keeping the island together. Over the course of the year, waves push sand over the grass, forming new beaches and protecting the island. Without the grass, the ocean would eat away at the beaches and then the island itself. Under-

Evening activity keeps the sandy roads busy on Calle Igualdad in downtown Holbox.
Chip Rankin

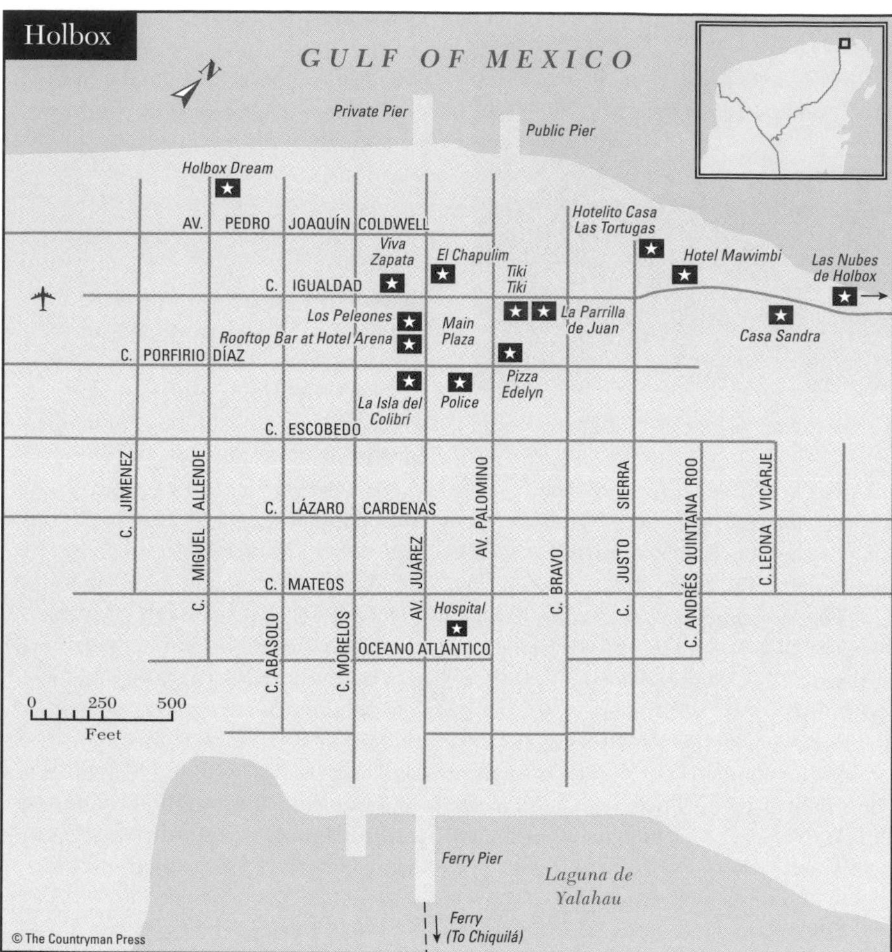

standing this, the local government has made it illegal to remove the grasses and disturb the natural process. However, you can still find beautiful beaches that are largely free of the grass, particularly along the shore immediately northwest of the town square, where the island's shore continues to curve away from true north.

Yalahao Lagoon, on the sheltered side of the island, features a mangrove swamp, flamingos, schools of dolphins, and a freshwater spring just up from the beach. It's a popular gathering spot for locals and tourists alike. In the times of the Mayans, it was believed to have curative properties, and natives would come from miles away to rejuvenate and refresh.

For people, life on the island is not complex. There are no cars, just motorized and electric carts, bikes, and mopeds. Locals operate the handful of restaurants, bars, and inns. But most go fishing and lobstering and sell their catches each day at the beach and to distributors on the mainland. Although ATMs have been popping up on the island, they often run out of bills, and many businesses still accept only cash. Tourists while away the day on the beach, explore mangrove canals in kayaks, go windsurfing, or head out on the water to sail, fish, and occasionally even dive.

The town of Holbox itself has an unusual and compelling energy about it, as locals live their lives among the tourists. Visitors are welcome enough, but the locals don't show a great deal of interest in them either. Although many of the islanders live simply, few would consider themselves poor. As one restaurateur said, even the family living in a simple dirt floor shack typically has a small fleet of four or more fishing boats, a truck on the mainland, and cash at its disposal. On Holbox, there's not a great deal for the locals to spend money on, so they forget about it. Regardless of the veracity of this observation, visitors will quickly note that children on Holbox don't ask for handouts, no one appears to be homeless, locals seem genuinely content, and few local shopkeepers try to hustle you into their shop to buy souvenirs. It's live and let live on island time.

At present, Isla Holbox finds itself at a rare, and usually temporary, equilibrium where its charms have manifested themselves, tourism infrastructure is present but small, and the tourists themselves are just a small percentage of the island's income, activity, and importance. If you like authenticity with a tropical twist, this is a place worth seeing. And that might also pose a problem for the very character that makes it so interesting.

Unfortunately, Holbox's current magnetism also likely foreshadows the dramatic growth that transforms once-sleepy villages into something wholly different—not unlike Cancún or Playa del Carmen itself. Already, the Mexican government has stated that hundreds of acres of untouched Holbox scrub will be given over to the development of large resorts. The introduction of carnivorous creatures to the island, such as the badger-like, egg-eating coati, has led to a dramatic decrease in Holbox's bird population. And the loss of plankton in the sea, resulting from the chemicals used to clean the BP oil spill, have changed whale shark migration patterns. This means that fewer whale sharks show up in the region and tours typically have to travel 45 miles over sometimes-rough seas to find them.

However, all is not lost. Holbox is clearly on the move. And given its own leadership's understanding of infrastructure preservation, such as the beach-replenishing seagrass, and lessons learned in the development of the rest of the region, Holbox has the chance become a special destination that manages to preserve its own unique character as it grows and matures.

Getting There

With the opening of a new connector road from Puerto Morelos, the ferry to Isla Holbox is a 2.5-hour drive from Playa del Carmen and a 3-hour drive from Cancún. The island is 7 miles offshore from the dock in the quiet town of Chiquila. The 30-minute, air-conditioned ferry ride costs 100 pesos for tourists and 70 pesos for locals. If you're reading this book, expect to pay full freight, at 100 pesos with no debate.

Parking is available at small, private lots across the street from the ferry, typically at 50 pesos per day.

If you take a chartered flight, the airstrip is just a few blocks from the town plaza. The company Aerosaab (Playa del Carmen, www.aerosaab.com) offers plane charters starting around $325.

Checking In

Best places to stay in and around Isla Holbox

Not long ago, overnight visitors to Holbox needed to be comfortable sleeping on hammocks and taking quick showers before the water ran cold. While this remains common, it's also easy to find rooms with cold air-conditioning, warm water, comfortable beds, and an artistic tropical style with a little panache. If you need Jacuzzi bathtubs and 4-star dining come nightfall, you're best off visiting the island on a day trip and returning to your upscale hotel in Cancún or the Riviera Maya.

BUDGET LODGING

The cheapest way to stay the night is to rent one of the Mayan-style beach *palapas* on the island's north side. For around $10, you get a place to put your things and a hammock under the stars or in a small hut. Bathrooms are communal and in poor shape. Renting a room in a local house is another low-budget solution. To go this route, ask any cab driver, waiter, or another local, and they're sure to know someone with a room for rent. This typically ranges from $15 to $25 and includes a private room, shared bathroom, and usually a meal or two with the host family.

You can also find home and room rentals online at **Airbnb** (www.airbnb.com), which has more than 15 listings, and on **VRBO** (www.vrbo.com) and **HomeAway** (www.homeaway.com), each with more than 10 Holbox listings.

MIDRANGE BOUTIQUE HOTELS

Travelers seeking more stylish comfort may choose from several local beachfront boutiques currently pushing the envelope in Holbox.

Guests at the ultra-relaxing, rustic-chic ★ **Hotelito Casa Las Tortugas** (Playa Blanca, www.holboxcasalastortugas.com) can swing in hammocks outside their 12 eclectically designed suites and bungalows or retreat inside to curl up in Egyptian cotton sheets. The boutique hotel has winding staircases, twisting pathways, colorful walls and tiles, and a private pool. It's home to a *mezcaleria* and *cevicheria*, yoga studio, and kite surfing school. The picturesque beachside restaurant and bar is sometimes open to the public, but at times is limited to hotel guests, depending on the provisions it has on hand.

The most removed hotel on the island, ★ **Las Nubes de Holbox** (Paseo Kuká on the corner of Calle Camerón, www.lasnubesdeholbox.com) has 28 very peaceful rooms and suites tucked away in thatch-roofed bungalows. *Palapa* roofs and traditional white stucco walls conceal upscale, air-conditioned interiors. Guests are welcome make use of courtesy bikes and kayaks, and a small private yacht is available to rent for an additional charge. In addition to three swimming pools, the hotel offers relaxing massage and facial treatments at Orquídea Spa, located onsite. Remote and serene, the hotel is a popular spot for destination weddings.

Helpful links: Isla Holbox

HolboxIsland.com. Highlights hotels, tours, transportation, and restaurants

Cancun.com/Holbox. Covers restaurants, attractions, hotels, shopping, and tours

HolboxWhaleSharkTours.com. Overview of the island, its attractions, and whaleshark tours

You can watch the sun set into the ocean from the palm-shaded beach at Hotel Casa Las Tortugas. Chip Rankin

The affordable Holbox Dream hotel sits along one of the best stretches of beach, just a few blocks from the town square. Chip Rankin

Designed and owned by a once traveling artist who decided to stay, the romantic 18-room **CasaSandra** (Calle de la Igualdad, www.casasandra.com) showcases hand-made décor reflecting Holbox's back-to-nature ambiance. Original art is on display throughout the charming boutique hotel, which sits northeast of downtown Holbox, across from the beach on a sandy road.

★ **Holbox Dream** (Pedro Joaquin Codwel Avenue at the beach, www.holboxdream.com) is situated on the best stretch of beach in Holbox, as the waves typically wash up less seagrass than they do on the beaches east of downtown. Small, simple, and charming, the hotel offers air-conditioned rooms with comfortable beds at a very reasonable price. Downtown is a short walk from the hotel, but also removed enough that travelers will feel far away from any of its modest bustle. In 2014, Holbox Dream doubled in size, adding about 20 rooms, a feature swimming pool, and new restaurant and bar. The hotel is an ideal pick for travelers wanting a boutique hotel experience at a reasonable price.

Local Flavors

Taste of the town—restaurants, cafés, bars, bistros, etc.

Mostly centered around the town square, restaurants welcome locals and visitors as they mingle and compare menus. Several restaurants display samples of their fresh fish and other dishes. Select shops along the square proffer fresh fruit smoothies and ice cream treats.

Perched above the southwestern side of the plaza, ★ **Restaurant Los Peleones** (Juarez Avenue across from the town square) celebrates Mexico's love of the *luchador* (masked wrestler) with a witty atmosphere and delicious food and drink. Owned by an Argentinian chef turned local, the small and charming restaurant serves fresh seafood, Argentinian-grilled meats, and a unique selection of pastas. Save room for Los Peleones' original and curiously tasty dessert creation: dark chocolate crumbles and nuts served on a thin layer of fresh olive oil, topped with fresh vanilla ice cream.

During the day, ★ **La Casa de la Tortilleria de Española** (Juarez Avenue across from the town square, directly beneath Los Peleones) pours coffee, tea, and lemonade and serves up healthy and vegetarian lunches.

Their most popular dish is the Spanish tortilla, which is really an omelet prepared with potatoes and cheese.

Found on the southern corner of the town square, across from the large Isla Holbox bandshell, **La Isla de Colibri** (Juarez and Porfirio Diaz Avenues) looks like an old Caribbean homestead whose town sprung up beyond its doorstop. The simple, local restaurant serves fresh seafood, Mexican dishes, and basic international fare for the faint of heart. Beneath its tin-roof, the edifice is stuffed with Mexican art and curios celebrating Frida Kahlo and other cultural influences. On a nice day or evening, take a street-side table, order a large, fresh margarita, and watch locals and tourists drift by. Visa and Mastercard accepted.

On a third floor patio overlooking the ocean, **La Parrilla de Juan** (Igualdad Street between Palomino Avenue and Bravo Street, one block northeast of the town square) is an Argentinian steakhouse with a decent assortment of wine. Like most restaurants on Holbox, freshly caught seafood is on the menu as well.

There is no set menu at **El Chapulím Mexican Bistro & Artisan Beer House** (Juarez Avenue just northwest of the main plaza). Instead, the owner prepares an original four-course meal each day based on what he finds fresh and available during his morning market run. Closed most Sundays and Mondays.

Tourists and locals stop in for fresh favorites at La Isla de Colibri, at the southern corner of Holbox's main square. Chip Rankin

Other popular stops include **Pizzería Edelyn** (eastern corner of the town square), serving up amazing lobster pizzas, ice-cold beers, and a lively atmosphere on a second-story terrace overlooking the town, and the inexpensive, open-air **Viva Zapata** (half block west of the main plaza), offering lobster, whole fish, shrimp, and traditional Mexican fare under a *palapa* roof and along the longest wooden bar in Holbox. The no-frills, outdoor **Las Panchas** (Morelos Street between Pedro Joaquin Codwell Street and the beach) is a favorite breakfast stop among locals—and tourists are welcome too.

Nightlife

When the sun goes down, the island quiets noticeably. Visitors stroll the square and the main streets and tend to linger over dinner with a few extra drinks. Many lights are dimmed, and candlelight provides much of the atmosphere. A few places on and around the square tend to be livelier, but only relative to the quiet town.

There are few dedicated bars on the island. However, most restaurants that remain open past the dinner hour are happy to serve drinks.

★ **Habana Nights** (half block west of the main plaza, next to Viva Zapata) is the most popular, thanks to its laid-back Caribbean atmosphere and big-screen TVs, especially during key soccer matches and sporting events.

The **Rooftop Bar at Hotel Arena** (Juarez Avenu across from the southeastern side of the town square, www.hotelarenaholbox.com) is pretty basic, but it emits its siren call to local nighttime revelers with club and dance music. It's the highest perch around with a view of the main plaza below.

Barquito Mawimbi (on the beach at the Wawimbi Hotel on Damero Street northwest of Sierra Street, www.mawimbi.net) isn't open late, but it's a favorite stop for tourists who are exploring the island and looking for beach bar away from their own hotel.

Mingle with friends, or maybe even make some new ones, at **Tiki Tiki** (Igualdad Street between Palomino Avenue and Bravo Street, one block northeast of the town square). The second story terrace overlooks the town square and has a bit of a clubby vibe, with lounge music and international bar options. You can usually catch a *futbol* match or other sports game on one of the televisions if you ask.

Activities

Beyond lounging on the beach and grazing at local restaurants, Holbox is best known as the home of the whale sharks, the largest species of sharks in the world, often growing as long as a standard 72-seat school bus. Fortunately, they are gentle giants, preferring to passively feed on plankton, so they are quite slow and docile.

Whale shark sightings near Holbox have dropped dramatically since the BP oil spill in the Gulf of Mexico. It's said that the chemicals designed to clean the oil have eliminated much of the plankton, prompting the mammoth whales sharks to chart a new course and migrate closer to Cancún.

However, from mid July to September, ★ **whale shark sightings** are still possible and visitors happily join them by swimming Holbox's waters. Many tour operators will still guarantee that they'll find the sharks or refund your money. Others warn that this might mean a 2½-hour boat trip to reach more fertile waters. When making your arrangements, be sure you understand exactly what is being promised and how long it may be expected to take.

On successful trips, the captain typically zeros in on a shark and slowly pulls the boat within several feet. Two at a time, snorkelers swim alongside for about ten minutes. The shark continues to move, so there's a fair amount of swimming involved to keep up, though most people are so engrossed in the experience that they don't notice how tired they're getting. Boats carry about ten people, so after an hour or so on deck, you'll have another turn to jump back into the water, continuing the interaction.

Some boat captains and tour operators offer private charters. Tours are available that include transportation from Cancún, Playa del Carmen, or even Cozumel. A top operator is **Holbox Tours & Travel** (www.whalesharktours.com).

Tours and private charters can also be arranged to visit the **Island of the Birds**, a natural habitat a few miles away, take **Sportfishing and Flyfishing** excursions, visit the **Yalahau Cenote**, and go horseback riding.

ISLA CONTOY (25 miles north of Cancún, by boat)

This bird sanctuary and wildlife refuge is offshore from the northeastern tip of the Yucatán Peninsula. There are no bars or restaurants, no hotels, no roads, and very few facilities. A small group of Mexican marines runs a lighthouse, museum, lookout tower, and outpost, but there are no other full-time inhabitants. It's a popular nesting ground for sea turtles, and occasionally naturists will camp out and care for them and watch for poachers, backed by the marines. There are a few rolling hills and a long deserted beach, ideal for strolling and snorkeling.

Getting There

Visitors can arrive by private boat or with a tour group, but proper authorization in required. The island (www.islacontoy.org) is managed jointly by the local NGO Amigos de Isla Contoy A.C. and by the Secretary of Environment, Natural Resources, and Fishing (SEMARNAT), who limit island visitors to two hundred per day. If traveling with a tour group, your permit is likely included, but visitors traveling on private watercraft must apply for permits at the park offices in Cancún or Isla Mujeres.

THE MAYAN COAST—SOUTH OF THE RIVIERA MAYA

South of the Riviera Maya, beyond Tulum and the nearby Si'an Kaan reserve, are some curious and quirky hideaways that few travelers venture see, including the stunning Lake of Seven Colors and the emerging town of Mahahual, which just may become the quirky, upscale getaway that today's toddlers favor in 20 years.

LAGUNA BACALAR

About 2½ hours south of Playa del Carmen is Laguna Bacalar, a freshwater lake just east of Highway 307 that feeds into Chetumal Bay. With crystal-clear water and gleaming white sands, it's a rare jewel in the jungle. The lake has a dramatic setting and varying depths, causing the colors to change from spot to spot—hence its nickname, the Lake of Seven Colors. It is a prime spot for snorkeling, bird-watching, swimming, and photography.

Checking In

Best places to stay in Laguna Bacalar

A full-service hotel with 33 rooms and suites (some air-conditioned), and incomparable views of the lagoon, **Hotel Laguna Bacalar** (25 miles north of Chetumal, just off Highway 307, www.hotellagunabacalar.com) is an ideal headquarters to explore the area. The crisp-white, turquoise, and pink hotel feels much like a charming throwback to 1950s Baja California. A terrace restaurant overlooks the lagoon, and a sundeck offers direct access to the *laguna* itself.

MAHAHUAL

When you arrive in Mahahual you'll immediately notice a laid-back atmosphere, but with a sense that things may be changing. More villas and small inns continue to pop up, and the town is slowly developing a rustic yet upscale tone, similar to

Playa del Carmen's early days. There are a few sandy streets and several open-air restaurants, and hotels and private homes are stretched out along the beach.

The shallow reefs of the Chinchorro Banks are known for being the healthiest in the area, with huge sea fans, sponges, anemones, sea cucumbers, arrow crabs, and seahorses. There are also hundreds of species of fish (including large barracuda), sea turtles, and even dolphins, which sometimes follow dive boats and play in the wake.

In 2000 Mahahual completed construction of a cruise ship terminal, and each month there seem to be more arrivals, steadily changing the face of the town. The cruise dock is only five blocks from the town center, and the streets become lined with new restaurants, bars, and souvenir shops. When the boats are in town, the beach is full of day-trippers snorkeling, swimming, riding WaveRunners, and enjoying the day. The rest of the time the village is mellower, with locals talking in the storefronts, tourists lingering in the beachside restaurants, and only a few people relaxing on the beach.

Getting There

To get to Mahahual by car from anywhere along the Riviera Maya, take Highway 307 south toward Chetumal. Fill up with gas when you go through the town of Carillo Puerto, as there are not many stations in this area. Once you pass the village of Limones (about 2½ miles south of Playa), you'll go about 2 more miles, and then you should see a sign for Mahahual and the Cafetal exit. Turn left and head east to the beach. From this point, Mahahual is still about an hour away. About halfway down this road, you ll arrive at a military checkpoint, so don't be alarmed if you see men in uniform carrying machine guns. They may search your car for drugs, but they are courteous and won't cause any problems—as long as you don't. The road is a fairly straight shot through the jungle, finally arriving at the small beach town of Mahahual. Most hotels, restaurants, dive shops, and other attractions are close to the area where the main road meets the beach.

To get to Mahahual by bus, from the Cancún bus station take a bus to Limones, either a direct route or a bus to Chetumal that stops there. Be sure to ask, as not all buses to Chetumal stop in Limones. From there, transfer to a Mahahual bus, which leaves every hour or so from Limones.

Checking In

Best places to stay in Mahahual

Surrounded by trees and flowering plants, **Balamku Inn** (3 miles south of the Mahahual town square on the main beach road, www.balamku.com) is a great escape for nature lovers, and the beach is perfect for tanning and relaxing.

Right in the center of town on the beach, the10-room **La Posaada de los 40 Canones or Forty Cannons Hotel** (www.40canones.com) may seem bustling for the area, but relative to more touristy destinations up the coast, is still ultra-relaxed.

On an excellent, remote beach up the coast from Mahahual center, the solar-powered ★ **Mayan Beach Garden** (El Placer, 15 miles north of Mahahual, www.mayanbeachgarden.com) offers suites and beach cabañas with ceiling fans and direct beach access.

HOBIE CAT
GETAWAY
2305130814-4

5

Activities

ADVENTURE ABOUNDS IN THE RIVIERA MAYA and wherever you are, most activities are no more than an hour away from any hotel in the area. Nearly every hotel tour desk can sell you tickets that include round-trip transportation. They're also easy to get to by rental car or even bus, so they make for good self-guided outings as well. Note: Secondary and local attractions are discussed in other chapters in this book, based on the area where they're located.

Nature Parks, Amusement Parks & Zoos

Once a sacred Mayan site, the Mayan-themed ★ Xcaret (Highway 307, km 287, 3 miles south of Playa del Carmen, www.xcaret.com) recreational park is far and away the top attraction in the area. True to its roots, it has several native ruins on-site, and each evening native dancers put on an incredible show of Mayan dances and rituals. There's an interactive museum, miniature models of many Mayan sites, and a petting zoo.

Visitors can go tubing or snorkeling through an underground river, watch horsemanship exhibitions, see native fish in a saltwater aquarium, watch butterflies in their natural habitat, go scuba diving, lounge on the beach, swim with dolphins, and even visit a re-creation of a native Mayan village. Near the village, an ancient ball court is set up where games of pok-ta-pok are played, with rules similar to those that were used more than a thousand years ago. In the game, players try to bounce the ball through an overhead hoop without using their hands or feet. It is said that in ancient times the losers were sacrificed to the gods. Tour buses from Cancún come in hourly, so it's best to arrive early to experience the park before it gets too crowded.

Next door, Xcaret's new park ★ Xplor (Highway 307, km 282, www.xplor.travel)

LEFT: An afternoon sail through Akumal Bay Riviera Maya Destination Marketing Office

caters to the active adventure set, letting them explore its grounds through the air, water, and land. Guests can enjoy 2½ miles of zip lines that include water landings, tour through the jungle on amphibious ATVs that they drive themselves, and swim or hand-paddle a personal raft though an underground river surrounded by striking stalactites and stalagmites. Book through a local tour agency, or just show up at the ticket office. All-inclusive available.

Learn about sharks at Xcaret Park.

Riviera Maya Destination Marketing Office

A 370-acre activity and nature park, ★ **Tres Rios** (Highway 307, km 300, 7 miles north of Playa del Carmen, www.tres-rios.com) offers an environment to learn while you have fun. There are mountain bikes for cruising through the jungle, canoe trips, jungle rivers, sea kayaks, snorkeling beaches, freshwater swimming holes, and beach hammocks. Hiking tours and horseback expeditions are offered and take participants through the dense jungle to see *cenotes*, tropical flora, wild animals, and deserted beaches. If you're interested in scuba diving, you can take a resort course that includes an hour of instruction and then an actual open-water dive, with an instructor at your side. Park areas are left as untouched as possible, giving visitors the feeling that they are seeing the land much as the Mayans did hundreds of years ago. All-inclusive available.

Nature park ★ **Xel-Ha** (Highway 307, km 245, 8 miles from Tulum, www.xelha.com) was once a Mayan seaport and later a popular snorkeling cove frequented by an adventurous few. Today it's one of the Riviera Maya's largest attractions. Meaning "where the waters are born," Xel-Ha features underground rivers where fresh and salt water come together, an animal nursery, cliff jumping, a tubing area, a dolphin discovery center, massage huts, ocean snorkeling, mountain bike trails, and a hiking area. All-inclusive available.

Mayan for "underground river cave," ★ **Aktun Chen** (Highway 307, km 107, between Akumal and Xel-Ha, www.aktunchen.com.mx) is a 1,000-acre nature park with a large cavern and jungle tour. The main, 600-yard-long cave is said to have been a natural bunker for the native Mayans, who sought its protection during serious storms. An hour-long guided walk through the park reveals badgers, iguanas, spider monkeys, tropical birds, and wild turkeys. There's also a motorized ATV tour, if you'd rather ride than walk. Along the way, you'll see many tropical flowers, coconut palms, and a gum tree called the chicozapote. The cave itself has amazing formations of stalactites and stalagmites, and an amazing underground *cenote*, more than 35-feet deep. Though the cave winds its way several hundred yards through the ground, there are frequent openings and areas where fresh air and the sun shine through, so it's not as claustrophobic as it may sound.

If you prefer fauna over flora, you'll enjoy **Crococun Crocodile Farm & Zoo** (Highway 307, km 323, near Puerto Morelos, www.crococunzoo.com). Formed in 1985 as a commercial croc farm where the animals were raised for their skins

Swimming With Dolphins at Xcaret

Ancient Mayans saw the dolphin as a sacred animal and a source of inspiration for the creation of myths and legends. Today, dolphins contribute to aquatic therapies and humanities disciplines, and experience has shown that they only lack the ability to speak

At Xcaret, dolphins are treated with care and respect, and their well-being is always the main priority. Biologists there, and area veterinarians, meet all the needs of the park's dolphins. They monitor their health, weight, and food, and conduct research on their behavior. In fact, biologists claim that the 40-year life expectancy of a dolphin can increase when living in captivity or semi-captivity (in extensive areas of its natural habitat). Dolphins have actually been born in captivity at Xcaret, and the way in which the baby mammals arrive into this world is quite a sight. They come out of their mother's womb tail first, so as not to drown, and they emerge like torpedoes to the surface as they take in their first breath. Their first year is a delicate time because dolphins are born without antibodies; however, their mothers feed them for one to two years, building these defenses.

Qualified dolphin trainers, who are constantly learning new skills, spend long hours with the dolphins, forming extremely strong, family-like bonds and communication abilities. Every single approach of the trainer receives an answer from the dolphin: a jump that soars more than 2 meters up in the air, a tail dance, a flipper greeting, a friendly sound, and underwater tricks.

Due to their high cognitive ability, dolphins understand every instruction their trainers give them. Dolphins have the ability to associate, and this allows them to translate signs and develop a series of perfectly synchronized movements. With a "target pole," which functions as an extension of their trainer's hand, dolphins learn to identify instructions until they develop a language that establishes a sophisticated communication with their trainer.

and skulls, it's been transformed into a preserve, where visitors' admission fees go toward rescuing the crocs rather than killing them. The park now has dozens of other animals, including white-tailed deer, spider monkeys, snakes, spiders, and birds. Except for 300 crocodiles, many animals are tame enough for kids to pet.

A fun little stop-off between Cancún and Playa del Carmen is the 150-acre **Yaax-Che Jardín Botánico** (Highway 307, km 33, just south of Puerto Morelos, www.ecosur.mx/jb/YaaxChe/). Set up like a museum, with everything clearly marked and explained, this botanical garden and nature preserve has hundreds of species of plants, trees, and flowers. From a hilltop overlook you can see the jungle canopy and the ocean beyond, and a small Mayan ruin called *El Altar* that dates from the 1400s. There's also a mock-up of an ancient Mayan homestead and a *chicle* camp, where farmers worked to process the rubber gum from the *chicle* tree. Look for the native tree called the *ceiba*, which the Mayans called *yaax chen*. Considered a spiritual icon, it was said to connect the three levels of the universe.

Popular with families and nature buffs, the privately run **Xaman Ha Aviary** (Paseo Xaman Ha, behind Plaza Playacar, Playacar) exhibits more than 50 species of tropical birds, including flamingos, toucans, macaws, and other favorites native to the region. Some are caged, while others roam free in their natural habitat. There are many iguanas, butterflies, turtles, brown squirrels, and freshwater fish. It's best to go in the morning when the animals are more likely to be moving about.

A small replica Mayan temple marks the entrance to **Kantun Chi** (Highway 307, km 266.5, 14 miles south of Playa, 1 mile south of Puerto Aventuras, www.kantunchi.com), an ecology and adventure park, across from the Barcelo Maya Hotel. Meaning "yellow stone mouth" in Mayan, Kantun Chi has nature trails, swimming holes, caves, and an animal sanctuary. Fauna include raccoons, spider monkeys, and white-tailed deer, along with several endangered local species, which the park is helping to bring back. It has four *cenotes* large enough for swimming and snorkeling, including one called Uchil Ha, or "ancient water," said to have been an ancient Mayan religious site. Visitors can go horseback riding, mountain biking, or hiking.

Keep your eye out for iguanas and you may make a new friend. The Wilkerson Family

Just across the highway from the Cancún airport, as you head to the Cancún hotel zone, you'll find the 18-acre **Wet'n Wild Cancun** (Boulevard Kukulcán, km 25, Cancún, www.wetnwildcancun.com). You can't tell from the road, but it's actually on a huge stretch of perfect white-sand beach. There are wave pools, water slides, a lazy river, tube rides, and many other freshwater attractions. Dolphin-swim programs are offered through Dolphinaris (www.dolphinaris.com), located at the back end of the park.

Cenotes

Cenotes are relatively small and the water does not circulate, so it is important that all swimmers and divers rinse off any mosquito repellent or sunscreen before entering the water. Remember to bring cash, as most individual *cenotes* have an admission starting around $10, with larger parks and excursions run upwards of $60. For general information about cave diving, see chapter 9.

CAMINO DE CENOTES

Across from the main entrance to Puerto Morelos, a new modern highway heads inland, beyond a tall archway etched with RUTA DE CENOTES at the top, at approximately km 321 of Highway 307. This road is a fairly straight shot for 25 miles, passing through the blue-collar town of Central Vallarta, past several *cenotes*, and on into Quintana Roo's interior. There are dozens of *cenotes* in the area, though most are still unaccessible. Check for signs as you travel the road, and you could be the first to visit a newly opened one.

Popular stops include ★ **Selvatica** (Ruta de Cenotes, km 19, www.selvatica.com.mx), the largest *cenote* in the area, which boasts a 160-foot-wide *cenote*, perfect for cooling off and swimming. The park also includes a 300-acre preserve, with bike riding, zip-lining, canopy tours, and lunch. Impromptu visits can also be accommodated. With 24 platforms, the 2-mile-long zip-line circuit is the longest in North America. This trip was named "one of the 35 great adventures of the world" by *Travel & Leisure* magazine.

At ★ **Siete Bocas** (Ruta de Cenotes, km 13) there are seven different lagoons, a couple of them large enough for swimming. There isn't yet a road connecting the *cenote* to the main road, so visitors have to walk 25 minutes down a jungle path to reach it.

A small sign marks the turnoff to the medium-size **Boca del Puma** *cenote* (Ruta de Cenotes, km 14), which has a camping area and room for snorkeling and swimming.

Cenote Verde Lucero (Ruta de Cenotes, km 16) has several different *cenote* openings, with undergound caverns connecting them. There's not much to see for snorkelers, but trained divers can traverse underground to the connected lagoons. The *cenote* is about a quarter mile from the entrance. You can park and walk or, if you want to brave it, drive your car right up to the edge.

Hidden Worlds Cenotes

Discovered in 1986, **Hidden Worlds Cenotes** (Highway 307, 30 miles south of Playa, 2 miles south of Xel-Ha, www.hiddenworlds.com) covers nearly 10,000 hectares of land, and the cave system runs for 42 miles, most of it underground. In business since 1994, it hosted the filming of the IMAX movie *Journey into Amazing Caves* and operates as a private scuba and snorkeling park, affording visitors an incredible underwater experience that feels more like being in space than

Cenotes offer a rare opportunity to snorkel in gin-clear freshwater. The Wilkerson Family

underwater. Visitors choose from several different *cenotes* and caves, depending on their experience, the time they have available, and whether they want to scuba or snorkel.

The first site is called **Dos Ojos** (Two Eyes), essentially two separate *cenotes* connected by a channel. This is the main site where most of the IMAX footage was shot, and is the third largest underwater cave in the world. Basic dive certification is required, and there is natural light the whole way. The water is unimaginably clear, and if not for the air bubbles, it really would seem like outer space, especially given the otherworldly scenery, unlike anything you would ever see on the land.

The next dive, the **Caverna de los Murcielagos** (the Bat Cave), has been known to bring divers to tears with its awesome beauty. The cave is as dramatic as it is exquisite, with a sublime combination of steep drop-offs, Disney-worthy stalactites, and elaborate features that have taken millions of years to develop. There are also hundreds of brightly colored tropical fish, elusive cave shrimp, and other critters. The depth is only 35 feet, making it especially safe for scuba newcomers and easily appreciated by snorkelers.

The relatively small and shallow **Hilario's Well** is best for snorkelers. During a one-hour guided tour, snorkelers encounter stalagmites, stalactites, and other truly awe-inspiring formations.

Other *Cenotes* around the Riviera Maya

One of the region's better known *cenotes*, ★ **Aktún-Ha or The Carwash** (just south of Akumal, off Highway 307), is frequented by scuba-diving groups from the United States and beyond. The Carwash is only 50 feet deep, but the caverns are wide and long (nearly 2 miles long), making it very popular for certified cave divers. During the summer the surface is covered with algae, but in the cooler months snorkeling is possible.

★ **Cenote Azul** (Highway 307, km 266), half the size of a basketball court, is on a small ranch bordering the highway. Look for the hand-painted sign along the road and slow down fast to avoid slipping on the gravel entryway. The lagoon is a short walk from the parking area and has a rope swing and 10-foot-high cliff, perfect for jumping into the water. An adjacent *cenote*, **El Jardín del Eden**, offers a similar experience and is a frequent stop for tour groups.

Part of an immense nature preserve and ranchers' cooperative, ecopark ★ **Cenote Dos Ojos** (Highway 307, km 242) offers several *cenotes* for exploring, snorkeling, and scuba diving. First discovered in 1985 by dive maven Mike Madden, it's been extensively explored and mapped. Most of the *cenotes* connect through underground caverns, which require advanced cave-diving certification to experience.

Cenote Ponderosa (Highway 307, 3 miles south of Puerto Aventuras), a *cenote* and cavern dive, is comprised of two separate *cenotes*, connected through an underground channel. Wide caverns are easy to maneuver and swim around, helping prevent feelings of claustrophobia. The main feature is an underground air dome called the Chapel, where divers can submerge and breathe natural air, even though they are under the water level.

Chaak Tun Ts'ono'ot (Avenue Juárez at 120th Avenue, Playa del Carmen), whose name translates from Mayan to "rain rock *cenote*," has multiple caverns and a stunning cave formation.

Popular with snorkelers and divers, ★ **Grand Cenote** (2 miles inland from the main intersection in Tulum on the road to Cobá) features amazing underwater stalactites, stalagmites, and other limestone formations. You can swim a ring around the middle island sundeck area. It makes for a great stop-off after a trip to the beach or a long drive back to Playa from Cobá.

A group of four *cenotes* and caverns, the **Taj Mahal** (Highway 307, 3½ miles south of Puerto Aventuras, just past Xpu-Ha) is known for a cavern called the Beam of Light Room. This spot is less crowded than many of the others, making it a good place to linger over a picnic lunch. The connected **Sugarbowl** *cenote* has a large cavern open to the daylight, which creates mind-numbing rays of light under the water.

Water Sports & Activities

With **Dolphin Discovery** (www.dolphindiscovery.com), you can interact with live dolphins at one of five locations (Villa Pirata, Isla Mujeres; Avenue Juárez, downtown Cozumel; Puerto Aventuras, on the marina; El Dorado Marina, Maroma; and Hotel Sirenis, Akumal). Several 45-minute packages are available, from viewing sessions where participants pet the creatures and observe tricks to swimming sessions where guests are pulled through the water by a dolphin. For all programs, the minimum age is 8. Children ages 8 to 11 must be accompanied by a paying adult. No pregnant women or people with physical or mental limitations are permitted.

★ **Ikarus Kiteboarding** (Quinta at 20th Street, Playa del Carmen; www.kiteboardmexico.com), which is PASA and IKO certified, offers lessons, equipment rentals, and sales of windsurfers, skateboards, and kiteboards. It also has bathing suits, backpacks, T-shirts, and other beach games.

A great trip for snorkelers of all levels who want to wet their fins in the Caribbean, three-hour ★ **Snorkeling Tours** (Tank-Ha Dive Center, Quinta between Eighth and 10th Streets, Playa del Carmen, www.tankha.com) depart on a 25-foot boat with a sun shade. Advance reservations are highly recommended and can be made by phone or by stopping by the Tank-Ha shop.

With **Atlantis Submarines** (Carretera a Chankanaab, km 4, Cozumel, www.atlantissubmarines.travel) guests see the amazing reefs of Cozumel, including Santa Rosa and Palancar, from the comfort of a chair. The air-conditioned sub goes 100 feet deep and passes many of the same sites that scuba divers visit.

Sub See Explorer (Boulevard Kukulcán, km 15.2, Cancún, www.aquaworld.com.mx) also offers an underwater ride through the reefs and undersea channels. Off the coast of Cancún, you can see living coral reefs, sea sponges, sea fans, angel fish, parrot fish, grouper, rays, sea turtles, moray eels, and other marine life.

Located off the west coast of Isla Mujeres, ★ **MUSA**, or **Museo Subacuático de Arte** (Isla Mujeres, www.musacancun.com), is an artistic snorkeling site ranging from about 10 to 20 feet deep. Featuring sculptures of people and common objects by artist Jason deCaires Taylor (www.underwatersculpture.com), it was started in 2009 to draw visitors away from the fragile coral reefs while providing infrastructure for new coral growth. Already stunning, plans call for it to become the world's largest underwater sculpture gardens. As of press time, deCaires

Yalku Lagoon is a great spot for beginner snorkelers. Gary Walten/locogringo.com

Taylor had submerged four exhibits, including "The Silent Evolution," featuring more than 500 life-size sculptures of human figures. Visits to the site are offered by local tour operators.

One of the top snorkeling spots in the area, ★ **Yalku Lagoon** (north end of Akumal Bay) has a mix of fresh and salt water, which provides a habitat for a wide variety of fish, including triggerfish, wrasse, parrot fish, needlefish, and sometimes sea turtles. The shoreline has several metal sculptures imported from Mexico City, plus a few picnic tables and stairways to the water. The bottom and sides are more rocky than sandy, so walking can be treacherous, but a pair of water shoes and a careful eye make it worth the effort. Float along in the cool water, watch the colorful fish, and listen to the tropical birds singing from the trees.

Horseback Riding

Once part of one of the largest and most prosperous commercial ranches along the Yucatán coast, **Rancho Punta Venado** (along Highway 307 in Paamul, 10 minutes south of Playa del Carmen, www.puntavenado.com) is now open to visitors. Occupied by Mayan natives 1,500 years ago, the ranch still exhibits evidence of their existence through stone fences, small dwellings, and other minor structures. In the 1950s, cattle baron Miguel Joaquin Ibarra purchased nearly 10,000 acres of land at this site and ran more than 600 head of cattle, in addition to farming coconuts, watermelons, limes, and cucumbers. In the 1970s blight struck the coconut crop, and Ibarra sold all but 2,000 acres. In 1988 Hurricane Gilbert hit, thinning the herd down to only 40 head. Some ten years later the ranch opened as a tourist destination, turning the working cowboys into riding instructors and expedition guides. Better care was taken during Hurricane Emily in 2005, and the only losses were to the structure and were quickly repaired.

The ranch has 30 *cenotes*, caves, pristine beaches, and unexplored jungle, and offers horseback riding, snorkeling, and ATV-adventure excursions through the property. With any paid expedition, guests can stay at the ranch all day and enjoy the other facilities, including the beach club, hiking trails, and snack bar.

Tucked away by Maroma Beach, 20 minutes north of Playa del Carmen, **Rancho Baaxal** (along Highway 307, km 51, by Maroma Beach, www.ranchobaaxal.com) is a small ranch with just 12 horses. Prioritizing the health and well-being of its horses above all else, the ranch offers a very personalized tour, which takes riders into the jungle and along the beach that the Travel Channel rated as one of the world's "top ten most beautiful beaches" four years in a row. Moonlight rides are also available.

Bike Riding

Bike rental is available in all urban areas, and you can likely find a bike rental option near the heart of most towns in the area. Many all-inclusive resorts also provide complimentary bikes for guest use, so double check with your hotel before you rent from a third party.

In Playa, **Playa Rida** (Eighth Street at 10th Avenue, www.playarida.com) offers some attractive cycling options, and **Hola Bike Rental** (www.holabike.com) offers additional rental options.

Parasailing, Skydiving & Plane Tours

Certified by the U.S. Parachute Association, **Sky Dive Playa** (Plaza Marina, Playa del Carmen, www.skydive.com.mx) offers tandem and solo jumps. Its rectangular parachutes have ram-air canopies, allowing for a very stable and controlled descent. Dives include instruction and have about 45 seconds of freefall, plus a six- to seven-minute parachute descent. Landings are on Playa's main beach.

At **Yucatan Explorer** (www.yucatanexplorer.com.mx), small lightweight airplanes take off from an open field near Xcaret for a 25-minute trip, heading north along the coast to Playa del Carmen, circling out over the water, and then back to the landing strip.

Offering sightseeing tours, private transportation, and air taxi service, **Aerosaab** (www.aerosaab.com) services Playa del Carmen, Cozumel, Holbox, and Chichén Itzá.

Well-respected **Riviera Maya Parasail Adventures** (Oasis Hotel, Puerto Aventuras, www.rivieramayaparasail.com) offers tandem and solo rides around Puerto Aventuras' bay and beachfront.

Organized Tours

Just a handful of group tour and travel-providers service the Riviera Maya, and they own the vehicles, employ the guides, set the itineraries, negotiate rates, and provide the actual tours. Sometimes they sell directly to the public, but primarily they rely on tour resellers to market their tours and book the majority of reservations. Nearly every hotel has a tour desk, and there are tour offices on nearly every block of Quinta in Playa del Carmen. Some restaurants have tour kiosks at their entrances, and tour representatives even walk the beaches carrying a notebook describing the trips they can sell. Authorized agencies and individuals have licenses and ID cards, and it's recommended that you verify tour representatives' credentials before giving them any money. Most sellers have the same catalog of 20 or so tours, though there can be some variation in the selection. Prices are generally fixed and do not vary much from one operator to another.

Most tours require advance reservations so that transportation and meals can be planned accordingly. If you're interested in a spur-of-the-moment trip, your choices may be limited, but there's usually something available. When a tour is reserved, a deposit or even full payment is normally required, and you'll receive a voucher that proves you have paid and tells you when and where to go for the trip. Most major tours include hotel pickup and drop-off, while others begin at a predetermined location. The balance of the fee is paid at the start of the tour if you have only put down a deposit.

Many tours and adventures can be purchased well in advance, through your local travel agent, through the web site where you booked your flight, or directly with the tour operator. This can be a good way to guarantee availability and set your itinerary before your trip even begins, but prices are generally the same whether you book in advance or not.

TOUR OPERATORS

Alltournative Expeditions (various locations along Quinta, Playa del Carmen, www.alltournative.com) specializes in natural and cultural tours, eco-adventure, and alternative adrenaline-rush activities, and trips can be custom-designed for large groups. Many tours stop at the company's crafts shop, where profits are shared with the indigenous communities who offer their land to be used for the adventure trip. Tours are adventurous, educational, and a great way to meet other travelers. Most of the activities require participants to be in relatively good physical shape. Many of tour locations are on private land and cannot be visited any other way.

★ **CancunVista Tours** (Avenue Cobá, 31, Cancún, www.cancunvista.com) offers some great combination tours for travelers who want to see and do a bit of everything during their stay. It also represents many of the standard water sports, adventure, and Mayan ruins tours offered by other agencies.

EcoColors (www.ecotravelmexico.com) appeals to environmentally conscious travelers who want to experience the Riviera Maya but don't want to alter it. Adventures include boat trips through Sian Ka'an, bird-watching, biking, kayaking, *cenote* swimming, and jaguar discovery trips. The company also offers guided trips to Chichén Itzá, Cobá, and the lesser-known ruins of Muyil.

A Mayan Legend

Following the great flood, the world was dark and full of chaos. Nothing moved and nothing existed. The sea and the sky were empty. On the second day, the gods became tired of dancing over cold waters, so they created a thin layer of solid land where they could rest while they finished their work. "Let there be land," they said, and a beautiful layer of earth rose from the ocean. On the third day, the gods called upon Chaac, the god of rain, who poured rich water into the cracks of the land, giving life to the plants, flowers, and trees.

As the rain continued on the fourth day, water filled all the cracks and basins, producing amazing lagoons and *cenotes*. On the fifth day, Kukulcán, the god of wind, flapped his wings, blowing warm breezes over the land, giving all living things a gentle dance. On the sixth day, Kukulcán turned his winds toward the sea, creating waves and forming Ixchel, the goddess of the moon and womanhood. Ixchel rose to heaven and gave birth to Itzámna, the lord of the skies, who created the day and the night and then painted the night with thousands of stars. "Let the trees have their own guardians," the gods ordered on the eighth day, and birds were created in astonishing varieties, including Mo, the scarlet macaw, who became the guardian angel of the skies. On the ninth day, Hunab-Ku buried a white knife in the land, and from it flowed all sorts of animals, including reptiles, jaguars, monkeys, and Huh, the iguana and guardian of the land.

Like a falling star, Ixchel descended from the night sky on the tenth day. She dove naked into a *cenote*, and the waters came alive with millions of fish, of all colors and sizes. The gods then picked the parrotfish, or Kay-Op, as the guardian of the waters. The gods rested on the eleventh day, but they were feeling cold, so they asked the sun god to help them. He came from the skies with his magic fire and heated the waters of the sea, the lagoons, and the *cenotes*, thus creating a warm and gentle climate.

On the twelfth day the gods created humans, the most perfect of living creatures. With their intelligence, speech, sight, smell, taste, hearing, and touch, they were the ones gifted with the right to enjoy all the magic the gods had made for them. The gods danced and sang, full of joy for what they had created, and then they returned to the heavens. Pleased with what they saw and the world they had created, they decided to name it Xel-Ha, or "the place where the water is born."

Budget tour company **SeaMonkey Business Tours** (www.seamonkeybusiness.com) offers many of the same tours as other agencies, but often at a discounted rate. The company's website has destination information, travel resources, and photos and descriptions of dozens of tours and activities.

Yucatan Explorer (south of Playacar, www.yucatanexplorer.com.mx) offers expeditions by land, sea, and air that tend to be a bit more extreme than those of other operators—in a good way. The ATV tours take about two hours and take participants deep into the Mayan jungle to swim and snorkel in a hidden *cenote*. They offer 12-man powerboat tours along the Riviera Maya coastline to secret snorkeling spots and ultralight plane tours that afford amazing views of the beachfront and jungle.

Boasting a catalog of "tours for people who don't take tours," **YucaTreks Far Out Adventures** (www.yucatreks.com) features intensive excursions to some of the area's top historical Mayan sites, *cenote*, and zipline experiences, and some lesser-known alternatives that most people have never even heard of.

POPULAR TOURS & EXPERIENCES

Unless otherwise specified, these tours can be reserved through the above tour operators or through local agencies. Availability, times, and prices can vary.

An active adventure experience, **ATV Tours** (Highway 307, between Playacar and Xcaret, Playa del Carmen, www.atvexplorer.com) offer a two-hour ATV ride through the jungle, stopping at a freshwater lagoon, caves, Mayan ruins, and other attractions.

Though there's no pillaging and plundering on the ★ **Captain Hook Pirate Dinner Cruise**, (Cancún, www.pirateshipcancun.com) there is plenty of eating, drinking, and laughing on this swashbuckling adventure. Board a 93-foot Spanish galleon replica and sail the waters of Cancún while enjoying a pirate-themed show and dinner.

Catamaran Sailing Adventures (Puerto Aventuras, www.fatcatsail.com) offers you the chance to sail through the Caribbean aboard a 41-foot catamaran: the Fat Cat. Launching at 9 AM, the first stop is the hidden beach of Xaac, where you can go snorkeling, climb the Mayan ruins, play on the beach, and grab a bite to eat before undertaking some more open-wataer sailing.

Catamaran cruising in Puerto Aventuras Philip Gamon

20 Kid-Friendly Spots for Families

1. 100% Natural restaurant (Cancún & Playa del Carmen)
2. Akumal Beach Resort (Akumal)
3. Barcelo Maya Resort Complex (Xpu-Ha)
4. Hard Rock Hotel (Cancún)
5. Crococun Crocodile Farm & Zoo (Puerto Morelos)
6. Dolphin Discovery swim park (Puerto Aventuras, Cozumel, Akumal, Maroma & Isla Mujeres)
7. Gran Bahia Principe resort (Akumal)
8. Grand Palladium Kantenah Resort & Spa (Kantenah)
9. Gran Porto Real resort (Playa del Carmen)
10. Iberostar Resorts (Playa Paraíso and Playacar)
11. La Cueva del Chango restaurant (Playa del Carmen)
12. Las Palapas hotel (Playa del Carmen)
13. Mayan Palace Riviera Maya (Playa Paraíso)
14. Mini Golf El Palomar (Xcaret)
15. Pericos restaurant (downtown Cancún)
16. Playa San Francisco beach (Cozumel)
17. Señor Frog's restaurant (Before 10 PM; Cancún, Cozumel, and Playa del Carmen)
18. Turtle Bay Café (Akumal)
19. Xaman-Ha Aviary (Playa del Carmen and Playacar)
20. Xcaret park (Xcaret)

A family that plays together stays together. Riviera Maya Destination Marketing Office

Chichén Itzá Deluxe (departs from Playa del Carmen and hotels along the Riviera Maya) is a good bet for a first-class visit to the legendary ruins. The trip includes a pass through the colonial city of Vallodolid, the entrance to Ik-Kil nature park, the entrance to the Chichén Itzá ruins, and a traditional folkloric show.

Playa del Carmen is a great spot for a sunset cruise. Brian E. Miller Photography/www.lomimonk.com

Mixing Mayan history and modern adventure, the **Cobá & Chimuch** trip includes a two-hour visit to the Cobá ruins, an authentic Mayan lunch buffet, and a trip to two different eco-parks for kayaking, rappelling, and zip-lining.

Unique, educational, and entertaining, ★ **Dos Palmas Mayan Ceremony Night** (www.dospalmas.info) includes Mayan cultural lessons, a Mayan jungle ritual with bonfire and torches, a *temazcal* steam bath ceremony, and *cenote* swimming. This activity must be reserved for a group of ten or more.

This traditional Mayan ceremony is performed at special events. Mike Stone

You don't have to spend the night in a sweaty, un-air-conditioned lodge to experience the incredible fly-fishing or light-tackle fishing in Ascension Bay. This all-day trip starts with a pickup from your hotel at 5 AM for the adventurous drive through the Sian Ka'an biosphere. Spend the day fishing for bonefish, permit, tarpon, snook, barracuda, and other game fish, plus have lunch on the boat. You'll be back at your hotel by 8 PM.

Marina Maroma Paradise (www.maromaparadise.com) offers a variety of exciting tours for adventure seekers, including combinations of ATV/speedboat trips, snorkeling at Paradise Reef, deep-sea fishing, and horseback riding.

Mayan Canopy Expedition, an all-day trip combining water fun and jungle adventure, includes a bike ride through a Mayan farm, zip-lining, a visit to the Xtabay *cenote*, snorkeling in Chikin-Ha *cenote*, and a visit to Aluxes *cenote* for a purification ritual.

An eco-friendly trip deep into the jungle offered by Alltournative Expeditions, the ★ **Pac-Chen Tour** (www.alltournative.com) visits Cobá, where you will have a guided tour of one of the most dramatic Mayan ruins, and the traditional village of Pac Chen, a lagoon-side town of 100 residents living much as their ancestors did centuries ago.

The ★ **Rio Lagarto and Ek Balam Tour** lasts a full day, taking travelers to the traditional town of Tizimin and to the Ek Balam ruins in the northern part of Yucatán State. The highlight is the visit to Rio Lagarto, a remote river where hundreds of flamingos make their home.

If you want to see a couple of Mayan sites but don't have much time, **Tulum & Cobá** is a good option, taking you to two of the best-known sites of the Mayan world.

The combo trip of ★ **Tulum and Xel-Ha** offers something for travelers who want to see the ruins but also want to do something active. First stop is Tulum, where visitors will have a chance to see the cliffside ruins and the ocean below. Next is Xel-Ha water park, where you can play in the water, snorkel, or lie on the beach.

Holbox Adventures coordinates the seasonal ★ **Whale Shark Tour** (www.holboxadventure.com) for travelers staying throughout the region. The tour offers the chance to swim and snorkel with the docile 50-foot-long whale sharks at Isla Holbox, north of Cancún. Tours include transportation to a dock north of Cancún and then the boat ride to Holbox. Not available year-round, this tour must be scheduled in advance, based on availability and presence of the sharks.

At the new evening dinner and entertainment option **Xoximilco** (Cancún) visitors board colorfully decorated canal boats known as trajineras for a three-hour dinner cruise through a dedicated system of canals. Along the journey, boats will stop at docks where musicians will play mariachi, grupo jarocho, marimba, bolero, and other traditional and regional Mexican music. The meal is all-inclusive and includes an open bar of tequila, beer, soft drinks, and aquas frescas.

Other Activities

★ **Bullfights at the Plaza de Toros** (Bonampak Avenue, downtown Cancún) are held every Wednesday at 3:30 PM and sometimes on Sunday. Depending on the day, there will either be a tourist-oriented show with folkloric dancing, Mexican rodeo, and a single bullfight, or a full bullfighting competition with two matadors and six bulls.

6

Mayan Ruins

IF YOU COULD travel back in time and see the Riviera Maya as it was centuries ago, you'd see a thriving civilization with a complex social, political, and religious community. From the Cancún hotel zone to the Playa del Carmen shoreline to the beaches and jungles of the Riviera Maya, there were hundreds of structures, religious temples, dwellings, stone roads, and even recreational facilities. When the Mayans abandoned their cities, the jungle reclaimed their buildings and many deteriorated. Some sites retained their spiritual significance and were occasionally used as ceremonial sites by the local population until not long ago.

Archaeologists began uncovering these sites in the early 1900s, and little by little, more sites were rediscovered, studied, and, in some cases, restored to their original splendor. Many have been declared federal property by the Mexican archaeological institution and turned into public parks where locals and tourists can visit, learning about Mayan culture and history and experiencing firsthand the places where the ancient Mayans lived, worked, prayed, and played. Many other sites remain buried, shrouded by jungle, sometimes just out of view. Some are too remote to be easily discovered, but new sites continue to be uncovered.

If you're investing the time to visit these sites, it's also worth reading up on the Mayans. Many tour guides seem to want to stimulate the crowd with tales of human sacrifice (which did indeed occur) at the expense of broader aspects of Mayan culture.

If you can't make time to visit any of the area's major sites, you can always peek through the fence on the east side of Quinta Avenida at 14th Street in Playa del Carmen to see an authentic, though quite unassuming, bit of Mayan history. Surrounded by a chain-link fence and official-looking signs declaring it a federal archaeological site is a small temple built at the base of a tree. It's not labeled, but it's rumored to be a small ceremonial site or even an ancient dwelling.

Make sure you bring some water and a hat when you visit any of the other ruins. The humidity and the sun will get to you faster than you think.

LEFT: Ek Balam is much less frequented than other sites. Dr. John Anderson

CHICHÉN ITZÁ

Mexico's best-known Mayan ruin site, Chichén Itzá, is 128 miles southwest of Cancún, a two-and-a-half- to three-hour drive from either Cancún or Tulum. Visitors can take the toll road, Highway 180D (cost is about $40 each way), out of Cancún or take the road from Tulum and head inland past Cobá and through Valladolid. The drive through the jungle is interesting, with many picturesque places at which to stop along the way. The beautiful town square of the colonial city of Valladolid is worth a few minutes' diversion.

Chichén Itzá is the jewel of the Mayan sites, easily reachable from the Caribbean coast, and its grandeur makes it the obvious choice if you have time to visit only one of the ancient cities. The site is amazing, and for first-time visitors can be a bit overwhelming. The structures are awe inspiring, and the restoration work makes it easy to picture what the city must have been like at the height of its splendor.

The area covers more than 6 square miles and is divided into two very distinct parts, and you can see classic Mayan as well as later Toltec-influenced

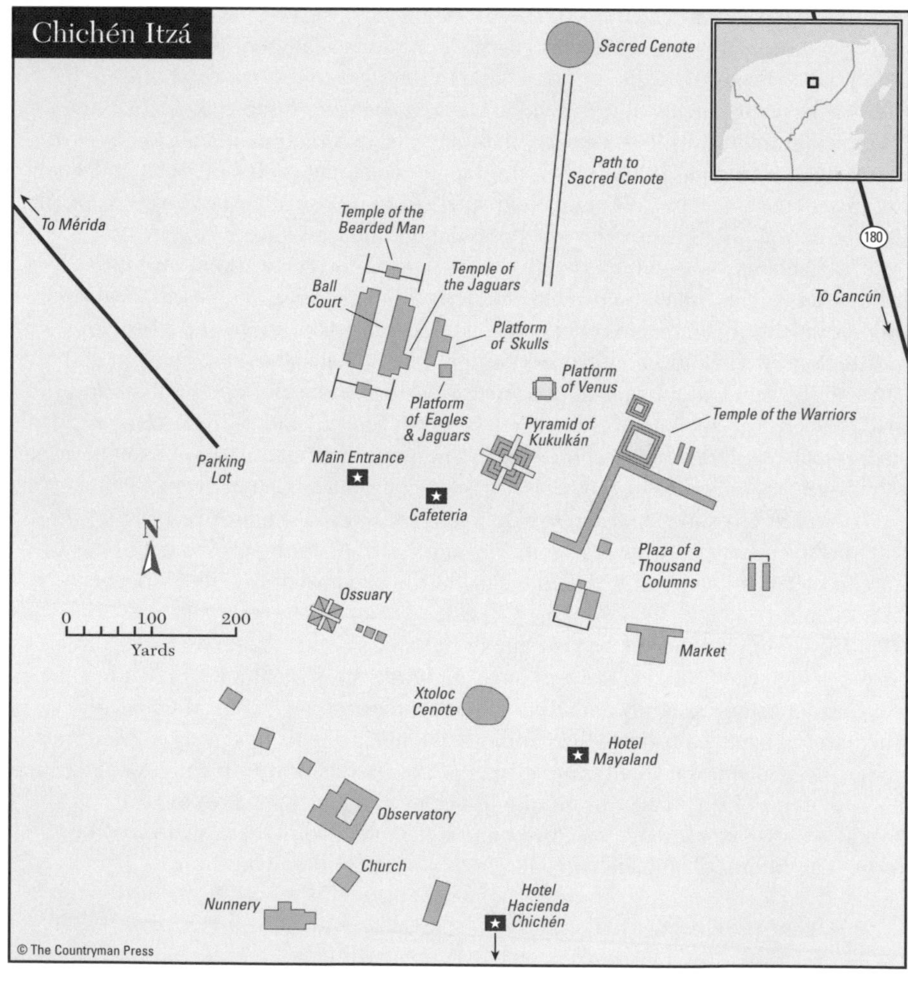

The awesome size of Chichén Itzá has made the site famous around the world. Dr. John Anderson

structures. Be sure to check out a map and see both—many tours cover only the later structures like the Pyramid of Kukulcán and the *pok-ta-pok* ball court that are typically seen on postcards. These structures are the largest here, particularly the ball court (270 feet long and one of 22 on the entire site), which is the largest in Mesoamerica. However, the large size of the newer city means you could easily miss the old city if you were unaware of it. These older structures also include examples of the softer *pu'uc* architecture (the church and its annex in particular) and display beautiful carvings not seen on later structures—they are not to be missed. A good plan is to head over to the older area and work your way back to where you started.

The Pyramid of Kukulcán and the Nunnery (where an explosion was used in the 19th century to access one side of the structure) are the two places where you can really see that the Mayans built these structures in successive additions in their religious time cycle. The temple interior is interesting as long as you're not claustrophobic, but don't spend your time standing in line for it if you haven't seen the rest of the site. The exterior features are more impressive.

Not mentioned on many tours, a museum on the grounds displays some of the small artifacts that weren't taken to other museums around the world. If you're visiting on your own, it's worth seeing, but if you're on an organized tour, your limited time is likely better spent outdoors.

There are night shows here with light and sound, but these are impractical for the traveler from the coast given the long drive back after dark.

The entrance fee is $10 per person, and tours (including transportation, snacks, and drinks) can be arranged through any local travel agency or tour desk.

TULUM

Given its proximity to the hotels of the Riviera Maya, Tulum (2 miles east of Highway 307, 40 miles south of Playa del Carmen) is one of the most frequently visited Mayan sites.

Tulum is unlike any of the other major Mayan ruins in Mexico in that it is right on the coast. Originally called Zama, meaning "sunrise" in Mayan, it faces due east. The beauty of the Caribbean Sea enhances the structures, and many people say this is what makes Tulum so appealing. The site, known as the Walled City, rose to prominence during the post-Classic period (AD 1000–1500), and it is the polar opposite of Chichén Itzá in terms of what makes it beautiful.

While Chichén Itzá has a sense of isolation about it, given its distance and the thick jungle surrounding it, Tulum has a sense of openness and airiness brought on by the ocean itself, and the ocean views are amazing. At the same time, being

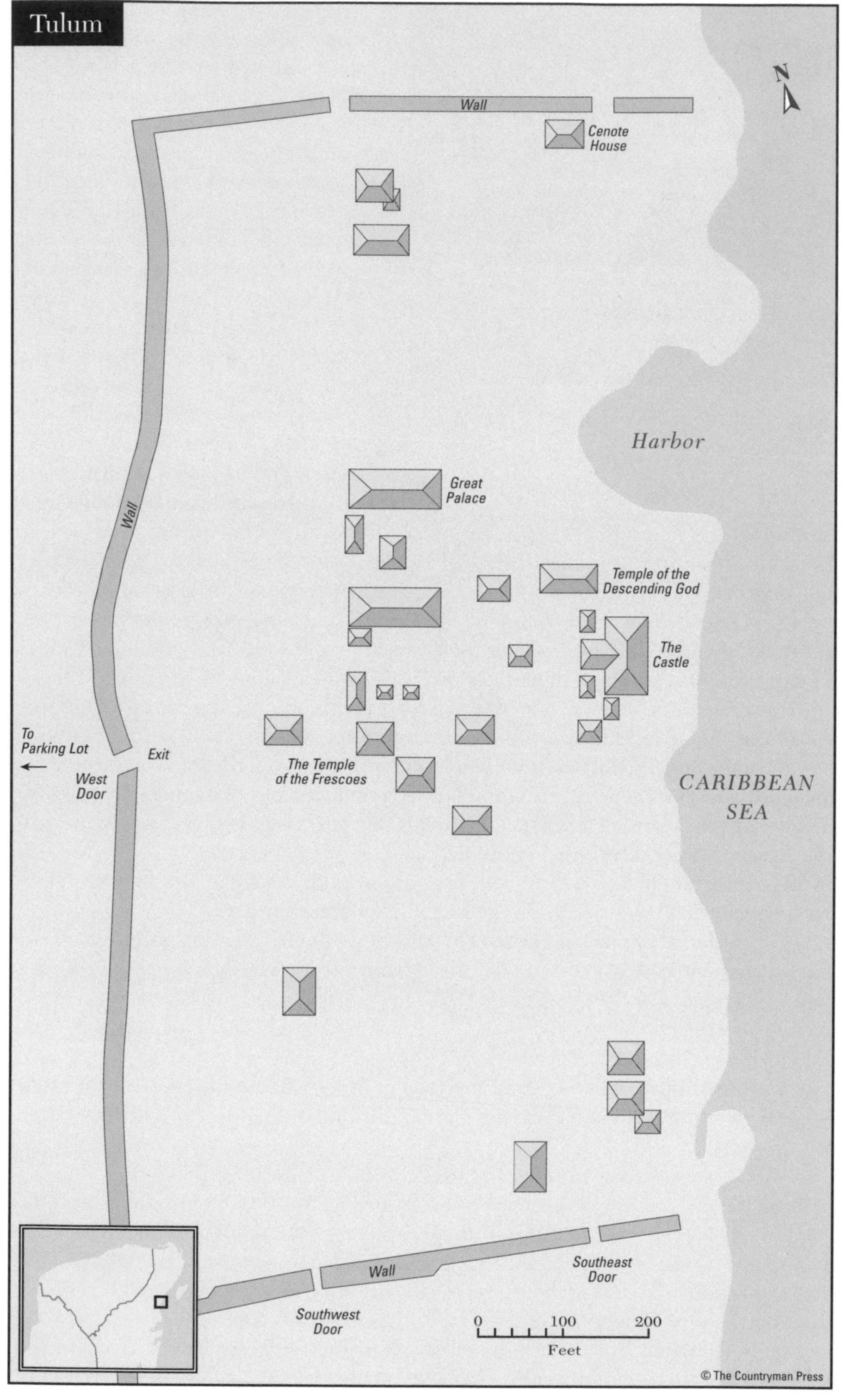
Tulum
N
Wall
Cenote House
Harbor
Great Palace
Wall
Temple of the Descending God
The Castle
To Parking Lot
Exit
West Door
The Temple of the Frescoes
CARIBBEAN SEA
Wall
Southeast Door
Southwest Door
0
100
200
Feet
© The Countryman Press

Off the Beaten Path

The ancient Mayan city of Ek Balam is one of the Yucatan's most extraordinary sites, but amazingly, it's also one of the least visited. Excavation began in 1987 and has uncovered a long stretch of perfectly preserved sculpturework on part of the main temple, which shows how elaborate the exterior of these ruins once was. The enormous toothed mouth of the Witz Monster, symbolizing the entry to the underworld, is surrounded by elaborate Mayan figures. Ek Balam makes a great side trip during a visit to Chichén Itzá.

next to the ocean leads to a great deal of erosion, and between this and the many hurricanes that hit the Caribbean, most of the detail of Tulum's structures has been lost. Some restoration work has been done, but the structures do not at all bear the crisp lines of those at Chichén Itzá. Instead, they are well-rounded, bleached limestone, and the few remaining detailed carvings are protected by woven structures to keep the rain off. As such, you won't get an accurate picture of the Mayans if it's the only ruin you see.

Since it is so close to the population centers, there are many more tourists for the size of the area than you would see elsewhere (this is also in part because it's a small area and is more difficult to find a place to retreat from large groups). The convenient access also means that many of the tourists are not particularly interested in the Mayans and come because it's close and "worth seeing." This can make for a somewhat less sacred atmosphere than one finds at the other sites.

But as a relatively small site, there is no problem finding time to see all the major elements of the Tulum ruins. This makes it a good first stop if you're visiting several ruins, and a choice to consider if you are traveling with small children or anyone with limited mobility. If you have your own vehicle, you can easily start off at Tulum early and go to Cobá the same day. In fact, most commercial tours combine visits with other activities in the area.

Free parking is available at Tulum's back gate. To get there, head south of the main highway entrance to the ruins and turn east at the Tulum crossroads, by the San Francisco de Asis grocery store. After 2 miles, the road will dead-end at the Tulum beach road. Turn left and the ruins are straight ahead, 2 miles down the road, past a wonderful public beach at Playa Maya. This gate is used for bicycle and walking access by travelers staying at hotels along Tulum beach. Park along the side of the road and walk the half-mile to the entrance booth.

Entrance is $5, and bilingual guide service is available.

COBÁ

In its heyday, Cobá city had 44 miles of urban sprawl, making it one of the largest cities in the Mayan civilization. It is located an hour inland from Tulum, on the road that starts at Tulum pueblo and passes several popular *cenotes*, such as Grand Cenote and the Carwash (see chapter 8), before yielding to the jungle.

The city of Cobá flourished during the Classic period (300–1000 AD) and was once home to more than fifty thousand inhabitants. It's the least excavated of the region's major ruins. Thick jungle encroaches onto the site and near the structures themselves, creating an atmosphere of discovery. (Chichén Itzá is also surrounded by jungle, but the area around the structures themselves has been largely cleared.) A number of the ruins at Cobá are partially reconstructed, but not in the finished way that one sees at Chichén Itzá, so unlike at other sites the ruins look like ancient, unrestored buildings. Because of this, things appear much as they would have looked when European explorers first arrived.

The city of Cobá was very large, and the excavated ruins are in groups spread across the jungle. Bicycles come included with many commercial tours (or can be rented for $2.50; tricycle taxis for two go for $7.50) and are advisable. If you're on an organized tour you'll have limited time here, and more of it can be spent exploring the ruins if you can move between the groups more quickly. However, if you have the time, the jungle walk is pleasant and relaxing.

The highlight of Cobá is Nohoc Mul, the largest pyramid in southern Mexico (138 feet tall), and it's considerably larger than the Pyramid of Kukulcán at Chichén Itzá. The fact it's surrounded by jungle rather than open space further magnifies the size difference. Like the Pyramid of Kukulcán, this structure can be climbed, but take great care: While the stone steps are stable, they are very irregular compared to the climb at Chichén Itzá. The view from the temple atop Nohoc Mul is beautiful, and you can see the tops of many other structures, the lake (rare in the Yucatán) on which Cobá sits, and also a vast canopy of surrounding jungle. The ball court here, one of the smallest in the Mayan world, is also an interesting counter to Chichén Itzá's massive court.

There are several other significant structures, including Xaibe (the Crossroads Pyramid), a rounded, tiered structure very different from any other structures on this side of the Yucatán and more reminiscent of Uxmal. There are also many stelae (standing stone markers) here noting important events in the Mayan history, and many are still detailed enough to see the forms carved onto them.

Tours to Cobá are still less common than to the other ruins, and so the area can be less crowded than the others. If you are looking for a place with fewer tourists, this is likely your best choice. A number of commercial tours combine a visit to Cobá with a tour of a local Mayan village, intending to both show the ancient architecture and expose the visitor to the Mayans in their modern lifestyle.

Entrance is $5, and guide service is available. Open 9–5 daily.

CHUNYAXCHE/MUYIL

Fifteen miles south of Tulum on Highway 307 and 7 miles from the coastline, the ruins of Chunyaxche/Muyil are located within the Sian Ka'an biosphere and are significantly less visited than the better-known temples of the Caribbean coast. Some researchers believe, however, that the site will some day rival Tulum in its scale and importance to the historical record. Inhabited from 300 BC until the Spanish conquest, the site has some 75 individual structures believed to be still hidden beneath the jungle vegetation. The University of the Yucatán is leading the excavation, though scarce funds have significantly delayed the project. Archaeological evidence indicates the site was built to honor Ix-Chel, the Mayan goddess of fertility.

Built on La Laguna freshwater lake, the site has narrow canals that lead to the ocean and once served as passageways for seafaring adventurers and traders.

Entrance fee is $5, and guide service is available.

Beware the Bewitching Call of X'tabai

According to Mayan legend, X'tabai (Ish-TAH-buy) was a beautiful woman and ensnarer of men known to live in the Yucatán jungle. Much like Greece's mythological sirens, she reportedly drew unsuspecting males to her with her beauty. After which, they were never seen again.

But rather than entrancing men through song, she is said to have possessed them as soon as they first spied her great physical beauty and flowing black hair.

Modern accounts contradict themselves as to whether she was a singular spirit or a race of females, but most stories claim X'tabai is connected to the beautiful ceiba tree found throughout tropical Latin America.

Known for its winding, tall, and wall-like roots, the ceiba tree has often been used in Mayan ceremonial art. From the roots, which depict the underworld, the tree connects it to the terrestrial world via its trunk and ultimately reaches up in every direction to the heavens through its branches.

Stories suggest that X'tabai removed men from the terrestrial world, though some speculate that she provided passage to the heavens, rather than to the underworld.

Today in the Riviera Maya, warnings of X'tabai still persist, though often with a knowing wink. Given that some reports question whether it was her deep eyes, her lustrous hair, or simply her willingness to expose her breasts that stunned the men, it seems like she might easily conceal herself in plain sight on the beaches of Playa del Carmen.

SAN GERVASIO

The center of Cozumel's Mayan World, San Gervasio was inhabited from 200 AD until the arrival of the Spaniards. It was of great spiritual importance and many Mayan women traveled to the island to make offerings and pay homage to the fertility goddess Ix-Chel.

Although there are no grand pyramids, the site features about 40 structures, including smaller temples, pyramids, and dwellings. Structures are congregated around a central plaza, much like a traditional Roman forum. Experts theorize that the structures were once larger due to additions and extensions made from wood and thatched leaves. Tiny red handprints still visible on an interior wall of one home named Manitas have prompted jokes that it was probably a village day care for visiting mothers.

Set in relative isolation, amid the Cozumel rainforest, the ruins remain overgrown today and are home to many tropical birds and large iguanas. Visitors can easily walk around the 2-square mile site.

The entrance is located on Cross-Island Road at km 7.5.

Entrance is $5.50 (free for children under eight) and guide service is available. Open 7 AM–4 PM daily.

7

Diving & Snorkeling

THE RIVIERA MAYA is home to some of the most unequaled dive sites in the world. It's one of the few places where you can swim with a green moray eel on a 100-foot wall dive in the morning, go free diving and snorkeling with dolphins after lunch, explore virgin caverns on a freshwater cave dive in the afternoon, and then pet sleeping sharks on a shallow-water dive that same night.

The Great Mayan Reef is the second longest living barrier reef in the world, and only Australia's Great Barrier Reef is larger. It starts in Cancún and extends just offshore along the eastern tip of the Yucatán Peninsula and all the way down to Honduras. From many towns the reef is only a short swim from the beach, making for excellent snorkeling without the need for a boat or special equipment. You can usually see the water breaking over the reef, which helps to pinpoint its location. The reef itself is razor sharp and extremely delicate, so touching it, bumping it with your equipment, or even kicking sand onto it can cause serious damage from which it takes years to recover. It is home to hundreds of species of live corals, fish, anemones, eels, rays, and other life forms, small and large.

The water itself is gin-clear, with horizontal visibility up to 150 feet in some areas. The prevailing current is north to south, though it varies widely depending on the weather and local geographic conditions. Water temperature ranges from a low of 75 in the

Small boats called *pangas* can be chartered for $200 for four hours.

LEFT: A unique snorkeling opportunity at Playa Mia in Cozumel Playa Mia Cozumel

winter months up to the mid-80s in the height of the summer. Many divers choose to dive without a wet suit, which lessens the amount of weight they are required to carry, making for a less-encumbered dive and more bottom time. Other divers opt for a spring suit, shortie, or Farmer John–style wet suit, which provides a good layer of warmth while still allowing for freedom of movement.

There are a variety of open-water dives available. Divers in Cozumel and Akumal frequently go on shore dives, either in small independent groups or with a dive master. In these locations the reef comes within 100 yards of the shore, enabling divers to reach excellent dive spots with a short underwater or surface swim. Cozumel is also known for its wall dives and drift dives, where the dive boat will stop at one end of a reef and let the divers out, follow their bubbles as they drift along with the current, and then be waiting to pick them up when they surface at the end of the dive. This type of diving can be very relaxing for the divers, who hardly need to swim as they're swiftly drawn along with the current, which travels up to 5 mph.

On other dives, where there isn't as much current, such as off the coast of Puerto Aventuras, Isla Mujeres, or Playa del Carmen, the boat will anchor, the dive master will lead the group on a dive, and then all divers will return to the entry point. Diving this way requires all divers to stay in sight of the others, ensuring that nobody gets lost underwater. If you don't have a dive buddy, you'll be assigned one on the boat before the dive begins.

Gear up at one of the scuba shops around town and plan an outing.

Open-water Dives

Experienced divers can go on self-guided dives right from the shore at many hotels, particularly in Cozumel and Akumal. You can bring your own gear or rent it at the hotel dive shop. Most shops have tanks available for around $10, allowing you to custom-create the dive profile that you want and then go for it. On these dives, the maximum depth is usually around 50 feet, but divers can see just as much variety and just as much beautiful underwater scenery as on boat dives.

Organized boat trips are another way to go. These trips are normally booked at least one day in advance so that the boat captain can prepare all gear and ensure there will be enough assistants on the boat to handle the group. These trips offer either one or two dives and can be in the morning, afternoon, or even night. Most boat rides will be 30 minutes to an hour long, giving you plenty of time to prepare your gear, document the trip in your log book, socialize with other divers, and even do some sight-seeing along the way. The boats range from 14-foot, open-hull *pangas* carrying just a couple of divers, all the way up to 40-foot yachts that can accommodate more than a dozen divers and have air-conditioning, a galley, a shower, and other luxuries. Divers can choose to go on a private trip or can join a group trip with other divers. Nondivers can accompany divers on the boat trip for a nominal fee, though this must be arranged in advance so the captain can plan for the extra space and refreshments.

There are several types of open-water dives common in the area. One of the most common is a reef dive, where divers swim or drift along the top of the reef. Off many beaches there is a steep wall within a few miles of shore, where the depth drops from around 80–100 feet to more than 1,000 feet, almost straight down, and on these dives either the divers swim along right at the edge of the drop-off, with the reef below them and the vast depths of the blue ocean just beyond, or they swim along the wall itself, with the reef to the side and the depths straight below. When wall diving this way, it is important for divers to watch their depth gauges closely since it's deceptively easy to go deeper and deeper without even noticing it. For recreational scuba diving the maximum depth is usually considered to be 120 feet. Plus, the deeper you go, the shorter amount of time you can stay, so most divers prefer to keep their maximum depth to around 80 feet, which gives them 30–40 minutes of underwater time.

Most dive boats carry sodas, water, and juice, and many stop for lunch between dives. Lunch can be taken on the boat, or the boat will pull up to the beach, where buffet meals are served. This is most common in Cozumel, though it's done in other areas as well.

Diving at night is a completely different experience than diving during the day, and is a real thrill. All divers carry their own lights and backup lights and also wear glow sticks to make them visible, even if their lights should fail. Octopuses, sharks, rays, squid, and other marine life are more prevalent at night since this is the time they normally feed. The same dive site will look totally different at night, with different colors on the coral, different types of fish swimming around, and a different sense of depth for divers since they can see only where they point their lights. On a clear night with a big moon, the divers can also see light from above and can sometimes see large fish or the dive boat silhouetted against the moonlight.

Cenotes & Freshwater Dives

A surprise to many first-time Riviera Maya divers is the presence of many freshwater dive spots, just as close and accessible as the saltwater ones. Throughout the Yucatán Peninsula, there are caverns and spring-fed lagoons called *cenotes* that offer unique dive opportunities for both amateur and experienced divers. The word *cenote* comes from the Mayan word *dzonot*, which was used to describe the sinkholes that formed after the collapse of the thin limestone earth revealed a cave underneath, which then filled with freshwater from the water table (quite near the ground in the porous crust of the Riviera Maya). Once a major source of drinking water for the ancient Mayan villagers, these *cenotes* range from the size of a kiddie pool up to that of a large lagoon covering several acres of land. Some are on private ranches and have been recently opened to visitors, and others are commercially operated as recreational parks and have resident dive operations, on-site instructors, and tour guides (see chapter 8).

The water in the *cenotes* is crystal clear and remains a fairly constant temperature of around 72 degrees. Most *cenotes* are fairly shallow, making even snorkeling and free-diving quite rewarding. Others have deeper holes, up to 50 feet deep, and are best explored with scuba gear. Since they are relatively small and the water does not circulate, it is important that all swimmers and divers rinse off any mosquito repellent or sunscreen before entering the water. The fish are colorful but fairly small, giving snorkelers and divers the feeling that they are diving inside an aquarium. The bottom is rocky and sometimes covered in algae, and the sides are craggy, making entry and exit a bit tricky, especially in areas that are less frequented by visitors. The major sites, though, have wooden docks and ladders, and can be easily entered, even by divers in full gear. With their shallow depth, clear water, and easy accessibility, *cenotes* make for great dives for beginner divers. They are sometimes even used for training classes since there is no wave action and no current, and it's easy to keep track of where all the divers are.

Caves and caverns, on the other hand, offer a completely different scenario. Diving in these situations should be done only by experienced and certified cave divers since they often require the use of specialized equipment, including redundant air systems, lighting systems, and navigation aids. Cave and cavern diving requires the diver to leave the open-water realm and enter restricted areas where there is no easy escape and no way to surface without retracing your path to the entry point. Without the proper precautions, this type of diving can be extremely dangerous, though it can also be rewarding for divers who know how to do it properly.

In these dives, divers carry extra air tanks and lights since they do not have the luxury of surfacing at any time should something go wrong. They also run lines of rope from their entry point so that they can always retrace their paths and will never get lost. Some caverns are quite narrow, requiring divers to actually remove their tanks from their backs and carry them in front of them so they can fit through. Others are wide enough to allow several divers through at a time and can even be enjoyed by relative newcomers to cave diving, as long as an expert guide is close at hand.

The Riviera Maya and the Yucatán are home to some of the world's best spots for this type of diving, and it's an amazing feeling to be surrounded by water as clear as air and to see the incredible cave formations, the underwater stalactites and stalagmites, and the fish that call this realm their home. Some of the dives involve entering the cave at ground level and swimming through a series of caverns prior to entering the more enclosed caves, which twist and turn their way for several hundred yards, sometimes opening up into wide rooms where divers can congregate and rest before continuing the adventure. With the proper preparation, equipment, training, and guide, it's easy to see why this can be one of the most incomparable diving experiences you will ever have.

Outfitters, Instruction & Certification

Each town has its own local dive shops, located around the town square, on the touristy streets, on the beach, or on-site at the larger hotels. Depending on the location, they offer NAUI and PADI training and certification, boat dives, shore dives, drift dives, reef dives, wall dives, night dives, *cenote* dives, and cavern/cave dives, as well as name-brand equipment and gear for sale or rent. All reputable dive shops and tour operators require divers to have a current certification, commonly called a C-card, prior to renting equipment or going on any guided trip.

Instruction and certification are offered at most shops, and many of the larger hotels offer free scuba introduction classes at their on-site pools. In this confined and safe environment, people new to the sport can practice using a mask and fins, snorkeling, and even breathing underwater from the scuba tank through the regulator. This can be a great way to experience the thrill of scuba diving for the first time, and it just may convince you to take a class and do it in the ocean.

Most dive operators offer a "resort course," which includes a bit of instruction on scuba theory and techniques, some time to practice in the pool, and then an actual scuba dive in open water with a certified dive master right by your side. Though the diver will not receive certification with this type of training, it is the best way to go from having no experience to going on an actual dive in only half a day. For safety reasons, the dive master will keep the dive above a depth of 30 feet and will monitor the diver throughout the adventure.

Many dive shops in the area offer full certification classes and even private certification classes. Though normal dive classes are spread out over a few weeks, a private instructor can take the student through a legal certification program in just a matter of days, including classroom lessons, pool practice sessions, and the open-water checkout dive. Some student divers take the classroom and swimming pool portions of the class at home and then just do their open-water certification dives while on vacation. If you plan on doing this, your home instructor will need to fill out a training referral form, and then your instructor in the Riviera Maya will complete the course with you and issue your C-card.

On group tours the depth and bottom time will be recorded by the dive master, and there will be time after each dive for participants to note the details in their log books. Dive operators use the recreational dive tables to plan the dives and determine the maximum depth, the required surface interval, and the available bottom time. Divers using their own dive computers may plan alternate dive profiles as long as they communicate with the dive master and boat captain so they know what to expect. The crew performs a head count at the start and end of each dive to ensure the safe return of everyone in the group.

While ascending from a dive more than 30 feet in depth, it is customary to perform a safety stop at 15 feet for three minutes. This is a precaution to help eliminate any cases of decompression sickness. If anyone does experience symptoms of "the bends," the crew will take quick action to get the diver to a medical facility and even to a hyperbaric chamber, if necessary. There are several chambers in the Riviera Maya, usually within a 30-minute drive from shore. Most dive operators charge a $1 insurance fee for every dive, which ensures that divers will be covered if they need to enter the chamber. Divers should remember not to dive within 24 hours of flying on an airplane, since doctors say the risk of decompression sickness and other diving ailments increases if you do so.

For most dives, except for extensive cave and cavern diving, no special training or licenses are required beyond the basic open-water scuba diving certification. However you decide to dive, remember what you learned in dive training class: plan your dive, then dive your plan.

Divers Alert Network

Divers wanting to be extra cautious should investigate the Divers Alert Network (DAN) (www.diversalertnetwork.com) before their visit. For a yearly fee, DAN provides diving safety information and offers air-evacuation insurance should a diver need to be airlifted back home for treatment of a diving-related injury.

CANCÚN

Known across the world as a mecca for water sports, Cancún is at the far northern tip of the Great Mayan Reef and doesn't have as much coral growth as the areas farther south. The water is as clear as a shot of tequila blanco, though, and some 500 species have been documented. Most of the dives, including **La Bandera, Punta Cancún** and **Punta Nizúc**, are fairly shallow and can be enjoyed by both snorkelers and scuba divers.

ISLA MUJERES

With an average underwater visibility of up to 100 feet and nearly 50 different dive sites within range of a 30-minute boat ride, Isla Mujeres, whose name translates to "island of the women," is also the island of the snorkelers and divers. Popular dives include **Camaronero**, a shrimp boat that sank in the late 1990s; the **Cave of the Sleeping Sharks**, where a brisk current allows sharks to temporarily halt their perpetual swimming and park themselves in an apparent stupor; **Los Marinos**, a sunken Mexican Navy vessel lying at only 70 feet; and **MUSA** (www.musacancun.com), a stunning manmade site featuring striking submerged sculptures (see chapter 8).

ISLA CONTOY

With white-sand beaches, shallow bays, and open-water drop-offs, this tiny island offers big variety for snorkelers and divers. Contoy isn't sheltered by the mainland, so the water can be rougher than elsewhere along the Yucatán coast. **Ixlache**, a very shallow reef popular with snorkeling tours and beginners, and the virtually untouched **Las Calderas** are the primary dives.

COZUMEL

One of the most popular dive destinations anywhere, Cozumel has enough world-class dive sites that you could stay there for a week, diving every day, and never go to the same spot twice. From shallow-water snorkeling spots to sheer walls that drop thousands of feet, Cozumel has superb dives for every skill level. The most popular type of diving is drift diving, which can take some getting used to but brings a whole new dimension to the diving experience. Most dive sites are on the island's southwest coast, facing the Riviera Maya mainland, where the reef runs parallel to the beach and the water is relatively calm, since it is sheltered from the open ocean. It's home to **Palancar Reef**, regularly ranked as one of the top five dive sites in the world.

Other popular dives include the **Santa Rosa Wall**, with an average depth of 90–100 feet, and the shallower Tormentos with a resident green moray eel, more than 6 feet long, sometimes known to eat fish right from the dive master's hand.

Dive Shop

Cozumel's **Studio Blue** (Fifth Avenue and Tenth Street, www.studioblue.com.mx) is a full-fledged dive shop with retail showroom, dive school, and snorkel and dive tours.

PLAYA DEL CARMEN & PLAYACAR

The unofficial capital of the Riviera Maya is also home to the greatest concentration of diving and dive-related activities and services. There are more than a dozen dive shops along Paseo del Carmen and in the water-sports centers of the larger hotels, particularly those in Playacar. Dive sites accessible by boat from Playa range from shallow reefs good for snorkeling to deep-water drop-offs best reserved for advanced divers. The **Buceo Mexico Hyperbaric Chamber** (10th Avenue and 28th Street), the leading facility in the treatment of diving accidents, including cases of "the bends," is open every day and is well known by all major dive operators.

One of the most popular dives in this area is **Las Barracudas**. This shallow-water reef is located just offshore from the Xcaret ecological park and is frequented by schools of large barracuda. Another site, **Chen Zubul**, is frequently visited by novice divers and is also popular for night dives. Nearby, **Moche Deep** is a deep-water reef with swifter currents, making it best for advanced divers only.

Dive Shops

The Abyss (Playa del Carmen and Tulum, www.abyssdiveshop.com) offers PADI and NAUI instruction, open-water dives, and *cenote* trips.

Open since 1983, **Cyan Ha Divers** (North of town, between Hotel Las Palapas and Mahékal Beach Resort, www.playadiving.com) has several boats, an on-site training pool, and PADI instruction, and it specializes in small groups, *cenote* dives, and reef dives.

Scuba Playa Dive Shop (10th Street between First Avenue and Quinta, www.scubaplaya.com) offers a variety of open-water and *cenote* dives.

An old Playa standby, **Tank-Ha Dive Shop** (Tenth Street between Quinta and 10th Avenue, www.tankha.com) has moved into a large diving facility located just off Quinta. It offers PADI and NAUI instruction, an on-site training pool, *cenote* dives, open-water dives, and reef dives.

Yucatek Divers (15th Avenue between Second and Fourth Streets, www.yucatek-divers.com) offers one- and two-tank dives, night dives, cavern and cave dives, and scuba instruction.

PAAMUL

This relaxing beach is home to some of the best diving in the area. With little in the way of tourism development, the reefs are still in pristine condition, and the sea life is prolific. The shallow bay offers excellent snorkeling since the reef is healthy and full of life, even in just a few feet of water.

Good for all certified divers, the 45-foot-deep **Horst's Reef** offers some small swim-throughs. Large coral heads, sea sponges, and abundant marine life can be spotted at the intermediate **Paraíso Shallow**. The beautiful **Xel-Ha Reef**, offshore from the park, is open for exploration provided divers follow Xel-Ha's preservation rules.

PUERTO AVENTURAS

Boats depart from the Puerto Aventuras Marina several times per day, shuttling divers to the nearby reefs. Though it's always best to book ahead, dives can sometimes be planned at the last minute if a boat has extra space available. Local dives include the deep, 75-foot **Los Caniones**, with steep canyons, groove formations, and plenty of fish; the easy-to-access **Brisa Caribe**, between the public marina and the Oasis beach; and the colorful **Mook-Che** reef, near Playa Xcalacoco.

Dive Shop

This full-service **Dive Aventuras** (in the Omni Puerto Aventuras, www.diveaventuras.com) offers all levels of instruction in multiple languages, including a 45-minute tune-up course for certified divers who haven't been in the water for a while.

AKUMAL

Akumal is a shallow bay with calm water, slow currents, and coral beaches. There are many good spots in the 20- to 40-foot range to dive, making it a good spot for beginning and intermediate divers who want the thrill of an ocean dive but aren't quite ready for deep walls and cave systems. More advanced divers will appreciate the deeper sites such as **Gonzalo's Reef**, famous for frequent close encounters with a sea turtle, which reaches a depth of 85 feet in some spots.

The beach at Akumal is nearly always wave-free. Gary Walten/locogringo.com

Other favorites include **Dick's Reef**, named for the retired owner of the original Akumal Dive Shop; **Motorcycle Reef**, named for the sunken motorcycle lying 60 feet below; and the appropriately named **Shark Cave**.

Dive Shops

Akumal Dive Adventures (on the beach next to Buena Vista Restaurant, www.akumaldiveadventures.com) offers snorkeling, cave dives, cavern dives, *cenote* trips, and dives in Akumal and other openwater sites.

Open since 1980, the Texan-owned **Akumal Dive Shop** (near the main gate to the Akumal development, www.akumal.com) offers dives in and around the Akumal area, plus certification classes, "bubblemaker" classes for kids, and sailing and fishing trips.

TULUM

Known for its Mayan ruins and relaxed atmosphere, the Tulum area also has some great snorkeling and diving sites, particularly **Tulum Reef**, within sight of the ruins.

Dive Shop

Tulum's first dive shop, **Acuatic Tulum** (on Highway 307 at Coba Sur, www.acuatictulum.com.mx) offers snorkeling, ocean diving, and *cenote* diving trips.

COSTA MAYA

The Costa Maya starts an hour south of Playa del Carmen and extends nearly to Mexico's border with Belize. The reef is especially healthy in this section because it sees fewer divers and cruise ships. The coral is healthier, the colors are brighter, and the fish are larger. It's also harder to reach, so expect longer boat trips.

Banco Chinchorro offers diving opportunities along it thriving and expansive coral reef. There are also dozens of viable, remote, and rarely visited dive sites at the protected biosphere reserve **Sian Ka'an**, a UNESCO World Heritage Site.

8

Golf

THOUGH THE MAYANS never used the wheel, they did have the ball, and it is believed that they took great pleasure in playing various games. Their most famous ball game was called *pok-ta-pok*, and it was serious business. The ball was about the size of a kickball, and the game was played on a large field about the size of a basketball court. Similar to basketball, the game's object was to shoot the ball through a hoop mounted above the playing surface. Considering that players weren't allowed to use their hands, though, scoring was quite rare and was considered a tremendous feat. Large numbers of villagers turned out to watch the games, which had great religious and ceremonial importance. Fans sang songs, acted boisterously, and even bet on who would win. The winners of the game were given a hero's welcome, and a celebration was held in their honor. As legend has it, the losers were put to death.

Today, the open fields, beachfronts, and carved-away jungles of the Riviera Maya make a perfect backdrop for the more "civilized" ball game of golf. There are 15 courses within the Riviera Maya, including courses in Cancún, Cozumel, and the town of Bacalar (south of the Riviera Maya). Some of the courses are par 3, but others are par 72 championship courses designed by some of the best golf architects in the business, including Jack Nicklaus, Robert Trent Jones, Jr., and Robert Von Hagge.

Most of the courses have beautiful views of the ocean and the tropical jungle. Iguanas, colorful birds, and other animals are commonly sighted. Most have multiple water and sand features, and several even have actual Mayan ruins next to the fairways.

Most courses have clubs for rent, and unless you're a real pro or planning on playing multiple rounds, the loaners are normally sufficient. Balls can be expensive (and the loss ratio can be high), so it's usually best to bring some of your own since they're cheap back home and fairly easy to pack. The larger courses have full-service pro shops with name-brand equipment and apparel, club repair, and instruction.

LEFT: El Cameleón is the PGA Tour site for the OHL Classic at Mayakoba. Mayakoba

Some of the courses operate with an all-inclusive concept, where the greens fee includes a cart, range balls, and all the food and drink you care to consume during your round. To keep the costs down, consider playing in the afternoon to take advantage of discounted twilight rates. Just make sure to bring a hat, sunscreen, and plenty of water.

The Riviera Maya is becoming more of a golf destination with each passing decade. For information on all area golf courses, check with the Mexican Caribbean Golf Association (www.cancungolf.org).

Golf Courses

RIVIERA MAYA

El Cameleón Golf Club at Mayakobá (Highway 307, km 297, north of Playa del Carmen, www.mayakobagolf.com) is the first course in Mexico to be designed by Greg Norman. It curls around the Fairmont Mayakobá hotel and along the beach of the 1,600-acre tourism development. Players enjoy unusual hazards, such as *cenotes*, mangrove swamps, and other tropical features. The course spans more than 7,000 yards and has five sets of tees. Two of the holes are right along the beach, while 15 holes have some sort of water hazard. There is a driving range and putting green, plus a well-stocked pro shop and steakhouse overlooking the 18th hole. A novelty in Mexico, all carts have GPS navigation and yardage systems, allowing players to keep score, monitor other players' scores, and order refreshments while on the course. This course is the site of the yearly OHL Golf Classic pro tournament, first played in 2007, marking the first PGA event in Mexico.

The 27-hole **Bahia Principe Golf Club** (Highway 307, km 250, www.bahia-principe.com), designed by Robert Trent Jones, II, is part of a massive real estate development with condos, private residences, and resorts. It's about an hour from the Cancún airport and 30 minutes south of Playa del Carmen.

Designed by P. B. Dye and opened in 2005, **Iberostar Playa Paraíso Golf Club** (Highway 307, km 309, Playa Paraíso, www.iberostar.com) is convenient for players throughout the Riviera Maya. It features 18 holes stretched across 6,800 yards, with wide fairways, deep sand traps, and undulating greens. Rental equipment from brands such as Titleist, Nike, and Mizuno is available.

Opened in 1994, **Playacar Club de Golf** (Paseo Xaman-há, 26 Fraccionamiento Playacar, Playa del Carmen, teetimesplayacar@allinclusivecollection.com) was designed by Robert Von Hagge and acquired by Palace Resorts in 2005. The course runs 7,202 yards and has many jungle, sand, and water features to keep golfers challenged and entertained. There are even a few actual Mayan ruins along the fairways and greens.

Grand Coral Golf Club (Playa del Carmen, www.grandcoralrivieramaya.com/golf/) introduced the region's first Nick Price–designed course in early 2011.

Part of the Puerto Aventuras development, the nine-hole, 3,236-yard, par 36 **Puerto Aventuras Club de Golf** (Highway 307, km 269.5, Puerto Aventuras, www.puertoaventuras.com.mx) was designed by Thomas Lehman and built in 1990. No credit cards.

The Jack Nicklaus–designed par 3 **Riviera Maya Golf & Tennis Club—Mayan Palace Golf Club** (Highway 307, km 310, Playa Paraiso, www.mayan

palace.com) opened in 2003. It spans 2,823 yards and has lots of water and sand features. The signature 17th hole skirts a large lagoon and has an island sand trap, making your approach shot crucial.

Cancún

Inaugurated in 2008 in a large-scale development just north of Cancún, the 808-acre, 18-hole, par 72 **Puerto Cancún Golf Course** (east of Bonampak Avenue, near where Kulkulcán Avenue meets downtown Cancún, www.puertocancun.com.mx/golf), designed by Tom Wesikopf, features 185 acres of water features, sand traps, and manicured greens. An additional course, designed by Tom Fazio and Nice Price, is being contemplated.

Designed by Greg Norman, the 18-hole, 7250 yards, par 72 **Playa Mujeres Golf Club** (Bonampak Avenue, Punta Sam, www.playamujeresgolf.com.mx) snakes through tropical mangroves, the beachfront, and a saltwater lagoon.

The Jack Nicklaus Signature Course, **Moon Palace Spa & Golf Club** (Highway 307, km 340, Cancún, www.moonpalacecancun.com) includes three separate courses, each with distinct environments (jungle, lake, and dune), totaling 27 holes and a par of 108. Total length is 10,798 yards. The layout requires golfers to navigate through native vegetation, wetlands, and a plethora of sandtraps.

Designed by Robert Trent Jones, II, 6,636-yard long **Cancún Country Club Pok-Ta-Pok** (Kukulcán Boulevard, km 7.5, Cancún hotel zone, www.cancungolfclub.com) is the destination's first course, opening in 1976. With 18 holes and a par of 72, it has several holes along the beach and a few Mayan ruins scattered about.

Near Cancún's southern end and designed by Isao Aoki, **Iberostar Cancún Golf Resort** (Kukulcán Boulevard, km 17.5, Cancún hotel zone, www.iberostar.com.mx) has 18 holes, is par 72, and has 6,767 yards of play. Opened in 1994, it features holes along Nichupté Lagoon, with peacocks, an occasional crocodile, and lots of iguanas. From the 15th and 16th holes, players have a great view of the Ruinas El Rey, Cancún's most important Mayan ruins site.

Designed by Nick Price, **TPC Cancún at Cancún Country Club** (Highway 307, km 388, Cancún, www.tpccancun.com/ing) is an inland course, located immediately south of the Cancún airport.

Cozumel

Designed by Nicklaus Design in 2001, **Cozumel Country Club** (Carretera Costera Norte, km 6.5 Interior, Cozumel, www.cozumelcountryclub.com.mx) has four sets of tees, with the longest being 6,734 yards. There are many sand and water features to contend with as the course skirts native mangroves and tropical swamps.

Angie

9

Fishing

FISHING HAS BEEN a way of life in the Riviera Maya since the indigenous inhabitants paddled their dugout canoes through the shallows, plunging their wooden spears into the water to snare their catch. They also fished with reed baskets or nets, woven with the same techniques used to make hammocks. In some areas fish were caught with bows and arrows or even poisons. These were thrown into the water, killing the fish, which floated to the surface for harvest. Later, the Mayans even used a pole and line, possibly even making a sport out of it.

With its variety of good fishing locations in such a relatively small geographic area, the Riviera Maya is one of the world's top spots for sportfishing and deep-sea fishing. The waters off the northeastern coast of the Yucatán are prime for finding numerous species and a wide variety of fishing conditions. From deep channels to wide flats and shallow reefs to rocky points, there's always a spot that's producing, no matter the time of year and the weather conditions, unless a major storm keeps the boats in port.

Fishing options range from a do-it-yourself, wade-fishing expedition to a full-day excursion trolling on a luxury yacht, complete with meals, drinks, guides, gear, and a video recording of all the action. From your hotel in the Riviera Maya, several distinct fishing spots are within easy reach. From the deep waters off Cancún to the north, through the reefs of Puerto Morelos, to the shallows of Cozumel, to the drop-offs near Playa, to the bays of Akumal and Puerto Aventuras, and all the way down to the flats of Sian Ka'an, each area holds something unique and exciting for fishing. And whether you're a novice who just enjoys being out on the water and reeling one in, a regular enthusiast in search of your first marlin, or an old pro going for a coveted grand slam, you can find what you're looking for in the Riviera Maya.

Fishing is great year-round, but if you're looking for a specific type of fish, then you'll need to take note of the seasons to make sure your target is around when you plan to visit. Many visitors come to Playa seeking the majestic billfish,

LEFT: Fishing boats along the Isla Mujeres waterfront

which produces a thrill like no other when it takes the bait and then jumps in the air for all to see. These beautiful creatures, weighing up to 500 pounds, are seen throughout the year, though the prime time is from March to July, when they ply the deep waters between Cozumel and the Yucatán mainland in abundant numbers. Each year, there are several billfish grand slams recorded, when a single group manages to boat a blue marlin, a white marlin, and a sailfish on the same trip. When fishing for these beauties, a strict catch-and-release policy is followed, so make sure to bring your video camera to capture the moments for bragging rights.

Tuna, mahimahi, bonito, bonefish, and wahoo prefer the warmer waters and generally are more active from March to August or September, though catches of each have been recorded in every month of the year. Due to the varied underwater terrain and year-round temperate climate, however, many fish species can be caught throughout the year, including barracuda, grouper, kingfish, shark, skipjack, snapper, and other reef and bottom fish. They're so abundant, in fact, that many chartered boats promise to prepare a meal on the boat or on a hidden beach, and they rely exclusively on the day's catch to supply the main course. Though certainly it has happened that bad luck strikes and the group is left to dine on crackers, salsa, and sides, the trips almost always end with a bounteous feast of ultrafresh ceviche or fried fish.

A Mexican fishing license is required for boat fishing, and the fees go toward worthwhile conservation and regulation programs. Reputable tour operators, such as those listed in this guide, include all required licensing in the prices of their tours.

PRIZED CATCHES OF THE RIVIERA MAYA

Often seen while snorkeling, hovering nearly motionless next to the reef, seemingly watching every move you make, the **barracuda** is one of the most feared of all ocean creatures. Given its muscle-packed body, large eyes, gaping mouth, and razor-sharp teeth, it's easy to see why. Their fearless nature makes them great fighters, and they're commonly caught while drift fishing or bottom fishing, all across the Riviera Maya's shallows and deepwater cuts. Caught year-round.

The largest of the billfish, the **blue marlin**, can reach up to 1,800 pounds in the deeper Atlantic waters, though they seldom grow to more than 500 pounds in the local region. Average catches are in the range of 80–120 pounds. Caught while trolling using artificial baits, the blue marlin will be landed only if the angler is strapped in tightly to the fighting chair and ready for an exhaustive struggle. Keeping tension on the line is the only way to keep the blues from spitting the hook while jumping into the air. Best months: May to September.

White and blue, with a beautiful pointed "horn," the **white marlin** (50–80 pounds on average) is famous for long fights and high jumps, often twisting its body when it's out of the water. Found in the highest numbers in the Cozumel channel, between the island and the mainland. Best months: April to August.

One of the most exciting sport fish around, the **sailfish**, is known for its long, protruding dorsal fin, which looks like a sail. It is also known to fly through the air once it's hooked, offering up superb photo opportunities. Mostly 30–50 pounds, they're caught by trolling through the drop-offs and deeper channels, and can be

Arrange a fishing trip directly with the boat captains at this booth in front of the Gran Porto Real in Playa del Carmen.

very hard to land since they twist and turn a lot while jumping and fighting. Best months: March to August.

Noted for their exceptional fighting strength, a surprise given they are relatively small in size, bonefish are taken with fly-fishing gear, though spinning tackle can also be used. The angler normally casts when the fish breaks the surface or is swimming just below. The strike is hard and fast, requiring a high level of skill and making for a thoroughly entertaining day of fishing. One of the best spots in the world for finding bonefish is in Ascension Bay, at the southern end of the Sian Ka'an biosphere. Best months: March to August.

A member of the sea bass family, groupers are strong fighting fish and quite abundant in the warm Caribbean waters. They come in various colors, from dark gray to bright orange. Scuba divers are fond of watching groupers eat, a process that involves a slow circling around the prey, followed by a quick kick of the tail fin and a hard swallow, which lets them suck in large pieces of food at one time. They are generally caught while bottom fishing. Caught year-round.

One of the best-tasting fish in the Caribbean, the mahimahi (sometimes called dorado or dolphin fish) has a big face with a high, protruding forehead and beautiful blue dorsal fin running the length of its back. The body is thick and strong and seems to glow with every color of the rainbow. Can be caught trolling or bottom fishing, depending on the water depth. Best months: March to September.

Members of the jack family, permit are broad fish with silvery blue bodies that range in size from 3–30 pounds. Great fighters with fierce striking power, they can be taken with flies and light tackle. They're common in the shallow flats of Ascension Bay and near Isla Holbox. Since they stay in the warm, shallow water, fishing is good year-round.

Long prized by natives for their liver oil, sharks are still commercially fished

Fishing Seasons in Playa

FISH	JAN	FEB	MAR	APR	MAY
Amber jack	high season	high season	high season	high season	high season
Barracuda	high season	high season	high season	high season	high season
Blue marlin	off season	off season	some catches	some catches	high season
Bonefish	some catches	some catches	high season	high season	high season
Bonito	off season	high season	high season	high season	high season
Bottom fish	high season	high season	high season	high season	high season
Grouper	high season	high season	high season	high season	high season
Kingfish	high season	high season	high season	high season	high season
Mackerel	high season	high season	high season	high season	high season
Mahi-mahi	off season	some catches	high season	high season	high season
Permit	high season	high season	high season	high season	high season
Sailfish	off season	some catches	high season	high season	high season
Shark	high season	high season	high season	high season	high season
Snapper	high season	high season	high season	high season	high season
Tuna	off season	off season	some catches	high season	high season
Wahoo	off season	off season	high season	high season	high season
White marlin	off season	off season	some catches	high season	high season

for their meat, teeth, and jaws. The English word shark is said to come from the Mayan xoc. A year-round catch, they can be caught while trolling, bottom fishing, or even wade fishing. Though attacks are very infrequent, sightings are somewhat common, especially by local fishermen and others who spend a lot of time on the water.

The Riviera Maya is home to yellowfin, blackfin, and skipjack tuna. Each is

JUN	JUL	AUG	SEPT	OCT	NOV	DEC
high season	high season	high season	some catches	some catches	some catches	some catches
high season	high season	high season	high season	high season	high season	high season
high season	high season	high season	high season	some catches	off season	off season
high season	high season	high season	some catches	some catches	some catches	some catches
high season	high season	high season	some catches	some catches	off season	off season
high season	high season	high season	high season	high season	high season	high season
high season	high season	high season	high season	high season	high season	high season
high season	high season	high season	high season	high season	high season	high season
high season	some catches	some catches	some catches	some catches	high season	high season
high season	high season	high season	high season	off season	off season	off season
high season	high season	high season	high season	high season	high season	high season
high season	high season	high season	off season	off season	off season	off season
high season	high season	high season	high season	high season	high season	high season
high season	high season	high season	high season	high season	high season	high season
high season	high season	some catches	off season	off season	off season	off season
high season	high season	high season	high season	off season	off season	off season
high season	high season	high season	off season	off season	off season	off season

quick and strong and can put up a great fight. Most often caught while trolling, tuna can be served grilled, in lime-marinated ceviche, or even raw. Can't beat that for fresh sushi! Best months: April to July.

Wahoo are long and thin, with a barracuda-like face and sleek body that can cut through the water at an incredible 45 mph. When a wahoo hits the bait, you better make sure the pole is fastened in the rod holder or securely in someone's

10 Hotspots for Manly Men

1. Bahia Principe Golf Club at Gran Bahia Principe resort (Akumal)
2. TPC Cancún at Cancún Country Club (Cancún)
3. Bullfights (downtown Cancún)
4. El Cameleón Golf Club at Mayakobá (Punta Bete)
5. El Rey Polo Country Club (Puerto Morelos)
6. Iberostar Playa Paraíso Golf Club (Playa Paraíso)
7. Pesca Maya fishing lodge (Punta Allen)
8. Playa Mujeres Golf Club (Playa Mujeres)
9. Puerto Cancún Golf Club (Cancún)
10. Tequila Barrel sports betting lounge (Playa del Carmen)

arms, or you'll end up losing your whole rig to the depths. Most often caught while trolling, wahoo can be cut into large steaks and are great for frying. Best months: March to September.

TOP FISHING DESTINATIONS

Akumal has been a sportfishing town for more than 30 years. One of the top guides in the area and 25-year resident, **Pillo** offers two-hour trips for up to four anglers (sometimes four more). Reservations can be made in person at Lot 40, near the Nah Kin Condos.

Recognized as the best place in the world for a permit, tarpon, and bonefish grand slam, **Ascension Bay** and **Boca Pila** are also prime spots for snook, barracuda, Spanish mackerel, and permit. The bay has various inlets, ensuring that your boat captain can find fishing no matter the wind direction. Anglers can visit on a day trip from the Riviera Maya or stay overnight at one of the many lodges found between Boca Paila and Punta Allen.

Excursions from **Cancún** promise day- and night-fishing expeditions to the reefs not far from shore, between the coastline and Isla Mujeres. Common catches include grouper, hogfish, mackerel, and snapper.

The lagoons, jagged shorelines, and flats of **Cozumel Island** offer up excellent bonefishing, which is most often done using fly-fishing tackle or a lightweight spinning reel. There's good bottom fishing along the northern coast near Passion Island and on the island's east coast, where the coral reef is not part of the federal reserve. Farther from shore, in the Cozumel channel, anglers troll for marlin, sailfish, and other large game.

The fishing mecca of **Puerto Aventuras** is the southernmost deep-water marina in the Riviera Maya, with many sportfishing and deep-sea fishing charters available. A walk around the marina reveals the dozens of well-equipped boats awaiting their next expedition.

Local Knowledge

ONCE YOU'RE ON THE GROUND, and sometimes even before you arrive, it's handy to know a little bit more about the practices and social norms of your destination. Think of this chapter as a handy reference to things you might need to know on the fly or may just require some additional cultural insight.

CALLING HOME

Don't dial direct from your hotel room! Even a quick call home from your hotel can carry a charge of $25 or more, due to high connection fees and even higher per-minute tolls. Most hotels offer local calls for around $1 each, about the same as in the States, but long-distance calls—especially international—are a completely different story. Some hotels offer and market free VOIP calls, but be sure you ask how they would like you to place these calls.

Of course, these days, most travelers have smartphones. If you don't already have one, most carriers will allow you to set up a temporary calling and data plan that will allow you to stay in touch with the folks back home. Many travelers download the popular Viber and Skype apps for Internet-based phone calls and text messages and WhatsApp for basic text messaging.

If you don't have a smartphone nor Internet access and a Skype or VOIP account, your best option is to buy a prepaid phone card (called LADA cards, or tarjetas LADA) and make all calls with it. Even then, it's best to make the calls from a public phone to ensure you won't be billed a connection fee, which is common even for "toll-free" calls placed inside hotel rooms.

Official Tourism Office

Stop in the state-run **Tourism Office** (15th Avenue between Fourth and Sixth Streets, Playa del Carmen) for free area maps, promotional information, tour recommendations, safety tips, and lists of approved vendors.

The author and his wife on a scouting trip near Playa del Carmen Jessica Loera

Post Office

Playa's main **post office** (Avenue Juárez between 15th and 20th Avenues) is open 8–5 Monday through Friday and 9–noon Saturday. Postcards are cheap and always appreciated by the folks you left back home. It can take weeks for mail to arrive, however, so don't mail any critical messages. Stamps can be purchased at many convenience stores or hotel gift shops. To send anything quickly or of any value, use private courier **Estafeta** (on Fourth Street between 30th and 35th Avenues, www.estafeta.com), Mexico's largest document and package delivery company.

Beach Etiquette

All Mexican beaches are federal property. No hotel can restrict access to the beach (from the water) or make their own regulations about what you can and can't do. That said, hotels don't have to allow you to cross their private property to access the beach, and they can prevent access to the hotel from their beachfront. Many hotels set up a cordoned-off semi-private area, supplying beach chairs or shade umbrellas for the exclusive use of their guests, which is legal.

Going nude, or even topless, isn't permitted by Mexican decency laws. Topless sunbathing is tolerated (and sometimes appreciated) by the local police in many areas, though, and many visitors to Playa del Carmen and the Riviera Maya—particularly Europeans—enjoy this freedom. To avoid any trouble with the law, it's best to restrict such European-style sunbathing to times and places when there are other people doing the same. In Playa, for instance, the beaches adjacent to the ferry dock are popular with local families and children, and tourists should be respectful of the local customs and refrain from going topless in these areas. Farther south of the dock, closer to the Gran Porto Real hotel, topless tanning becomes more of the norm, and visitors should not have any problem, except for an occasional passing gawker. To the north, most beaches are topless-friendly, though it is uncommon in front of the family-oriented hotels.

Elsewhere in the Mayan Riviera, local attitudes will dictate whether or not topless sunbathing is acceptable. On most beaches it's no problem, though in some areas it's frowned upon. The general rule is that the more locals or families, the less appropriate it is to go topless. Full nudity is generally frowned upon in all but a few specific areas, namely in front of the nude resorts, such as Hidden Beach, Desire Resort, and Playa Secreto.

The Mayan Riviera still has some relatively deserted beaches, accessible only by a four-wheel-drive vehicle and a bit of courage. Though these beaches do see occasional patrols from the Mexican Army or local police, discreet travelers can generally enjoy the freedom of being one with nature, however they choose to define it.

YEARLY EVENTS CALENDAR

January 1, New Year's Day.

Early January, The BPM Festival in Playa del Carmen. This 10-day gathering brings the world's hottest DJs to Playa, where they perform on the beaches, in the clubs, and around Playa. One of the largest events of the year, performers, patrons, and partygoers dominate the town at this massive annual event. (www.thebpmfestival.com)

January 6, Day of the Three Kings. A traditional day of Christmas gift-giving, marking the Christian holiday of Epiphany, when the three wise men arrived to give gifts to the baby Jesus.

January 10, Quintana Roo's Constitution Day. Banks are closed, but not much else happens.

January 11, anniversary of Quintana Roo's restatement as a territory.

February 5, Constitution Day. A federal holiday, but there's not much social celebration.

February 14, Day of Lovers and Friends. Similar to Valentine's Day in the United States. Street vendors sell flowers and balloons; restaurants offer special romantic meals for couples.

February 24, Flag Day. A ceremony is held in Cancún and Cozumel at the sites of their giant flags.

February–March, Carnaval. Fluctuates with the Christian calendar. It's mostly celebrated in Cozumel and Playa del Carmen, where school children dress in colorful costumes and parade through the streets. In Playa, there's a week of festivities and impromptu parades, capped by a long procession down Quinta and up 12th Street to the municipal park, where a live music stage, food vendors, midway games and revelers keep the party going late into the night. Mostly locals, but tourists are welcomed.

Mid-March, Wine and Food Festival Cancún–Riviera Maya. Great chefs and sommeliers from Europe and the Americas gather to celebrate food, wine, and spring at this region-spanning event. (www.crmfest.com)

March 20 or 21, vernal equinox. This marks the first official day of spring, when daylight and night are the same length. It's celebrated at Chichén Itzá, where the shadow of the serpent Kukulkán snakes down the side of the temple when the sunlight hits it just right.

March 21, birthday of Benito Juárez. Former president and reform-movement leader, Juárez pops up frequently in the Riviera Maya, in street names, building names, and statues. All banks and government offices are closed, but most tourist businesses stay open.

March or April, Easter and Holy Week. Known as *Semana Santa* (Holy Week) in Spanish, this is a very popular travel time for Mexican families since schoolchildren get two weeks' vacation. The holiday, which celebrates Christ's resurrection, is traditionally celebrated even more than Christmas.

Late April–Early May, Sol a Sol Regatta. Annual sailboat race from St. Petersburg, Florida, to Isla Mujeres (www.regatadelsolalsol.org). Live music, street festival, and celebrations.

Late April–Early May, Akumal Comedy Festival. An annual event with comedians from the United States performing multiple shows at venues in Akumal, Tulum, and Playa del Carmen. (www.akumalcomedyfestival.com)

May 1, Labor Day. National holiday.

May 5, Cinco de Mayo. Celebration of Mexican independence from France during the 1862 Battle of Puebla. Not as widely celebrated as the September 16 holiday marking independence from Spain, but most tourist bars make a show of it just the same.

June 1, Navy Day. Honors sailors lost at sea. Celebrations vary by municipality.

Last weekend of June, Playa del Carmen Sportfishing Tournament. This major fishing tournament helps fill hotels and restaurants, but the town doesn't get too involved.

Mid-July, I Love Cancún Gay Pride Parade. Everyone's welcome at this mid-summer's evening parade along Cancún's malecon (www.cancunprideparade.com).

August, Dia de la Asuncion Festival, Oxkutzcab, Yucatán (date varies). Week-long Assumption Day celebration near Loltún Cave, about three hours from Playa.

Second weekend of August, Ferragosto Italian food festival (date varies). Restaurant specials and a yearly "largest pizza in the world" exhibition, where Quinta restaurants pitch in to create (and then serve) a pizza spanning some six blocks through town. Coincides with a similar celebration in Italy, so Playa's Italian population celebrates all weekend at the many Italian-owned restaurants and bars.

August 17, Isla Mujeres Founding Day. Locals celebrate the date of their town's founding with parades, parties, live music, and street dancing. Underwater ceremony at Los Manchones Reef, where a large bronze cross is attached to the coral.

September 1, Presidential State of the Union Address. Mexicans love politics, and many stay riveted to their TVs to watch the speech. Bars and stores are not allowed to serve alcohol until it's over, but it usually turns into a party afterward.

September 16, national holiday marking Mexico's independence from Spain in 1821. Widely celebrated with parades, fireworks, and street parties. Much more important to locals than Cinco de Mayo.

September 22 or 23, autumnal equinox. Marks the first day of fall. Date varies by year.

September 27–October 13, Fiesta de Cristo de las Ampollas in Mérida. Religious festival honoring a sacred relic housed in the main cathedral.

October 12, Dia de la Raza, or Columbus Day. Celebrated throughout Mexico as a day to honor the many types of people that comprise its population.

October 31, All Souls' Day. Festivities inspired by the Halloween celebration in the United States.

November, Riviera Maya Latin Jazz Fest (date varies). This three-day festival brings together jazz musicians from around the world for concerts, dancing, and all-night parties (www.rivieramayajazzfestival.com)

November 1–2, Day of the Dead. Mexico's predominant Halloween-time holiday honors the dead. Friends and relatives gather at the graves of loved ones to celebrate their lives and honor their deaths.

November, OHL Golf Classic (date varies). The PGA descends on the Mayakobá resort for its only tour event in Mexico. Spectator tickets start at $10. (www.ohl classic.com)

November 20, Mexican Revolution Day. Marks Mexico's 1910 Revolution. It's mostly a federal holiday, with little local observance.

December 8, Feast of the Immaculate Conception. Religious holiday celebrated throughout the Riviera Maya.

December 24, Nochebuena, or Christmas Eve. A religious and social holiday with parades and street parties.

December 25–January 2, Christmas week. Weeklong festival with candlelight processions, Catholic mass, nightly parties, and religious ceremonies.

December 31, New Year's Eve. Many bars offer drink specials and all-you-can-eat specials. At the stroke of midnight, it's good luck to eat 12 grapes, one for each month of the new year. Nightclubs stay open until dawn.

BOOKS FOR RIVIERA MAYA TRAVELERS

Try these great reads in preparation for your trip while you're lying on the beach, or to ease your transition back to the real world.

Don't Stop the Carnival by Herman Wouk. This meandering tale may change your mind about wanting to open a hotel in the Caribbean.

Incidents of Travel in Yucatán by John Lloyd Stephens and Frederick Catherwood.

Top Five Places to Pop the Question

Courtesty of Brenda Alfaro, owner of Ajua Weddings (www.ajuaweddings.com)

1. The cliffs at the Mayan ruins of Tulum
2. On a private sailboat in Soliman Bay
3. On the beach at Playa Maroma
4. On top of the rocks at the Xaman Ha Beach in Playacar
5. In the canals of the Sian Ka'an Biosphere

Originally published in the 1840s, it's an amazing account of the life and times of the Mayans.

Cinnamon Skin by John D. MacDonald. A boat-bum detective travels to Cancún and the Riviera Maya to solve a crime for a friend.

A Salty Piece of Land by Jimmy Buffett. A cowboy moves to Sian Ka'an to become a fishing guide. Many Riviera Maya and Buffett song–inspired references.

A Tourist in the Yucatán by James McNay Brumfield. An action-adventure mystery set among the Mayan ruins.

Where the Sky Is Born: Living in the Land of the Maya by Jeanine Lee Kitchel. Thinking of moving to the Riviera Maya or curious what it would be like? Learn from someone who's done it.

Chaos in Cancún by Susan Murray. This detective novel for teens takes its main characters on a whirlwind tour through the Riviera Maya. Includes some fun references to local spots that kids will find entertaining.

Wicked Spanish by Howard Tomb. This tongue-in-cheek language guide will teach you some naughty phrases and fun sayings to try out on bartenders and fellow bus riders.

The Ruins by Scott Smith. A group of friends on holiday to Cancún and the Riviera Maya stumble across a mysterious secret in the Mayan jungle and struggle to get away. It may make you think twice about hiking in the jungle!

Captains Outrageous by Joe R. Lansdale. A comedic and bumbling tale of intrigue, with travels from east Texas to the land of the Mayans.

The World Is Blue: How Our Fate and the Ocean's Are One by Dr. Sylvia A. Earle. A fascinating, simple and clear explanation of our impact on the seas, including the Great Mayan Reef, and what must be done to counter it.

SPANISH CLASSES

As a sign on the wall of the Señor Frog's bar says, WE DON'T SPEAK ENGLISH, BUT WE PROMISE NOT TO LAUGH AT YOUR SPANISH. Not only is learning a bit of the local language a good way to win the favor of the locals you meet, but it can also be a lot of fun.

Programs in Playa del Carmen include **Playalingua** (www.playalingua.com), **Solexico Spanish School** (www.solexico.com), and **International House** (14th Street between Quinta and 10th Avenue, www.ihrivieramaya.com).

WEDDINGS IN PARADISE

If your idea of the perfect wedding is exchanging vows during a beachside ceremony with the sun going down, tropical flowers forming the aisle, a Mexican trio providing romantic music, and your guests dancing the salsa while they sip tequila, then getting married in the Riviera Maya may suit you.

Though most weddings in the region are fairly casual outdoor affairs, the facilities and services exist to put on a spectacular formal ceremony for hundreds of guests, complete with all the traditions and comforts of a wedding in your own hometown. Both civil and religious ceremonies can be planned, depending on the couple's preference.

There are several independent wedding planners in town, in addition to the on-staff planners at the larger hotels. They can assist with all of the details, from cakes to flowers, from hotels to photography, and from rehearsals to receptions. Due to the legal requirements for foreigners getting married in Mexico, it is recommended that the couple arrive in Playa del Carmen at least three business days prior to their wedding day to file the necessary paperwork.

LEGAL REQUIREMENTS FOR GETTING MARRIED

At least two days before the ceremony, the couple must go to the local courthouse and present:

1. A valid tourist card (your temporary visa, issued at the airport).
2. A notarized copy of each person's birth certificate (must have a raised seal).
3. An official Spanish translation of the birth certificate (should be done locally by a court-approved translator).
4. A health certificate certifying blood type and AIDS/STD status. (The tests must be performed and certified by a court-approved facility.)
5. The proper court documents if either person is divorced or widowed.

Best Places to Host a Wedding Reception or Other Special Event

Kartabar, Playa del Carmen. A trendy spot for food and drinks in the middle of Playa's party zone (see chapter 4)

Belmond Maroma Resort & Spa, Punta Maroma. Hosts upscale events that your guests will be proud to attend (see chapter 6)

Viceroy Riviera Maya. Rent out the entire facility and enjoy your own private village with stunning vistas and soothing forests. (see chapter 6)

Rancho Punta Venado. A private beachfront ranch with all the necessary facilities (www.puntavenado.com)

6. Two witnesses, with valid passports showing name, age, address, and nationality.
7. Basic fees, which total about $475.

MEDICAL CARE

The vast majority of Riviera Maya visitors never need to think about medical care during their stay, but accidents do happen—even while on vacation.

Medical facilities in Cancún, Cozumel, Isla Mujeres, and Playa del Carmen are modern and more than sufficient for most moderate emergencies and standard medical care. Most are operated by the Red Cross, or *La Cruz Roja*, and truly are first-class facilities, by any standard. Many of the doctors are U.S. trained and can provide care equivalent to what can be received at an average facility of a similar size in First World countries. A fairly large modern hospital called Hospiten opened in 2007, just south of Playacar, on Highway 307 in Playa del Carmen. The emergency medical first responders in the region are especially well trained and equipped, and they are well versed on procedures related to scuba-diving accidents, falls, car wrecks, animal bites, broken bones, and other common incidents. There are also many private clinics with English-speaking doctors who can treat nonemergency cases and make house calls to hotels or other locations.

The farther you travel from the main cities, the fewer medical facilities you will find. In Akumal, Puerto Aventuras, and Tulum there are small clinics, though emergency services lag behind those of the larger cities in terms of quality and reliability.

Common sense and common precautions will prevent most accidents, and taking good care of yourself, including drinking plenty of water and moderating your alcohol intake, will reduce your chances of getting sick. After all, even though the medical facilities are generally quite good, they're not as nice as the beach.

A large iguana catches some rays at Tulum. Dr. John Anderson

EMERGENCY RESOURCES

Find up-to-date phone numbers and addresses at the websites listed below.

Directory Assistance: 020

Police, fire, or ambulance: 066 (free call from any phone)

Cancún Hyperbaric Chamber: www.sssnetwork.com

Hospiten Hospital: www.hospiten.es

Playa del Carmen Hyperbaric Chamber: www.sssnetwork.com

Medica de Carmen Hospital: www.medicadelcarmen.com

Angel MedFlight Ambulance Service: www.angelmedflight.com

LOCAL TRANSPORTATION RESOURCES

Find up-to-date phone numbers, departure and arrival schedules and more at the websites listed below.

Cancún Airport: www.cancun-airport.com

Bus station: www.destinosxado.com

Cozumel Ferry Office (Ultramar): www.granpuerto.com.mx

Cozumel Ferry Office (Mexico Water Jet) www.mexicowaterjets.com.mx

LOST CREDIT CARDS

American Express: www.americanexpress.com

MasterCard: www.mastercard.us

Visa: www.visa.com

LONG-DISTANCE SERVICE

AT&T: www.att.com

Sprint: www.sprint.com

T-Mobile: www.t-mobile.com

Virgin Mobile: www.virginmobileusa.com

Numbers Game

Country code for the United States: 01

Country code for Mexico: 52

Area code for Cancún: 998

Area code for Playa del Carmen: 987

Prefix for dialing Mexican mobile phones: 044

AIRLINES

Aeromexico. www.aeromexico.com

AeroSaab (charter): www.aerosaab.com

AirCanada: www.aircanada.com

American: www.aa.com

British Airways: www.britishairways.com

Delta: www.delta.com

JetBlue: www.jetblue.com

Magnicharters (charter): www.magnicharters.com.mx

United: www.united.com

CONSULATES

Consulate offices are open weekday mornings and by appointment.

United States: www.usembassy.gov

Canada: www.canadainternational.gc.ca

United Kingdom: www.ukinmexico.fco.gov.uk

Index

C

D

G

H

I

Q

R

S

T

U

V